The Family Guide
New Revised Edition

The Family Guide
New Revised Edition

Lesley Lababidi

In collaboration with
Dr. Lisa Sabbahy

Contributions by
Jayme Spencer
Kelly Zaug
Janice Hill-Garing

Photographs by
Saadiah Lababidi

Plans by
Mohammed Suwaifey

The American University in Cairo Press
Cairo • New York

To

Our Cairo Kids

Lesley's: Omar, Saadiah, and Zane

Lisa's: Marwa, Sally, and Sherif

and to all the Cairo Kids who take the challenge to know this ancient city

New revised edition 2006

Copyright © 2001, 2003, 2006 by
The American University in Cairo Press
113 Sharia Kasr el Aini, Cairo, Egypt
420 Fifth Avenue, New York, NY 10018
www.aucpress.com

Additional photographs by Neil Hewison, Lesley Lababidi, Lisa Sabbahy
City maps by Lesley Lababidi

Dar el Kutub No. 19334/02
ISBN 977 424 791 4

Designed by AUC Press Design Center

Printed in Egypt

Contents

Maps and Plans

It is our duty to proceed from what is near to what is distant, from what is known to that which is less known, to gather the traditions from those who have reported them, to correct them as much as possible and to leave the rest as it is, in order to make our work help anyone who seeks truth and loves wisdom.

—Abu'l-Rihan Muhammad al-Biruni,
AD 973–1050

Acknowledgments

One of the most satisfying results of writing is meeting new people. Writing does that: it takes you onto paths that would never have been taken and individuals come forth with knowledge, encouragement, and a helping hand. We hope that in this space all the individuals who guided this book's progress in one way or another are remembered. If we have inadvertently left out a well-deserved thank you, forgive us—for although not in print, your help is forever within these pages and in our hearts.

This book would not have been possible without the confidence of Mark Linz, director of AUC Press, who recognized its importance and uniqueness. Our journey began with the introduction to AUC Press editors Pauline Wickham and Neil Hewison, who started to lead us through the maze. A special thanks to Moody M. Youssef and Rehab Farouk for their patience and ingenuity with the layout and design. More thanks to Neil Hewison and Kelly Zaug who edited both first and second editions. And now, we're back with another up-to-date, revised, and absolutely fabulous third edition. Again, Neil's support and encouragement brought the team of Nadia Naqib, Abdalla Hassan, and Aida Nasr who took over the daunting job of editing and ensuring every detail is in its proper place. Not withstanding, the Press staff, all, have been supportive, helpful, and enthusiastic in the production of *The Family Guide*. Thank you.

We are grateful to Mark Linz for contacting Dr. Zaki Hawass, who generously allowed us to view the Coptic Museum before its public opening. Thanks to Yousra, Madame Fatma Mahmoud, and Madame Saly for their time and warm welcome. Thank you to the inspectors at Saqqara and the curatorial staff at the Imhotep Museum for all their help.

Over the past six years, Saadiah Lababidi generously gave of her time to photograph Cairo, and where needed, Neil Hewison and Lisa Sabbahy contributed to the photo gallery. Thank you to Dr. Sherine Mahmoud Ramadan for allowing Saadiah to photograph the aqueduct from her balcony. We are grateful to Mohammed Suwaifey, whose detailed drawings illustrate the text. The drawings of young artists, Kareem and Adham M. Youssef, are sprinkled throughout the book. Thanks to Yara Idriss and Rasha Soliman for their help in checking ticket prices and telephone numbers, and Abeer's fascinating tour through Qasr Amir Taz. Thanks to Hany Amr for the Petrified Forest excursion. The Khan al-Khalili experts include shoppers Jeremy, James, Luke, and Mathhew Spencer and Joseph Viste.

Friends gave extra encouragement, all helping to move this book forward. Ultimately, it is our families we thank for their patience, especially when Mom could not relinquish the computer or fix dinner due to exhaustion. With their support, love, and patience, and with all who joined with us, this book reflects the joy and excitement of stepping out to discover Cairo.

Introduction

"Who needs another guidebook?" was the first of many questions that I mulled over in my mind while designing a book proposal. Arriving in Cairo sixteen years ago, I found that many expatriates who had been in the country for some time had a wealth of travel information about Egypt. Most adults took advantage of the rich history Egypt offered by visiting ancient monuments, sites, and cities; but beyond these visits, exploring Cairo with children remained the responsibility of schools and special interest groups. In New York City or Paris one might take the family to a museum or an art gallery on a Saturday afternoon, but in Cairo few people thought such outings were of interest. My question was, "Why?"

I looked back on my years of raising teenagers in Cairo. We spent many wonderful weekends exploring museums and galleries throughout the city and realized that learning about the many facets of Egyptian culture and history enriched our lives. We came to appreciate James Russell Lowell's words, "The wise man travels to discover himself." I began to expand our family discoveries to a larger circle and attempted to organize bimonthly excursions for youth of different nationalities. My vision was to encourage this group to use their creative tendencies in art, writing, and photography while visiting Cairo's treasures, and eventually to compile a book with their comments. Unfortunately, this premature idea failed to garner interest, and again I wondered "Why?"

Cairo: The Family Guide is an attempt to answer these questions, and to create a starting point for families and young people to begin exploring Cairo. Written to inspire frequent and informal outings, this guidebook will help you begin to appreciate Cairo for its exceptional diversity. The book is designed to be used over time: perhaps one morning while shopping in Dokki with your four-year-old you have an extra hour to slip into the Agricultural Museum; or roam through the Fish Garden and Aquariums in Zamalek. Perhaps on the weekend you find your teenagers with nothing to do—this guidebook has many suggestions on how to spend those hours.

As you flip through its pages you will notice that the book is divided into sections covering the city's major, well-known districts. After a short historical overview of each area, accompanied by a map, the reader is introduced to places of interest with a note on the history and significance of each site and a description of the place and what to do there. At the end of the entry, exact directions, landmarks, opening hours, telephone numbers, and tips are given. The objective of each chapter is to provide knowledge of what is recreationally, culturally, and historically available in every locality. Highlighted facts pertaining to the area or site are sprinkled throughout the text. In the appendix, there is a reading list for children of all ages, additional information about community service, city libraries, Web site and activities directories, and sports facilities for children with special needs.

This book represents the accumulated scholarship of experts in various fields. Dr. Lisa Sabbahy collaborates by bringing her expertise in Egyptology, anthropology, and archaeology to the book, and she has designed self-guided tours with age appropriateness in mind through the Egyptian, Islamic, and Coptic museums, the Citadel, pyramids, and much more. Jayme Spencer, co-author of a guide to Khan al-Khalili, writes about the Khan and places of interest in the surrounding area for the curious kid, no matter what the age! Geologist Janice Garing walks you through Wadi Digla's geological wonderland, and Kelly Zaug has assembled a list of books about Egypt for children and teenagers who want to know more about Egypt.

Those of you who march to a different beat or just don't know where to begin will find suggestions, encouragement, and unlimited opportunities to explore communities outside your own. This guidebook is written for Egyptians and residents who have left tourism to the tourist yet still hear the call to explore their city. It is a book for those who think discovering Cairo is more of an annoyance than a pleasure, for parents who want to take their children on cultural excursions, or for teenagers who would like to see Cairo without their parents.

Cairo is a story of people's experiences, their visions, their glories, and their defeats. As Cairo's personality unfolds with all its inherent and complex characteristics, a familiarity develops and we are reflected and recreated in the times and the cultures. This book emerges from our passion to investigate, to broaden, and to share what we have learned about this city. We hope it will expand your knowledge of Cairo and stimulate a sense of adventure. We invite you to explore the journeys and stories of others and discover your own personal reflection in Cairo.

Lesley Lababidi
2006

How to Explore Cairo

The Basics

Getting better acquainted with our surroundings in this ancient city will be more successful if you begin your journey prepared. Here are a few suggestions to help ensure your excursion is rewarding.

Attitude

The best advice in exploring Cairo—or any other city in the world—is to leave your expectations at home, keep your eyes and mind open, and enjoy the experience as it unfolds. Museums and historical sites are doorways; each person has their unique memory of an experience. Do not try to insist that the children have fun or must learn. A day that promotes curiosity and adventure leads to an excitement at—or at the least an acceptance of—trying another place on another day. Being allowed just to observe the surroundings often simulates the delights of learning and a quest for knowledge. The most important question might be, "What did you notice today?"

Age Appropriateness

An enjoyable afternoon means something entirely different to a six-year-old than to a thirteen-year-old. Throughout the book, we have tried to be sensitive to age groups, those ages most likely to enjoy the site or outing. However, taking into account maturity development, parents need to use their discretion. The objective is not to force a bored child to see everything in a museum, but to introduce the subject matter in increments so that your daughter or son can begin to appreciate their surroundings. There is always another day to return. If boredom and irritability do set in, simply end the

Qalyubiya

CAIRO

Nile

Matariya

Zeitun

al-Qubba

Heliopolis

N

Shubra

Imbaba

Abbasiya

Bulaq

Ramses

Madinet Nasr

Zamalek

Gezira

Ataba

Agouza

Downtown

Opera

Garden
City

Abdin

Khan al-Khalili

Islamic Cairo

Mohandiseen

Dokki

Sayyida Zaynab

Roda

Citadel

Kerdasa

Old Cairo
al-Fustat

City of the
Dead

Giza

Muqattam Hills

Giza
Pyramids

Petrified Forest

Nile

Wadi Digla

Maadi

Harraniya

Saqqara

*The Districts
of Cairo*

visit. Tempers and frustrations flair when a child is forced to see all of the museum or zoo, so go for some ice cream and return another day. Be sure to allow your child to discuss the one positive point of the trip and focus on that interest.

Adolescents and teenagers often display boredom when included in family outings. One suggestion is to let them invite a friend to go along. Let

Camels on University Bridge

teenagers do some of the research on the area you will visit and even be the guide or the official photographer. When all else fails, stop for a snack at one of the many restaurants throughout the city!

Many museums are more appropriate for the older child and teenagers than for a youngster. These museums and restored houses relate to Egypt's national leaders, thinkers, and artists. While not of interest to everyone, these sites introduce a student to the development of this country's independence. They are especially important to visit when studying the history, art, and literature of the Middle East, and are significant when comparing their subjects' accomplishments to what was happening in the rest of the world.

How to Use This Book

Museums and places of interest are divided by the areas of Cairo. A brief overview of each area is in effect an orientation to the historical development of the land and the people who inhabited, conquered, colonized, changed, and expanded Cairo. Maps for each section pinpoint the sites, museums, and points of interest that are discussed. Side panels contain tidbits of information pertaining to the subject matter in each section that add background to further develop an understanding and appreciation of the place, person, or historical time. At the end of each section, the important information that pertains to that particular place is provided, such as how to get there, what to take, hours, prices, and tips to

Egyptian children

make the trip more accessible and enjoyable. The Ministry of Culture and the Supreme Council of Antiquities close museums and historical monuments for renovation without notifying the public so have an alternative plan in mind when setting out.

How to Find Out

The problem in Cairo is not lack of activities and entertainment but knowing when the events happen. How many times have you heard about something that you and your family would have liked to attend but the date has passed? To help solve these annoyances, make it a habit to collect the major monthly magazines such as *Egypt Today* at the *beginning* of each month and scrutinize their listings. *Al-Ahram Weekly* has a weekly update, *Community Times, Community Service Association, Maadi Messenger,* and the *Croc* guide are good sources, and the *Egyptian Gazette.* There are some helpful Web sites, too:
www.egycalendar.com – calendar of conferences held monthly in Egypt.
www.croc.filbalad.com – Arabic/English guide to restaurants and events.
http://groups.yahoo.com/group/wazzup_in_Cairo – people of Cairo inform
    each other of events, workshops, openings, exhibitions, and performances.
http://weekly.ahram.org.eg – good section of weekly event listings.
www.egypttoday.com – monthly listing of events in an online magazine.
www.aucegypt.edu/tools/calendars.html – monthly calendar of events.

Cultural centers and embassies often invite guest artists, scholars, and musicians to perform. There is rarely a calendar of events, so it pays to put your name on their mailing lists. In addition, many centers and galleries have mailing lists, so put your name on all of them! Keep your eyes peeled on bulletin boards and ears open when others tell what they have enjoyed. You will develop sensitivity to what is 'on' in Cairo.

What to Take

The normal list of necessities can be kept in a 'See Cairo' bag. Pre-moistened towels, tissue, toilet paper, sunscreen, and sunglasses are the basics. Add to your bag plenty of bottled water, and small change for tipping. It never hurts to add pencils, colored pencils, and drawing paper for the artist, a simple camera for the photographer, and a journal for those who express themselves in the written word. Everyone should have comfortable walking shoes; leave the sandals at home.

To respect the culture of the country, dress conservatively: elbow-length blouses, knee-length skirts, trousers, and loose-fitting clothing are all appropriate. When dressing discreetly, there is no question in your mind of the suitability of your attire and you will therefore enjoy a comfort level of knowing

*Licorice juice
vendor*

no one will be offended. An added benefit to dressing modestly is that if you and your family find yourself wanting to enter a mosque, no one will have to wait outside.

When entering a mosque, remove your shoes or cover them with the cloth booties provided (a small tip is appropriate). Shorts or short-sleeved clothes for men or women are not acceptable. Mosques are a place of worship and contemplation throughout the day, so please be sensitive to the quiet atmosphere. Do not enter a mosque while prayer is in progress unless you intend to pray.

Traffic

Beware of the street and the cars. One of the most dangerous threats to life and limb in Cairo is being a pedestrian on the streets of the city. Drivers pay little attention to people crossing streets. There are few crosswalks, crossovers, and pedestrian tunnels—when there are, use them, but otherwise be vigilant. It is better to wait than to think someone will stop, only to be sorry.

Photography

Egyptians are among the best-humored people in the world, and their country is probably one of the most photographed. However, if you want to take a photograph of a person, it is necessary to ask permission. At many museums, there is a fee for camera and videos. Do not use your flash inside ancient temples or tombs—it is forbidden, because the bright light damages the ancient colors. If visiting prehistoric caves, *do not* spray water onto paintings. This will destroy them.

Holidays

The Islamic (Hijri) calendar and the Gregorian calendar are both officially followed in Egypt. The Coptic calendar is also in use among the Coptic Christians. The Islamic calendar is lunar, with 12 months of 29 or 30 days, and is 10 or 11 days shorter than the Gregorian calendar. The Coptic calendar is a solar calendar with 30 days in a month and five days in the thirteenth month.

In observing Islamic holidays, the dates follow the Islamic calendar, so each year they fall 10–12 days earlier than the year before. Often the precise date of the holiday is not announced until the sighting of the moon the night before.

Islamic Holidays

- Islamic New Year.
- Birthday of the Prophet Muhammad.
- Eid al-Fitr: three-day feast held at the end of Ramadan.
- Eid al-Adha: four-day feast held seventy days after Ramadan, and celebrating the prophet Abraham's obedience to God. God told Abraham to sacrifice his son, and when Abraham obeyed, his son was replaced by a sheep. The pilgrimage to Mecca takes place at this time.

The Month of Ramadan

Ramadan is the ninth month of the Islamic calendar and is the holiest month, commemorating the revelation of the Quran to the Prophet Muhammad through the Archangel Gabriel. Pious Muslims fast from sunrise to sunset, with no food, drink, sex, cigarettes, or impatience. Although Muslims are more tolerant here than in many other countries, it is impolite to eat or drink in public areas, in a Muslim home, or in front of a fasting Muslim. Some restaurants remain open, and they are the appropriate places to eat in public during the day. Keep in mind, also, that the hours of every establishment, shop, and government office are affected by the change of schedule in Ramadan. People stay up late at night and opening hours are later and shorter for museums and galleries. This is the time of year that musical events celebrate Ramadan nights. The venues are fabulous historical monuments or gardens, and admission is free.

Coptic Holidays

- Christmas: 7 January.
- Easter: timing varies—it may fall on the same day as Western Easter or any time from one to five weeks after it.

Egyptian Holidays
- Shamm al-Nasim (smelling the breeze), a pharaonic holiday, the first Monday after Coptic Easter.
- Sinai Liberation Day: 25 April.
- Revolution Day: 23 July.
- Armed Forces Day: 6 October.

Sweet pastries for sale: basbusa and kunafa

Visiting Monuments and Places of Interest

It is best to check on opening times before starting out. Thursdays and Fridays are now the official weekend days, so many of the smaller museums are closed, but this is not necessarily the rule. Some are closed on Sundays and others are closed on Mondays, so check at the end of each entry.

If you are going to the Saqqara or Giza pyramids it is advisable to take a photocopy of your passport. At some monuments, there is a special price for residents and students, so take proof of your status and it might save you money. The Ministry of Culture announced in November 2000 that entry to historic mosques would henceforth be free of charge to all except groups arriving on organized tours. However expect to tip the shoe custodian. Although entrance fees are correct at the time of updating the information, prices may be increased.

Keep in mind that exhibits can change and sites or parts of them can be closed. Do not lean on walls or touch ancient painted walls for any reason. If everyone did this there would be no ancient Egyptian paintings left.

Egyptian schools provide field trips for their students throughout the school year. Some museums are more popular for school visits than others, but if you do not like crowds, it is a good idea to go on school holidays. Sometimes schoolchildren are curious about the origins of other visitors in the museum and they enjoy practicing their newly acquired language skills, so be prepared for some well-meaning greetings and questions in your language. However, sometimes this attention bothers younger children.

Parking is a tremendous problem. The perimeter around hotels and monuments are closed to traffic and parking. At the end of each entry we address the best means of transportation and if there is parking availability.

Street Food
Many people will tell you that if you are new to Cairo or have a delicate stomach, it is not a good idea to eat from street vendors, with the exception of sweet potatoes, which are baked to perfection in a wood burning stove.

Juice stands have seasonal juices available. Fresh mango, guava, orange, and carrots make refreshing drinks during a trip through the hot and dusty Cairo streets. If you are worried about the cleanliness of the glasses, pack your own plastic cups.

Summer in Cairo
Being a tourist during the summer months is not an easy job. More difficult is trying to interest children in the sights of Cairo when they are worn out from the heat. If you want to visit a museum, a few, like the Mr. and Mrs. Muhammad Mahmoud Khalil Museum, Abdin Palace, and Modern Art Museum are air-conditioned—otherwise visit the site as soon as it opens. Take plenty of water and plan to rest in a cool spot. For the Pyramids, early morning trips are necessary; otherwise, sightseeing may be unappealing to you or your children if the only memory is heat and exhaustion. A late-afternoon felucca ride is a remedy for calming nerves and offers time away from all the technical wonders of today's world.

While many Cairenes search for relief from the summer's heat on Egyptian beaches, the cooling evening breeze fans music over the ancient Citadel walls and wafts across the Opera House grounds for those who remain in Cairo. Staggered throughout June, July, and August, performances by local and international musicians at the Summer Music Festival enhance the summer months with shows from folk to classical music. The Opera House hosts a festival for dance and theater in June, as well as music and exhibitions along the banks of the Nile. In mid-August, the Ismailia Music Festival, which features dance troupes from around the world, extends performances to the Cairo

Feluccas in Garden City

Opera House. This is an opportunity to sample music and dance from nations you may never visit.

We, the public, are fortunate to have the pleasure of watching performances in ancient monuments and public gardens. It is to the credit of ministries to integrate communities with historical sites by way of music and art. So take advantage of the summer events. In September the Experimental Theater Festival opens with local and international productions. The unique experience of attending a performance from Belarus or Burkina Faso, for example, is a reason to participate. The entrance fees are nominal, but the most daunting problem that may arise is finding out when all this takes place: you need to be a detective. Keep your eye open for newspaper announcements, study the 'what's on' section in magazines, visit the ticket office at the Opera House.

For a lasting memory of Cairo summers, buy a necklace of *full* flowers at a busy roundabout or intersection. In the twilight hours, an old man or a child will run up to your car and extend the chain of sweet, fragrant, pearly blossoms through the window. Three strands cost one Egyptian pound (the best bargain in town). Put them around your child's neck and yours too!

What's New in the Third Edition?

The third edition of *Cairo: The Family Guide* has been produced with tender loving care. Hundreds of hours go into visiting areas—museums, houses, galleries, and centers—mapping out routes, watching for changes, crosschecking facts and information, and proofreading and organizing the data. As of May

2006, all information is up-to-date. The telephone numbers have been checked twice. We have new photographs to go along with twenty-three significant additions, and we have excluded anything that has closed. Unfortunately, renovation at Taha Hussein's House and the Islamic Museum are not complete as this edition goes to print, so we are unable to provide you with updated tours; however, this is something to look forward to in the fourth edition!

In the first edition of *The Family Guide* few museums, galleries, or even individuals had their own Web site. Today, it seems that everyone does. Like telephone numbers, we have included Web site addresses at the end of each entry whenever available. Furthermore, there is a Web directory of all the sites and a few extra ones in the index. "ACTIVE in Cairo" is new in this edition. The listings provide information for art, music, dance, and language lessons.

Picks for 2006 is another new feature. This edition gives you a fresh perspective of Cairo's offerings. Some of the places we were enthusiastic about in prior editions have changed. So the idea came about, "Why not highlight this year's favorites?" The following not only allows you a preview of what you will find in this book but also it highlights places off the beaten track, which you might think about including in your next excursion.

Picks for 2006

Lesley Lababidi: I love the Post Office Museum; it is like finding money in your pocket—a very pleasant surprise. The Museum is a treasure of postal memorabilia, which is immense and well organized. You will journey through the world of communication from ancient Egyptian times to the mid-1950; not to be missed is the commemorative stamp office.

The Modern Art Museum at the Opera House and the Mahmoud Mukhtar Museum complement each other. Both revolve around visionary aspects of art through themes of individualism, enlightenment, nationalism, and rich heritage of the Egyptian civilization. The Modern Art Museum houses over 12,000 pieces of contemporary works of art in a serene yet enormous space, representing the depth and breadth of the artistic movement in Egypt from 1900 to the present. Like looking through a magnifying glass, a visit to the Mahmoud Mukhtar Museum amplifies these themes. Mahmoud Mukhtar was a pioneer and visionary; his works embody this independent nature that began with the revival of sculpture in Egypt. Much of his work is dedicated to deepening national awareness in an era that ignited Egyptian national identity.

Last but not least is the newly renovated Qasr (Palace) Amir Taz, built in AD 1352. Just seeing the magnificent *ma'qad* begins a time-warp experience.

The peeling back of old masonry to reveal frescos and woodwork traces the changes from Bahri Mamluk to Ottoman periods. A surprise discovery of the only surviving waterwheel from the Bahri period, its aqueducts and cisterns indicates a sophisticated system of water use.

Lisa Sabbahy: I enjoyed the relaxed and friendly atmosphere of the new Fustat Handicrafts Center (across from the Fustat Ceramic Center), and was most impressed by the new *Paralititan stromeri* display at the Geology Museum, as well as their new labels throughout the Vertebrate Gallery. The new Imhotep Museum at Saqqara is a gem. It exhibits masterpieces from pharaonic Egypt that have been in storage until now. The first on-site museum in the Cairo vicinity, its objects and themes revolve around the relics and archaeological materials just from Saqqara. The presentation is effective and beautiful.

Jayme Spencer: Whenever visitors come to town, I immediately plan an outing to al-Azhar Park for sunset. This has become one of my favorite things to do. Even on a not-so-good day, the park is green, spacious, clean, and affords a spectacular view. With this overview of the area (sometimes even the Pyramids are visible), friends have a better understanding of the layout of the city.

Kelly Zaug: My number one favorite is still *The Day of Ahmed's Secret* by Heide and Gilliland. It's just such a good, sweet story and the illustrations by Ted Lewin capture the light and hustle-bustle of Cairo so well.

The second is a new picture book, *Goha, the Wise Fool* by Denys Johnson-Davies. The Goha stories the author collected are very funny and truthful, and the artwork is fabulous. Every story is illustrated by an image of Goha done by a family of tentmakers in al-Khayamia Street. It's a real cultural treat. In fact, the original pieces by Hagg Hamdy and his son Hany are currently on display in a gallery in New York City.

Central Cairo

Central Cairo broadly encompasses the downtown area, with the Nile to the west, Midan Ramses to the north, Sayyida Zaynab to the south, and Khan al-Khalili and the Citadel to the east. It's an area infused with history. When the Arabs first came to Egypt in AD 640, they settled in a place that they called Fustat, just north of the area now known as Old Cairo. The succeeding Abassid and Tulunid dynasties, each built themselves a city, moving progressively farther to the northeast to catch the prevailing breeze. Finally, the Fatimid Caliph al-Mu'izz ordered the building of his princely city, and in AD 969 al-Qahira—'the Victorious'—was founded. It is from this fourth and final ruling city, built around the area now called Khan al-Khalili, that modern Cairo gets its name.

In the late twelfth century the great Ayyubid ruler Saladin built the Citadel and rebuilt the walls of the Fatimid city. It was not until the middle of the nineteenth century, however, that the city really spread west from al-Qahira and the Citadel, as the swampy area next to the river was filled in and settled. During the late 1860s, Khedive Ismail initiated a momentous expansion as he planned and built a Europeanized downtown.

One thousand years ago, the Fatimid walls of al-Qahira were perceived as impenetrable by those who lived outside of them. Today, many Cairenes and expatriates find central Cairo equally impenetrable, since crowds, 'no parking' signs, and traffic build their own wall. Fortunately, there are solutions. Recently, the Metro has expanded, pedestrian areas are being developed, and taxi service is always available.

No matter how you get to central Cairo, it will be well worth your effort. From the mighty Egyptian and Islamic Museums to small and obscure

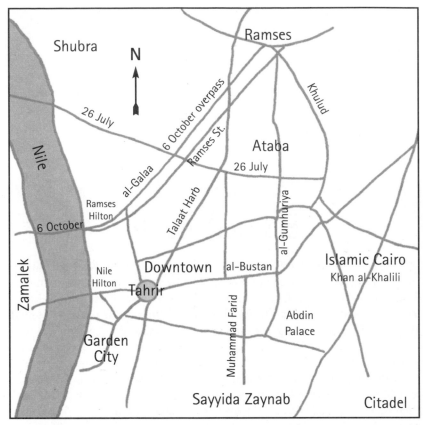

Central Cairo

museums tucked away from the energetic city, from modern art galleries nestled in quiet side-streets to royal palaces and antiquities, from shopping in the souks to fashionable boutiques, central Cairo provides endless excursions for family entertainment and education. Try an initial visit and you will return many times looking for another gallery or a hidden museum.

If your family likes quiet and peaceful weekends or wants to escape to wide-open spaces during vacations, an outing to central Cairo may seem overwhelming to begin with. Nevertheless, you will often discover that behind an ancient wall tranquility and beauty are stumbled upon away from the bustling streets. Some of the most refreshing moments can be spent sitting cross-legged in the calm of an ancient interior while outside the whirling street life never ends. Whether you are interested in Islamic history, traditional crafts, collections of ancient and modern art, or sipping stong tea at a traditional café, many family adventures can be spent visiting this area and still you will see only a fraction.

Downtown Cairo

Imagine standing in Midan al-Tahrir one hundred and fifty years ago. What would you see? If it were the end of July, you would probably be in a boat during the annual inundation of the great Nile. It was not until after 1863, when the French-educated Khedive Ismail came to power, that the swampy plains were turned into a complex of modern buildings and boulevards, echoing the architectural style of Paris. Ali Pasha Mubarak, Ismail's Minister of Public Works, was entrusted with the planning and building of this new district, to

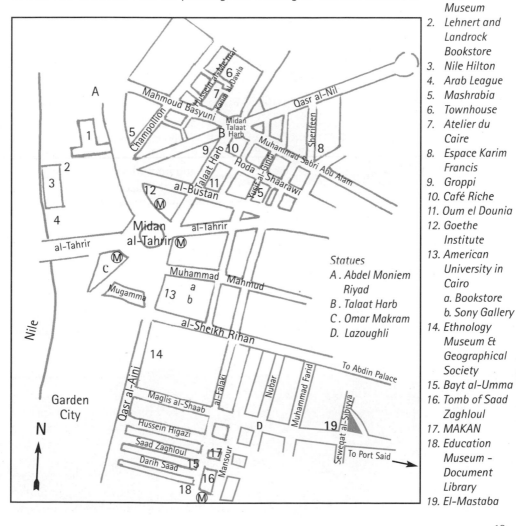

Statues

A . Abdel Moniem Riyad
B . Talaat Harb
C . Omar Makram
D . Lazoughli

Muhammad Farid Street

be known as Ismailiya. Cairo was to have a series of large *midans*, or squares, connected by boulevards radiating out from them like spokes from a wheel. This layout was difficult to superimpose on the crowded, eastern section of Cairo, but is clearly recognized in the downtown area. Downtown Cairo then became an elegant area for smart Cairenes and foreigners, and a residential area for the wealthy.

The grand square, Tahrir ('Liberation'), was formerly known as Midan Ismailiya. When Gamal Abd al-Nasser became president, the government renamed many streets and squares. Midan al-Tahrir is the hub from which to begin exploring central Cairo. As you stand facing the Nile, you will easily note the enormous structure on your left, the Mugamma, a daunting gray building of government offices. To your right, the russet-colored Egyptian Museum with the treasures of the pharaohs awaits you. Turn 180 degrees and you will see, just past the well-groomed roundabout, Talaat Harb St., the main street of entry to the downtown area.

Downtown Cairo

The Egyptian Museum

The Egyptian Museum

The Egyptian Museum, with over 120,000 pieces, houses the largest collection of ancient Egyptian art in the world. For the most part the collection is made up of items from tombs, the most famous, of course, being the treasures from the tomb of Tutankhamun. The museum building itself dates from 1902. In December 2002, a gala celebration was held for the centennial of the Egyptian Museum. The original Egyptian Museum, located in Bulaq, was founded in 1863 by Auguste Mariette, the Frenchman who a few years earlier had become the first director of the Egyptian Antiquities Service. Mariette died in Bulaq in 1881, and his remains were moved to the Cairo Museum in 1902. His sarcophagus and statue can be seen on the west side of the museum's garden.

The museum is huge, so it is best to plan beforehand which exhibits or areas you wish to visit. Two hours are probably as much as most people can absorb. Below are three itineraries, one appropriate for older children or young adults, one good for a family of all ages, and one especially designed for very young children.

Where: Midan al-Tahrir.
Metro stop: Sadat Station.
When: 9am–7pm daily, including Friday and holidays.
Ramadan Hours: 9am–3pm.
Entrance fees: Foreigners: LE40, students LE20; Egyptians and citizens of Arab countries: LE2, students LE1. Special entrance fee for the Mummy Room (purchase ticket inside the museum at the Mummy Room): Foreigners: LE70, students LE35; Egyptians: LE5, students LE2.
Telephone: 578-2852 for information.
Photography: No cameras, video, flash, or laser beams.

Facilities: Bathrooms are on the second floor, both east and west sides. The cafeteria is located outside, entered from the garden, as are small shops selling books, slides, postcards, and jewelry. There are two gift shops immediately inside the entrance of the museum. There is a Lehnert and Landrock Bookstore opposite the museum gates. Be prepared to lift strollers or wheelchairs, as there are many stairs to negotiate.

Parking: There is no parking. It is best to take a taxi or park in Omar Makrum garage, right off Tahrir Square.

Web sites: *www.egyptianmuseum.gov.eg*
AmarnaProject:
www.mcdonald.cam.ac.uk/Projects/Amarna/home.htm
Database for collections including prehistoric Egypt to the present:
www.globalegyptianmuseum.com – Global Egypt Museum (GEM) database of worldwide museum collections of objects from prehistoric to present in Egypt, includes activities for kids. In eight languages.
http://www.bibalex.org/English/researchers/cultnat.htm and *http://www.cultnat.org* – CULTNAT from Bibliotheca Alexandrina and Ministry of Communication and Information Technology, Center for Documentation of Cultural and Natural Heritage.

Activities: The Supreme Council of Antiquities (SCA) started an initiative to raise public awareness particularly with children. The approach aims to heighten their interest in their culture and history to strengthen their love of Egypt and respect for their heritage. Call SCA, 3 al-Adel Abu Bakr St., Zamalek (Headquarters), Tel. and Fax: 735-8749 to inquire about programs.
Web site: *www.eternalegypt.org*
Archaeological cultural season: Lectures

about Egyptology, Greek and Roman archaeology, Islamic and Coptic archaeology.
Cultural Seminars to raise awareness of challenges serving cultural heritage.
Documentary Films, weekly
Archaeological Education for adults in the Egyptian Museum School
Higher Antiquities School
Museum Friends Associations Festivals and Conferences
Mobile Exhibitions for Monuments
Cultural Development Program for children and children with special needs
Museum schools for children
Young Golden Pharaoh Festival

In the Future: Scheduled to open in 2009, the Grand Museum of Egypt, a complex of 38,000 square meters and to cost over $550 million, is a vision of precise geometric design to pay homage to human genius of the ancient Egyptians. The site is set between the Giza Pyramids and the fertile Nile Valley. It will house over 150,000 ancient Egyptian artifacts and be the home of the treasures of Tutankhamen and the colossal statue of Ramesses II (now standing at Bab al-Hadid, in front of the railway station). The building design was chosen in an international competition that attracted over 1,500 entries. The Irish firm Heneghan Ping Architect was selected for their unique approach to connect modern and ancient times and their precise use of geometry as used by ancient Egyptian architects. Dr. Mohamed Saleh, at the 2005 International Council of Museums Conference, explained that a line drawn from one edge of the roof of the Grand Museum would touch the tip of the pyramid Cheops. The building will be covered in translucent alabaster that will glow at night. For more information go

to: *www.gem.gov.eg.*
The Egyptian Museum will remain in use to house art works of pharaonic civilization.

Pharaonic History

The three main periods of ancient Egyptian history are referred to as Kingdoms. These were times when Upper and Lower Egypt were united under one ruler. The Intermediate Periods that come between them were times of instability and political disunity. Rulers are divided into dynasties, which for the most part indicate a family bloodline. Pharaonic history began with the First Dynasty in about 3100 BC, and ended with the coming of Alexander the Great in 332 BC.

Early Dynastic Period (Dynasties 1–2)
Old Kingdom (Dynasties 3–6)
First Intermediate Period (Dynasties 7–11)
Middle Kingdom (Dynasty 12)
Second Intermediate Period (Dynasties 13–17)
New Kingdom (Dynasties 18–20)
Third Intermediate Period (Dynasties 21–25)
Late Period (Dynasties 26–31)

The Ptolemies, who were Macedonian Greeks, ruled Egypt after the death of Alexander the Great until the death of Cleopatra VII (the famous Cleopatra), when Octavian, the nephew of Julius Caesar, who then ruled as the emperor Augustus, took Egypt as a Roman province.

Itinerary One
Famous Exhibits from the Old to the New Kingdoms
(for older children or teens)
The rooms on the ground floor of the museum are arranged chronologically and clockwise. Directly inside the front door are pieces from the Predynastic and Early Dynastic Periods. Turn left inside the main door and begin with the seated statue of King Djoser, the Third Dynasty king who built the Step Pyramid Complex at Saqqara. As you continue along this corridor, you will walk among pieces from tombs of the Old Kingdom, as well as some royal statuary from pyramid complexes. Turning right at the end, you continue through the Old Kingdom (also in rooms off the corridor), the Middle Kingdom, and by the end of the corridor, the New Kingdom. Turn right again and continue about halfway down to the newly restored statues of the deities Amun and Mut from the temple of Karnak in Luxor, and the Amarna room is on your left. This contains pieces from the city of Tell al-Amarna in Middle Egypt, built by the

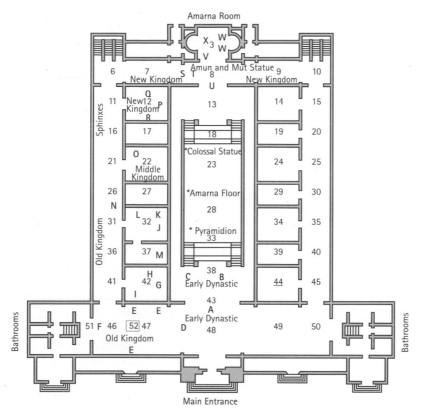

Amarna Room

X 3 W W

V

Amun and Mut Statue

6 7 S 8 9 10
New Kingdom New Kingdom
U

Q
11 New 12 P 13 14 15
Kingdom
R

Sphinxes

16 17 18 19 20

O
21 22 *Colossal Statue 24 25
Middle 23
Kingdom

26 27 *Amarna Floor 29 30
N 28

31 L 32 K * Pyramidion 34 35
J 33

Old Kingdom

36 37 M 39 40

38
H
41 42 G C B 44 45
I Early Dynastic

E E 43
A
Early Dynastic
51 F 46 52 47 D 48 49 50
Old Kingdom
E

Bathrooms   Bathrooms

Main Entrance

Egyptian Museum, Lower Floor

pharaoh Akhenaten in the latter part of the Eighteenth Dynasty. After touring this room, this is a good time to stop: you have toured a major portion of the museum's pieces, and covered a good chunk of pharaonic history.

Walk straight ahead back to the main door through the huge atrium in the middle of the museum, which houses pieces too large for other parts of the building. These pieces are marked on the museum lower-floor plan and are described at the end of Itinerary Three. On your way out you might take a look in Room 44, the first downstairs room on the east side. It is used for temporary exhibits that are changed fairly frequently. You never know what you might find!

If you still have the energy, however, you might go upstairs to the Treasures of Tanis Jewelry Room (room 2), just next to the largest Tutankhamun shrine (see museum upper-floor plan). Six royal tombs of the Twenty-first and Twenty-second dynasties were located inside the enclosure walls of the temple of Amun at Tanis in the northeastern Delta. Tomb III, of King Psusennes of the Twenty-first Dynasty, was discovered intact in 1939. A beautiful gold mummy mask and 140 pieces of jewelry were found. The antechamber of the tomb was reused in the Twenty-second Dynasty for the burial of King Shesonq II in a silver, falcon-headed coffin, along with a magnificent collection of gold and silver vessels.

A: The palette of King Narmer was traditionally regarded as pictorial evidence of the forceful unification of Upper and Lower Egypt and the beginning of pharaonic history with the First Dynasty. It is now accepted that Narmer ruled Egypt in the Predynastic period before the First Dynasty, and what is shown on the palette commemorates the king victorious, but is not related to the unification of Egypt.

B: Looking toward the Atrium, on the right far side of this case are small, square, bone labels inscribed with the earliest ancient Egyptian hieroglyphs yet known. They were found in early royal tombs at Abydos, dating from about 3300 BC–3100 BC, the period right before the First Dynasty. The labels name or number the object to which they were attached. Also in the case are slightly later, and larger, ivory labels. They often give the king's name as well as mentioning an important event.

C: Game boards and game pieces can be seen in this case. In the left corner is a game board in the shape of a coiled snake; the ancient Egyptians called this game "Mehen." The ivory lion game pieces in the middle of the case belonged to this game. Although the rules of this game are not clear to us, the red and white marbles in the case were thrown, and the lions moved along the coils of the snake accordingly.

The Ka

The Ka was the closest thing in ancient Egypt to what we would consider the 'soul.' The ka was born with you, and was your double. After death, the ka resided in the tomb with the corpse, and needed to be fed and taken care of. Almost all the statues you see from tombs in the Old Kingdom section of the museum are ka statues placed in the tomb for the ka to inhabit. In most private tombs, the ka statue was placed in a small room behind the false door of the tomb, where the daily offerings would be put. Sometimes the workers cut the stones, leaving a small hole or slit through which the ká statue could see, smell, and hear.

D: This seated statue of King Djoser was found in a small, enclosed room, called a serdab, in the funerary temple of his Step Pyramid Complex at Saqqara. The statue was meant for his soul, or *ka*, to inhabit, and see, hear, and smell the offerings and rituals for his afterlife. The inlaid eyes were made of semiprecious materials, but were chiseled out by robbers.

E: There are three separate triads of King Menkaure, the builder of the Third

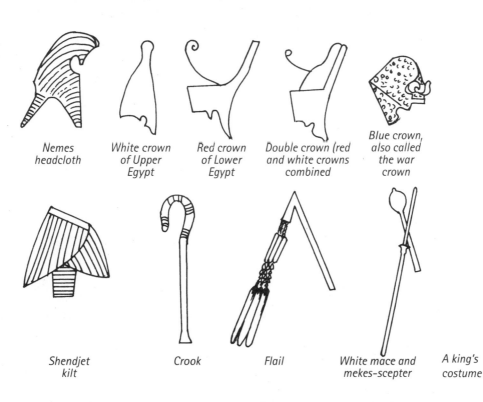

Nemes
headcloth

White crown
of Upper
Egypt

Red crown
of Lower
Egypt

Double crown (red
and white crowns
combined

Blue crown,
also called
the war
crown

Shendjet
kilt

Crook

Flail

White mace and
mekes-scepter

A king's
costume

Pyramid at Giza, with the goddess Hathor (wearing horns and disc) and a woman representing a district in Upper Egypt (wearing emblem on a pole). Typical of males in Egyptian art, the king strides forward (with the left foot), while females stand with feet together. Since the goddess was more than an ordinary woman, her feet get to take a tiny step! The king wears the tall, conical white crown of Upper Egypt, the royal beard, and the royal kilt.

In case 52, in the middle of the corridor between these triads, are limestone statuettes of servants producing food. These were placed in the tomb to provide for the deceased. The two most common forms of statuette grind wheat for bread, and strain beer mash into large jars. Bread and beer were the staples of the ancient Egyptian diet.

F: In the last case at the end of the corridor where you turn right, is a limestone statuette of a dwarf named Khnumhotep. He was an overseer of linen. He is shown as an older man, with short gray hair and a long kilt. In the same case is a wooden figurine with a humpback, perhaps representing a person suffering from Pott's disease or tuberculosis of the spine.

G: This statue depicts King Khafre, the builder of the Second Pyramid at

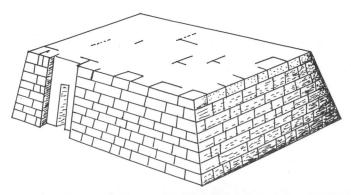

Mastaba (after Arnold, 1994)

Giza, with the falcon god Horus on his shoulders. The wings of the falcon blend into the stripes of the king's linen headdress. Notice the uraeus, or coiled cobra, on the king's forehead protecting him. The king wears the royal beard, which is tied on. Look at the straps on his cheeks. Also notice the rolled-up handkerchief that he has in his hand: this was a sign of his status. The lily of Upper Egypt and the papyrus of Lower Egypt are entwined on the side of the king's throne. This design symbolizes that the two halves of Egypt are unified under the rule of the king.

H: This is a standing wooden statue of a nobleman named Ka-aper, which was found in his mastaba tomb at Saqqara. He is shown as an older man, with little hair, overweight, and wearing a long kilt that covers his legs. When the statue was discovered in 1860 it was dubbed Sheikh al-Balad (meaning 'village headman') because to the workers who found it, it looked like the headman of their village.

I: This seated statue from Saqqara shows a scribe writing on a papyrus roll, with his stretched-out kilt as a writing surface. He would have had a reed pen in his right hand. Notice the materials used for his inlaid eyes: copper (which has turned green), quartz, and rock crystal.

J: This seated couple are Rahotep, a son of King Sneferu, and his wife Nofret, from their mastaba tomb at Meidoum. The colors have not been restored: all the paint is original. Examine Nofret's skin; it is light-colored, while Rahotep's is dark. This is another convention of ancient Egyptian art: the man is portrayed darker, as he would be active outside in the sun, while the woman would be mostly indoors and not be suntanned. Notice Nofret's real hairline under her wig. The Egyptians usually had short natural hair and wore a wig over it, but they did not try to pretend the wig was their own hair!

K: Limestone statue of a man named Seneb and his wife and children found in the mastaba tomb at Giza. You will notice that Seneb was a dwarf, and the children below him fill in the empty space where his legs should be. Notice

Osiris

In Egyptian mythology, Osiris once ruled as king of Egypt. He was murdered by his evil brother Seth, and afterward came alive again in the underworld, and ruled as king. Following this pattern of death and rebirth, every dead king became Osiris when he died. Since Osiris came alive again in the underworld, his cult is tied to fertility. He is shown with black skin, representing dark, fertile soil, which brings forth new life, or green skin, representing green growth or sprouts.

the artistic conventions for portraying children: they are nude, and hold a finger to their mouth. Boys have their hair pulled to one side of the head.

L: This painting of the so-called Meidoum geese was once part of a large decorated mastaba-tomb wall at Meidoum, and the geese formed a decorative band below a scene of hunting in the marshes. The colors for this painting were made from powdered minerals, and they were mixed with egg white so that they would adhere to the wall.

M: This side-room contains the remains from the tomb of Queen Hetepheres, the mother of King Khufu (who built the Great Pyramid at Giza). She was originally buried at Dahshur, but her tomb was robbed in ancient times, and what was left moved to a shaft tomb by the Great Pyramid. Against the back wall is a case containing a tiny ivory statuette of King Khufu, which was found in Abydos in 1903. This is the only known representation of this king!

This is a good place to have a seat and rest.

N: Seated statue of King Nebhepetre Mentuhotep, the king who fought and reunified Egypt at the beginning of the Middle Kingdom. He is shown with black skin because he is deceased and has become Osiris, the god of the dead, who is always depicted with black or dark green skin. The king wears the red crown of Lower Egypt.

O: In the center of the Middle Kingdom room is the burial chamber of the treasury official Harhotep, which was found at Deir al-Bahri on the West Bank of Luxor. The horizontal bands of inscription painted on the walls are religious formulae, and all the objects the deceased might need are depicted in another horizontal band. The smaller vertical lines of writing are Coffin Texts, which give magical protection and help the dead reach the afterlife.

Looking over to the left side of the room you will see two 'block' statues, one limestone and one dark granite. In a block statue the body is shown as a cube, with only the head, arms, and legs depicted. Block statues were also popular in the New Kingdom, and you will see another one in the next room.

Placed all around the burial chamber are ten virtually identical, limestone, seated statues of King Senusret I. They were found buried near the king's pyramid temple at Lisht, and originally must have been set up within the temple.

Ahead on your left in the corridor are gray granite sphinx statues of Amenemhet III of the Twelfth Dynasty. It was common in ancient Egyptian art to portray the king as a powerful, crouching lion. These sphinxes are our favorites, as they have a mane instead of the king's head cloth, and look like the lions in the Wizard of Oz. The ancient Egyptians liked them also, as four later kings 'borrowed' them by re-carving the inscriptions with their names.

P: In the center back of this room of New Kingdom monuments is a small chapel to the cow goddess Hathor that was found next to Queen Hatshepsut's Deir al-Bahari temple in 1906. An earthquake had covered it up in ancient times. The cow goddess is protecting Tuthmose III by embracing him from behind; if you look on the sides of the cow, the goddess is suckling him as well.

Q: These blocks of stone with decoration in carved relief come from the funerary temple of Queen Hatshepsut on the West Bank of Luxor. They were part of a large wall scene showing the arrival of her soldiers in the land of Punt (on the coast of Ethiopia or Somalia) to trade for incense and myrrh. On the right, notice the very overweight Queen of Punt standing behind her husband. Can you tell from studying the King of Punt that he is not an Egyptian? To the left is a man with a stick driving the queen's donkey, which has a padded saddle. Above the donkey the hieroglyphs say: "The donkey that carries his wife."

R: This block statue found at Karnak Temple depicts the official Senmut holding Queen Hatshepsut's daughter, Princess Neferure, whose tutor he was. The statue has been reduced to a square block formed from Senmut's cloak, from which only their two heads protrude. The hair of the princess is braided to one side, and she has a uraeus on her forehead to indicate her royal position. The surface of the block forms a flat surface for Senmut's inscriptions.

S: This case of Amarna pieces has a head and three statuettes of King Akhenaten's daughters. They were found in a sculptor's workshop in Tell al-Amarna. The elongated shape of their heads may represent youth, in the sense of just having been born. Their heads might also be egg-shaped, because in ancient Egyptian mythology the egg symbolized creation and birth. Also notice that the royal females are shown with dark skin. Perhaps since they spent their time worshipping the Aten in unroofed sun temples, they had great tans! In the corner of the case is an unfinished statuette of the king sitting with a daughter on his lap, kissing her.

The Amarna Period

The Amarna Period is the name given to the reign of King Akhenaten in the latter part of the Eighteenth Dynasty, roughly 1358–1340 BC. This king closed the cult temples of the traditional deities and moved the royal residence to the site now known as Tell al-Amarna in Middle Egypt. He was devoted to the cult of the Aten, the disk of the sun. Scholars now suggest that this deity was simply his deified father Amenhotep III. The most striking aspect of the Amarna Period is perhaps its art style, with the royal family depicted with long, thin faces, sagging stomachs, and fat thighs.

T: In the front center of the case is a square, limestone stela of King Akhenaten and his family. It was found in a chapel in a villa at Tell al-Amarna. Note the relaxed manner in which the king and his wife sit, playing with their daughters. In the middle shines the Aten sun disc, its rays coming down and ending in hands, which protect the royal family and feed them ankh symbols of eternal life. The king hands his oldest daughter an earring, whose design parallels the disc and rays of the Aten above.

U: Stop and take a look at this model of a typical nobleman's villa. Many such villas were excavated in the Southern Suburb of the city of Tell al-Amarna.

V: On your left as you enter the Amarna Room is a case with small, rectangular clay objects that you might normally overlook. These are letters that were sent to the king of Egypt from other rulers of the ancient Near East. They were discovered in the Records Office at Tell al-Amarna. The letters are in a language called Akkadian, the language of ancient Mesopotamia, which was used for international correspondence. Akkadian is written with symbols known as cuneiform, made by pressing a sharp pen into a wet clay tablet. The tablet was then baked, and becomes virtually indestructible.

W: On the two sides of the alcove on your right stand colossal statues of King Akhenaten which were discovered in the ruins of an enormous, open sun temple he built outside the back gate of Karnak Temple in Luxor. He built several such temples at Luxor before he moved to his new city at Tell al-Amarna in the fifth year of his reign. Note how the king is portrayed with a long, horsy face, and fat abdomen and thighs.

X: This is the famous Cairo Museum head of Nefertiti. It was found in a sculptor's workshop at Tell al-Amarna. It is sculpted out of brown quartzite, and the details of her face have been added in ink. The head was either left unfinished, or else it was simply a trial piece.

The Aten

Mummification

A ncient Egyptians wanted to live again after death, so they needed their bodies preserved and recognizable. To stop decay, the brain was removed immediately, but not preserved. The liver, intestines, stomach, and lungs were also removed and were mummified separately and placed in four 'canopic' jars. The heart was left in the body as it was considered the essence of intellect, feelings, and soul. The body was then heaped with natron (basically baking soda) for forty days, which removed all the moisture and fat. Afterward, the body was washed, carefully wrapped in linen, placed in a sarcophagus, and put in the burial chamber of the tomb.

Itinerary Two
The Treasures of Tutankhamun and the Royal Mummy Room
(all ages family visit)

King Tutankhamun ruled Egypt in the Eighteenth Dynasty. He took the throne at the age of eight, about 1330 BC, and ruled for ten years. Scholars still have no idea what caused his early death. Not originally meant for King Tutankhamun, the tomb in the Valley of the Kings in Luxor was hurriedly readied when he died, and stuffed with all the objects he owned in his life, as well as those he would need in the afterlife. The British archaeologist Howard Carter discovered the tomb in 1922. Although the king's actual burial was intact, other parts of the tomb had been robbed twice in ancient times.

Most of the mummies in the Royal Mummy Room are the bodies of pharaohs of the New Kingdom, which were found reburied in two caches—hiding places—on the West Bank of Luxor. About 1000 BC, priests of Karnak Temple collected the mummies from their plundered tombs in the Valley of the Kings. The priests rewrapped and then buried the mummies again in these two caches for safekeeping. Altogether, more than fifty mummies were saved in this way, and eleven of them are now on display in the mummy room. The mummies are arranged in chronological order as you walk around the room. The first mummy is King Seqenenre Ta'o of the Seventeenth Dynasty, who died during a battle with the Hyksos, who had invaded the Egyptian Delta. At the end in the middle of the room are two mummies of queens dating to the Twenty-first Dynasty.

The mummies in this room, unwrapped to show their heads and hands, might be frightening to some children. If you are unsure, it might be wise to gauge their reaction by proceeding first to the still-wrapped mummies in Itinerary Three, and then decide if a visit to the mummy room is appropriate.

A: Start by standing in the middle of the Tutankhamun chariots, which puts you out of the flow of foot traffic—all the groups tour the Tutankhamun

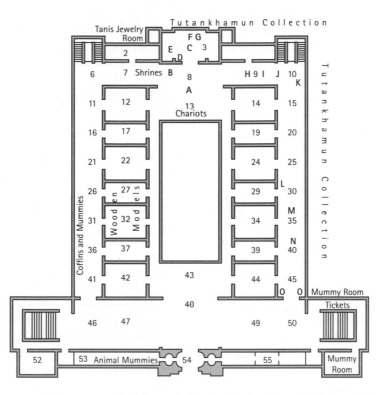

Egyptian Museum, Upper Floor

treasures, so it gets crowded! Four of the six chariots found in the tomb have been restored and are displayed here with their equipment. The chariots with decorated, gilded sides are assumed to have been for ceremonial purposes, while the plainer, more practical chariots were used for hunting. From here you can either just look at or walk along the shrines.

   B: These four gold-covered wooden shrines were built up around the stone sarcophagus of the king. The burial chamber of the tomb used for

Tutankhamun's Mummy

Tutankhamun's mummy had originally been placed inside three nested human-shaped sarcophagi, which were in turn inside a rectangular stone sarcophagus, and then surrounded by four golden shrines. His mummy is now back in his tomb in the Valley of the Kings. It lies inside the outermost of the three human-shaped sarcophagi, which has been placed back in the bottom half of the stone sarcophagus. This has been covered with glass so that you can see inside.

Tutankhamun was so small that only a meter of space was left between the largest, outermost shrine and the tomb walls. The shrines were taken into the tomb in pieces and put together inside. They are decorated with religious texts meant to guarantee the rebirth and afterlife of the king.

C: The fourth and smallest shrine puts you at the entrance to the Tutankhamun jewelry room. The most famous piece, his mask, is right in the middle. The mask was made out of two gold sheets, which were pounded into shape and then pounded together. Details on the head have been inlaid with lapis lazuli (a dark blue stone that comes from Afghanistan), glass, and semiprecious stones. The mask weighs almost 11 kilograms. Walk around and look at the back of the mask. The hieroglyphs are Spell 151 of the Book of the Dead, which protects the king by equating different parts of his body with different deities. For example, the vertical line of hieroglyphs on the right side of the king's pigtail says: "The top of your head is Anubis, the back of your head is Horus."

If the Tutankamun jewelry room is impossibly crowded, you can see comparable pieces in the Treasures of Tanis jewelry room next door, which displays pieces from intact royal burials of the Twenty-first and Twenty-second dynasties—see the introduction to *Itinerary One.*

D: Tutankhamun's mummy was ornately covered with more than one hundred pieces of gold jewelry, much of which he also wore in life. This jewelry fills the cases in the other half of the room. In this case are objects that were made specifically for the mummy: finger and toe covers, and sandals, all made from sheet gold.

E: The innermost and smallest human-shaped sarcophagus, which held the mummy of Tutankhamun, is made of solid gold and weighs 110 kilograms (notice the handles on the lid to help position it when the king was buried). It fits into the next larger sarcophagus, displayed right next to it. This second, or middle, coffin was made of wood, covered with gold, and then inset with tiny pieces of colored glass. Both coffins show the king as the mummiform god Osiris, hands crossed on the chest holding the crook and flail, the symbols of rule. The two goddesses of Upper and Lower Egypt, shown as vultures, wrap their wings around the king's body and protect him. On the solid gold coffin, the figures of the goddesses Isis and Nephthys cover and protect the king's legs as well—you can see Isis again on the flat foot end kneeling and spreading her protective wings.

F: Tiny coffins in the middle case held the mummified lungs, liver, stomach, and intestines of the king. These coffins in turn fit into the canopic jars and shrine that are just outside in the corridor. The canopic coffins are made of beaten gold and inlaid with colored glass, just like the second sarcophagus on the other side of the room.

G: At the left end of the rightmost case is Tutankhamun's writing equipment. The flat palettes hold reed pens and two circular cakes of hardened, powdered ink. The pen was dipped first into water and then scraped on the ink. The ancient Egyptians wrote in black and corrected in red, as many people still do today.

H: The canopic coffins displayed in the jewelry room were put into these alabaster canopic jars, and then set into the alabaster canopic chest. The jar stoppers take the form of the king's head. This alabaster chest was, in turn, placed into the gilt shrine, protected by four goddesses, one on each side. Observe the sled runners under the chest and shrine: ancient Egyptians used sleds to drag heavy objects across the sand. On the wall behind the canopic chest is an unusual object—Tutankhamun's linen loincloth.

I: This statue of the jackal-god Anubis on a shrine was found in the tomb guarding the canopic shrine. Notice the poles to carry it. The shrine and statue are of wood covered with gold, or in the case of the jackal's body, with black resin. The toe nails of the jackal are silver. The shrine has compartments inside to hold materials related to mummification.

J: Three funerary beds like these were part of the equipment of a royal burial. The beds take the form of a cow, a lion, and a composite animal made of a hippo, lion, and crocodile. These beds had symbolic meaning relating to religious myths that revive and raise the king up to heaven so that he might live again. Observe the foot boards on the beds; ancient Egyptian beds had foot boards rather than head boards.

K: This case displays the tiny coffins of Tutankhamun's two daughters. Their mummies were placed into inner and outer coffins of wood and sheet gold, and then put together in a wooden box in the Treasury of the tomb. One child was probably stillborn at about five month's gestation, while the other apparently died shortly after birth. Just to the right of this case is one with a lock of hair from Tutankhamun's grandmother, Queen Tiye. The lock of hair was in a tiny coffin and nestled into the other three coffins displayed.

You now go down the long east corridor of the museum, filled completely with more pieces from the tomb of Tutankhamun. You will pass model boats, a number of beds, alabaster lamps, throw sticks, bows, and chairs of various materials.

L: The ancient Egyptians loved games; especially two board games called Senet and Twenty Squares. The two games are similar, in that the aim is to get your pieces around the squares and finish before your opponent does. Either sticks or 'knucklebones' were thrown to determine how many squares to move. Tutankhamun had four of these boards in his tomb. Notice the size of the king's two 'portable' games.

You will pass two cases of shawabti figures on the west wall, as well as cases of sticks and staves. Shawabti figures were placed in the tomb to do any labor required of the deceased in the afterlife. Tutankhamun had 413 of them in his tomb. Notice the smaller cases of tools by each of the shawabti cases. These little hoes and baskets of metal and faience were for the shawabtis to use while digging and carrying dirt.

M: Tutankhamun's gold throne is a fantastic piece of furniture. It is made of wood, covered with gold, and inset with glass, semiprecious stones, and silver. Tutankhamun, wearing a fancy festival crown, is shown relaxing while his wife rubs ointment on him. Above the couple shines the disk of the Aten, the deity worshiped by Akhenaten, who was probably Tutankhamun's uncle. Tutankhamun had been born at Akhenaten's city, Tell al-Amarna, and ruled there for three years before leaving and reopening the traditional cult temples, which Akhenaten had closed. This throne was crafted while Tutankhamun was still at Tell al-Amarna (see *Itinerary One* for more Amarna information). On the outer arm of the chair, the cartouche still has his original name as king Tut-ankhaten.

N: You will pass gilt statuettes of the king and deities of the afterlife. Thirty-five of these figures were wrapped in linen shawls and packed into small boxes resembling shrines and put in the Treasury of the tomb.

O: At the very end of the corridor stand the two 'guardian' figures of Tutankhamun, which were found on either side of the entrance into the burial chamber. The statues are of wood, covered with bitumen to blacken them, and then decorated with gold leaf and bronze. The two statues are identical except for the difference in head cloth. They are black because the deceased king was identified with Osiris, the king of the underworld, who is always shown with black or dark green skin.

At the end of the Tutankhamun exhibit, turn left and you are at the ticket booth and entrance for the Mummy Room. The Mummy Room itself is darkened, and visitors are expected to talk quietly as they walk around and view the mummies.

The Royal Mummy Room

1: Seqenenre Ta'o (Seventeenth Dynasty). This king probably died on the battlefield, with no one to mummify him right away. Forensic pathologists have shown that Hyksos weapons made the gruesome wounds on his face and skull. The Hyksos, from Syro-Palestine, had invaded the Egyptian Delta, and we know from historical texts that the Egyptians in Upper Egypt had begun to resist them during Seqenenre's reign.

2: Amenhotep I (Eighteenth Dynasty). This king's mummy is still inside the original cartonnage case in which it was buried, placed inside a larger coffin. Notice the flowers that came from the original burial.

3: Queen Merytamun (Eighteenth Dynasty), the wife of Amenhotep I. Her tomb had been robbed and her mummy unwrapped in antiquity. X-ray evidence shows that she had scoliosis, or curvature of the spine.

4: Tuthmose II (Eighteenth Dynasty). He was the son of Tuthmose I and husband of his half-sister Queen Hatshepsut. Notice that his arms are crossed on his chest. This became the fashion for royal mummies from then on.

5: Tuthmose IV (Eighteenth Dynasty). This king was the father of Amenhotep III and grandfather of Akhenaten. He was the king who as a young prince fell asleep under the Giza Sphinx and dreamed that if he cleared the sand away from the Sphinx, he would become king of Egypt.

6: Seti I (Nineteenth Dynasty). He proclaimed a 'renaissance' in his reign, and is responsible for the building of the Hypostyle Hall at Karnak, the Temple of Abydos, and the longest tomb in the Valley of the Kings. The very dark color of his skin is from all the resins put on the body.

7: Ramesses II (Nineteenth Dynasty). Son of Seti I, Ramesses II is probably the most famous king of ancient Egypt. Confirmed by x-ray evidence, he died at about the age of 83. He had advanced arteriosclerosis and gum disease. His hair, which certainly must have been white, was dyed with henna when he was mummified.

8: Merneptah (Nineteenth Dynasty). By the time Ramesses II died, twelve of his sons had already died before him, and Merneptah, his thirteenth son took the throne. He was about 70 years old when he died.

9: Ramesses V (Twentieth Dynasty). He took the throne as an older man and had a short reign of about five years. His skin has eruptions on it, and he might have died from smallpox.

10: Queen Nodjmet (Twenty-first Dynasty). At this time, embalmers took great care to make the mummy look just like a living person. The embalmers made up the queen's face and glued on eyebrows. They stuffed her cheeks and neck with sawdust to fill them out.

11: Queen Henettawi (Twenty-first Dynasty). Notice her artificial eyes and the wig she wears. Her chubby cheeks come from all the packing that was put inside.

12: Tuthmose III: Son of Tuthmose II, he shared the throne with Hatshepsut for twenty-two years and then ruled another thirty-two years on his own. Tuthmose III was a great military man and builder of the Egyptian empire of the New Kingdom.

T hese wadjet eyes on the side of the coffin were to enable the deceased to 'see' out. The body inside was laid on its side. A headrest supported the mummy's head so that the face of the mummy lined up with these eyes. This side of the coffin faced the east, symbolically the land of the living, and the direction in which offerings would be placed.

Itinerary Three
Mummies, Models, and Big Pieces
(for young children)

If you are at the main entrance of the museum, the section for mummies (not the same as the mummy room, described above) and models is upstairs on the left. Go up the stairs on the west side and immediately turn left. Coffins and mummies are in the corridor running north, and the wooden models are in rooms 37, 32, and 27 (the second, third, and fourth rooms) going off it on the right. These three rooms and the coffins and mummies in the corridor just outside them offer a perfect visit for young children. They can move from case to case as they wish, and the objects are self-explanatory.

The models were put in the tomb to provide anything the deceased might need in the afterlife. You may have visited mastaba tombs at Saqqara with the scenes of daily life carved on the walls; these wooden models serve the same purpose. The models portray the deceased counting his cattle, men fishing with nets in the river, the weaving of cloth, a woman carrying offerings, carpenters at work, even soldiers who would have served the tomb owner.

In the first room, Room 37, there are coffins and two large models of troops of soldiers. One model shows archers from Nubia, and the other Egyptian soldiers with spears and shields. In the next room are many pieces of models that show the making of food and plowing. Inside the door on both sides are cases of headrests. Believe it or not, these are the ancient Egyptian equivalent of pillows. The Egyptians slept on their side with their head resting on one of these. All of these headrests were found inside coffins where they supported the mummy's head.

In the corridor just outside Room 32, there are perhaps the best mummies. There is an Early Dynastic burial, with the deceased in a fetal position, wrapped in linen and placed in a small coffin woven from reeds. To the left, there are Ptolemaic mummies dating almost three thousand years later. Look at the difference in how the body is treated, and how decorated the later mummies and their coffins are.

The most interesting models are probably in the third room, Room 27. These all come from a tomb of a nobleman, Meketre, at Thebes. They are from the Middle Kingdom. On the right and inside the door, the tomb owner sits in a small pavilion and inspects his cattle being driven past him. On the left is a complete model of a house with a garden and workshops for weavers and carpenters. There are also large riverboats, as well as two smaller boats with men catching fish in a net.

When you are done in this section, your children might find the animal mummies fascinating. The Animal Mummy Project room is upstairs, and is in Room 53. Walk in between cases of Predynastic pottery and straight ahead, at the entrance of the room is the mummy case of the mother of an Apis bull. This bull was a sacred form of the god Ptah of Memphis. The Apis bull and his mother were kept in the enclosure of the Ptah temple at Memphis, and when they died they were mummified and buried at Saqqara. Behind on the right is a case containing a mummy of a Mnevis bull, the sacred animal of the sun god Re. These bulls were buried in Heliopolis. Note the board that the mummy is on, and the metal clamps that were used to hold the mummy onto it. The back half of the room contains many more mummies. The case on the right displays two enormous crocodiles from the temple of the crocodile god Sobek at Kom Ombo in Upper Egypt. Each crocodile measures approximately five meters. Also in the case is a giant Nile perch, Latus niloticus, the sacred fish of Esna in Upper Egypt. Across on the opposite side is a wonderful example of mummified animals that were pets. The dog and monkey were discovered in a small tomb (KV 50) in the Valley of the Kings, and are thought to have been the pets of King Amenhotep II of the Eighteenth Dynasty. The last two cases on the left and right of the room contain mummies of animals, which pilgrims visiting a sacred spot, bought and offered to a deity. Examples of these votive mummies include cats, dogs, ibises, snakes, and shrews. The case against the back wall has three mummified rams encased in gilded cartonnage. They date to the Ptolemaic-Roman Period, and were discovered on the island of Elephantine at Aswan where there was a cult of Khnum, the ram god.

Web site: *www.animalmummies.com/project.html*

Book: *A Zoo for Eternity* by Dr. Salima Ikram. Published in Arabic/English. To purchase contact the Supreme Council of Antiquities in Zamalek, tel. and fax: 735-8749. Sometimes, the book is also at AUC Bookstores.

Walk downstairs to the Atrium to see the 'Big Pieces,' which are in the center of the museum. In front of you, there is a dark stone pyramidion (the stone that capped the top of the pyramid) from the pyramid of Amenemhet III at Dahshur. All around the room are stone sarcophagi from royal burials. The first one on the right is set up with a mirror so that you can see the underside of the lid. The sky goddess Nut stretches out so that she formed the vault of heaven over the deceased king. In the center of the Atrium is a painted pavement taken from a palace of King Akhenaten at Tell al-Amarna. Note that on one side there is a strip designed with captives and bows. They represent the "Nine Bows"—the traditional enemies of Egypt. This strip ran all through the palace's pavement, so that the king would walk upon it and always appear to be treading on his foes. At the far end of the Atrium is the monument small children will find the most amazing: a gigantic limestone statue of King Amenhotep III and Queen Tiye with three of their daughters. The statue was found in pieces on the West Bank of Luxor, and reassembled in the museum.

Hoda Shaarawi

While Talaat Harb and Mustafa Kamal campaigned against the writings of Qasim Amin, who stressed that the key to Egyptian progress was through female education, Hoda Shaarawi organized veiled women to demonstrate in support of the Wafd Party, which campaigned for Egyptian independence from Britain. Having grown up in a harem and received a formal education at home (she spoke French and Turkish fluently), and married against her will at a young age, Hoda Shaarawi courageously removed her veil as she stepped from a train in 1923. She continued to fight for women's social, economic, and political rights, and established the Egyptian Feminist Union. Read more in her autobiography *Harem Years, The Memoirs of an Egyptian Feminist* (AUC Press, 1998).

The Downtown Art Galleries

The best way to explore downtown is to start with a specific aim in mind. Our favorite reason is to check out the contemporary art galleries, all within pleasant walking distance of each other. Galleries and several cultural centers have recently banded together in an attempt to create programs and exhibitions that will interest the younger crowd. Already, art classes from many of Cairo's schools have discovered the importance of introducing their students to the diversity of contemporary art encountered throughout these galleries.

Reviewing the ever-changing art exhibits is a great way to explore the downtown area. In three hours you can easily see all the galleries and include a stop at one of the traditional-style restaurants or fast-food chains for lunch before returning home. Keep in mind that this outing is more suitable for older children and teenagers. In addition, some sidewalks are uneven and broken, and many of the galleries are up staircases.

Did you know there are gargoyles in Cairo? While you are walking between the galleries and minding the traffic and your step, look at the façades and balconies of the buildings. Downtown architecture—influenced by the styles of Europe blended with Islamic or pharaonic—is intriguing, especially for older children. The carved stone and ironwork balconies, enhanced by geometric and arabesque designs, decorate the windows of most downtown buildings. And, to see the gargoyles . . . you will find them off Talaat Harb, on Hoda Shaarawi St. and Yusif al-Gindi St., about a block from Felfela Restaurant.

The major Metro stop servicing the downtown area is Sadat Station. It is an easy walk to the galleries, with many restaurants in between. Do remember, though, that some galleries close in the afternoon by 2pm, reopening in the evening. The exhibits are always changing, so be sure to watch the weekly newspapers, monthly magazines, and bulletin boards for up-to-date information. See 'How to Find Out' for suggestions.

South on Yusuf al-Gindi toward the library of the American University in Cairo (AUC), there is a rattan and bamboo furniture workshop. Young apprentice boys learn their trade from aging men, who welcome onlookers. Watching them bend the cane with the heat of a gas torch is particularly interesting for all ages. On several occasions, we have backtracked to Hoda Shaarawi St. (named for the woman who became famous for unveiling publicly in 1923: see box on page 40), to stop for nourishment at Felfela Restaurant. This restaurant is sure to intrigue youths of all ages. Seated on the tree-trunk tables and surrounded by aquariums and stuffed animals, you can try Egyptian cuisine at moderate prices.

Gargoyles on Yusif al-Gindi St.

41

François Champollion
and the amazing story of the Rosetta Stone

In 1799 a group of French engineers, mending the walls of an old fort during Napoleon's military campaign, discovered the Rosetta Stone in the ancient port of al-Rashid (Rosetta). The irregularly shaped granite stone weighing 762 kilograms became the key to unlocking the secrets of ancient Egypt. Scientists realized its value immediately, as the text on the stone was written in three languages: ancient hieroglyphs, demotic (a later dialect of ancient Egyptian, written in cursive form), and Greek. After two years, the British forced the French out of Egypt and the Rosetta Stone ended up in the British Museum. However, it was a Frenchman, François Champollion, who deciphered the Rosetta Stone. Probably he never saw the actual stone but relied on lithographic-style prints made from it, and succeeded in deciphering the hieroglyphs in 1822.

Champollion had been a precocious child. By the age of 13, he had learned Arabic, Greek, Hebrew, Syriac, Chinese, and Coptic. A great scholar and admirer of the Egyptian people, he set his genius on deciphering the hieroglyphs. Following his success in deciphering hieroglyphs in 1822, the French king Louis XVIII rewarded him a gold box, after which Champollion did visit Egypt, staying for two years. He died in France at the early age of 42.

Mashrabia Gallery

Champollion St., named after the famous French Egyptologist who was first to decipher the language of the hieroglyphic inscriptions, is home to the Mashrabia. The clue to finding this gallery is the mashrabiya windows, which are easily noticed from the street, although the entrance to the gallery itself is hidden between two buildings on a narrow alley. Turn into the alley and about twenty feet farther along, you will see a stairwell to your left. Take the stairs to the second floor; the gallery is on your right. Do not be put off by the gloomy atmosphere of the approach, as it by no means reflects the interior of the gallery. In the gallery is a small gift shop for paintings, cards, and catalogues. Be sure to put your name on the Mashrabia's mailing list.

Where: 8 Champollion St., off Midan al-Tahrir.
Tel: 578-4494.

Metro stop: Sadat Station.

When: Open Saturday–Thursday 11am–8pm. Closed Fridays. During Ramadan and summer, the hours may change.

Activities: Frequent exhibitions of famous and budding artists. Be on the look out for lectures and youth programs.

Facilities: Small gift shop.

Parking: The large parking lot across from the gallery is for public use in the evening only.

Townhouse Gallery of Contemporary Art

You are in for a special treat when you visit this gallery. Not only is the gallery worthy of your complete attention but also the street approaching the gallery will captivate your imagination. You are on the right track when the aroma of freshly roasted coffee coaxes you forward. Just upon entering Hussein Pasha St. and on the right, there is a small shop specializing in coffees. An immense metal tray filled with steaming, freshly roasted coffee beans set outside to cool occupies the sidewalk. Inside, you are welcome to stop and to observe the roasting and grinding process of coffeebeans.

As you walk toward the end of the street, a dilapidated palace that was used as a school is on your left. If you ask local residents the name of this building, the response is "Champollion Palace," because they believe Francois Champollion stayed there when he visited Cairo after 1822. Actually, the palace on Champollion St. was built by the architect, Antonio Lasciac, in the late nineteenth century for Prince Said Halim Pasha, the grandson of Mohammed Ali. The palace was converted into Al Nasriya School for Boys after World War I, formally a school for the elite. Just looking at the ornate walls and statues in the corners and niches, you can almost imagine the elegant people who once lived within. (There is good news for this old palace— the Ministry of Culture will soon begin renovations.) Straight ahead at the kink in the road is the Townhouse Gallery. You might pass mechanics working on a car before you enter the building, which before 1948, was a part of the Jewish quarter.

Four old flats as well as two garages across the alley, have been converted into areas for imaginative art displays. The current director, an innovator in promoting art, allows the observer to participate in the art experience through exploring art themes, musical programs, unique displays, and discussions with the artists. Lectures and tours of the other downtown art galleries are also organized. Be sure to add your name to the gallery's mailing list. Don't miss the Townhouse Gallery on Site, reconverted garage workshops provide fabulous space for large art exhibits.

Where: 10 Nabrawy St., off Champollion St.

Tel: 576-8086.

Metro stop: Sadat Station

When: Open Saturday–Wednesday 10am–2pm and 6–9pm, Fridays open 6–9pm. Closed Thursdays. During Ramadan and summer, the hours may change.

Web site: www.thetownhousegallery.com

Activities: Young people are welcome to come and sketch and talk to the artists. Art programs, drawing classes, and tours are organized throughout the year.

Facilities: A book and art shop located on the first floor. Also on the first floor is a toilet. Library open Saturday to Wednesday 10am–9pm, Friday 6–9pm. Parking available behind the building.

Townhouse Gallery on Site:
End of Abou al-Feda St., Zamalek, at Café Ciabatta. Tel: 735-0014.

Atelier du Caire

Tucked away beneath the shade of a magnificent tree, surely a remnant of a long-ago garden, is a charming gallery. The main room for exhibits is on the ground floor but make sure you take the winding stairway, as there may be another interesting art display on the second floor.

Where: 2 Karim al-Dawla St., off Mahmoud Basyuni St. Tel: 574-6730.

Metro stop: Sadat Station.

When: Open Saturday–Thursday 10am–1pm and 6pm–12 midnight. Friday 6pm–12 midnight. Check on Ramadan and summer hours.

Espace Karim Francis – Downtown

There are two routes to walk when approaching Espace Karim Francis; both are equally interesting because of the many shops along the way; the long way around is by Qasr al-Nil St.; the more direct route by Sabri Abu Alam St. Upon reaching al-Sherifeen St., you will find the pleasant feature is that it has been turned into a pedestrian area accentuated by lampposts, benches, and little gardens. The Egyptian Stock Exchange is located on this street. It is a refreshing experience to walk in Cairo without the worry of traffic. There is no sign on the exterior of the building to advertise Espace Karim Francis but sometimes there is a sign just inside the entrance. You will pass an antique wooden, caged elevator that still works, which might be of interest to young eyes. The stairway is dim, but the gallery, on the third floor, is a bright haven. Watch for frequent and unusual art exhibits, lectures, and video presentations.

Where: 1 al-Sherifeen St., off Qasr al-Nil St.
Tel: 391-6357.
Metro stop: Sadat Station.
When: Open Friday–Wednesday 2–9pm.
Closed Friday.
Check for summer and Ramadan hours.
Zamalek Gallery: Karim Francis–La Bodega
157 26th July St., 3rd Floor, daily except
Monday. 4–11pm. Tel: 736-2183.

Oum el Dounia

As a rule, *The Family Guide* does not write about commercial shops except if their philosophy falls within three categories: one, there is a good book section about Egypt; two, quality, traditional items that youth like; three, the products come directly from the people who produce them. Oum el Dounia meets all our categories with flying colors. The storeowners visit all the regions of Egypt to insure that items on sale represent quality, local artisanship. Watch for monthly art exhibits.

Where: 3 Talaat Harb St., 1st floor. Tel: 393-8273.
When: Open daily 10am–7pm.

Groppi and Café Riche

Between the downtown art galleries, you will pass through Midan Talaat Harb. It is worth taking a few moments to walk into Groppi which in the 1920s was considered an elegant, Parisian-style patisserie and tea room. For many decades Groppi was 'the place' to be seen. Historian Samir Rafaat writes, "Whenever pashas, beys and resident-foreigners traveled to Europe they took cartons filled with Groppi chocolates with them. During the Second World War, it is said King Farouk freighted by air to London, via Khartoum, Entebbe, Dakar, Lisbon, and Dublin, a lacquered box emblazoned with the royal arms of Egypt and Great Britain. Inside, to the delight of Great Britain's Princesses, Elizabeth and Margaret were 100 kilos of Groppi chocolates." Additionally, not far from the Groppi's tea room is Groppi's tea gardens, which was a popular haunt for British soldiers during both world wars. Today, both are a shadow of their former glory; yet, Groppi's tearoom is still a good place to stop for a warm croissant with fig or mango jam and cappuccino, and the tea garden is still a tree-covered oasis in the middle of Cairo.

Café Riche

Whereas Groppi was 'the place' to be seen before independence, Café Riche, although opened in the early 1900s, became to embody the spirit of the revolution by being a hang-out for Egyptian intellectuals and writers after 1952. Umm Kulthum began her singing career there. Naguib Mahfouz was a regular during the 1960s, and in 1978, Naguib Surour declared, "The whole world is Café Riche." Café Riche is situated on Talaat Harb Street, although in the past few years there was a revival of the old spirit, but for reasons unbeknownst to most, it is open for business, sometimes.

Downtown Cultural Centers

What is the best way for teenagers to experience another culture without traveling? Cultural Centers! Cairo is host to a rich variety of cultural centers from around the world. The centers mentioned here are in the downtown area, but there are many active cultural centers throughout Cairo.

The programs vary from dance, music, theater, photography, lectures, and poetry to language classes and special Ramadan evenings. The most annoying problem is finding out what's on after it has happened! Most centers have mailing lists, so put your name on them, and keep an eye on listings for events.

The students we know have taken advantage of the many and varied programs throughout the year that the centers offer. All cultural centers provide pamphlets and booklets about their countries' history, culture, government, and often, tourism. Some centers have libraries to browse. Another source of interest is to interview the cultural attaché about his or her country.

There is something satisfying about researching a project or paper by going

*Midan
Talaat Harb*

to a cultural center. Our girls, in particular, clearly preferred finding out about a country by visiting the cultural center rather than sitting in front of the Internet, which they agreed spits out the information efficiently and quickly but is devoid of the spirit of the country. They commented that there is nothing like the flavor of authenticity.

Centre Français de Culture et de Cooperation

1 Madrasat al-Huquq al-Faransiya, Mounira. Tel: 794-7679, 794-4095. They offer French language courses for all levels. Cultural activities, exhibitions, performances, theater, and films are organized and a restaurant is on the premises as well as a library. In Heliopolis: 5 Shafiq al-Dib St., Ard al-Golf. Tel: 419-3857. Offers French courses, films, library, and exhibitions. Open 9am–8pm. Closed Fridays and Saturdays.

Talaat Harb

Why is there a statue of Talaat Harb in the center of downtown Cairo? He is best known for founding Bank Misr (Egypt) in 1920, but he was also a leading advocate of economic independence for Egypt in the climate of growing industrialization of the country under the British Protectorate. Concerned to secure Egypt's economic voice, he succeeded in encouraging investment by the landowning class in new Egyptian industries. He also established EgyptAir and Misr Studios. Talaat Harb was a strict Muslim who was opposed to interest-bearing loans, an innovator, a poet, a staunch patriot, and a campaigner against women's emancipation.

47

Cervantes Institute (Spanish Cultural Center)
20 Adly St., Kodak Passage, Downtown. Tel: 395-2326, 395-2627. Offers Spanish courses. In Dokki, the Institute is located at 20 Boulos Hanna St. Tel: 760-1746, 337-0845. Offers an array of lectures, exhibitions, and music to the public. Open 8:30am–3:30pm. Closed Fridays and Saturdays.

Goethe Institute
There are two in Cairo. Downtown: al-Bustan St. Tel: 574-8261. The Goethe Institute has an activities schedule each month providing films, lectures, exhibitions, concerts, and free library membership. In Dokki: the language department at Midan al-Misaha offers courses in German. Tel: 748-4500. Open 9am–2pm and 5-8pm. Closed Sunday.

Hungarian Cultural Center
13 Gawwad Hosni St., Abdin. Tel: 392-6692. Open 10am–2pm. Closed Fridays and Saturdays.

Indian Cultural Center
23 Talaat Harb St., Tel: 393-3396. Offers courses in Hindi and Urdu. Exhibitions, recitals, yoga, and Indian-cooking classes are just a few of the courses on offer. Open 11am–7pm. Closed Fridays and Saturdays.

Japanese Cultural Center
106 Qasr al-Aini St., Cairo Center Building, 3rd Floor, Downtown. Tel: 792-5011. Take a course in Japanese and be prepared for your trip to Tokyo. Also offers films Thursdays at 6pm. Open 8:30am–4:30pm. Library hours: 9am–4pm. Closed Fridays and Saturdays.

Swiss Cultural Center (ProHelvethia Center)
Swiss Embassy, 10 Abd al-Khaleq Tharwat St., Downtown. Tel: 575-8284, 575-8133. Sponsors art and photography exhibitions and music recitals. Open 8:30am–3:30pm. Closed Fridays and Saturdays.

The American University in Cairo
Have you ever wondered about the establishment of the American University in Cairo (AUC)? How did an American university come into being during the time Egypt was under British rule? It all started with a handful of Americans attracted to Egypt with the desire to promote higher education. Through years of turmoil, collection of funds, and political debate, Charles Watson, the first president of the AUC, was the driving factor in the realization of a commit-

ment to American presence in higher education. In 1919, Watson finally acquired the small palace that Khedive Ismail had built for his minister of education, Ahmad Khairy Pasha. The palace, situated on Midan Ismailiya (now Midan al-Tahrir), had been acquired after Khairy's death by a Greek named Nestor Gianaclis, who used the palace as a cigarette factory and rented rooms to the Egyptian University (now Cairo University). In 1919, the British arrested Saad Zaghloul, demonstrations for independence produced an unsettled atmosphere, and the value of land fell. This was Watson's chance to purchase the property. Soon thereafter, the doors of AUC opened to Egyptian and Middle Eastern students; the tuition fee was $80 a year. If you want to know more, consult Lawrence R. Murphy's *The American University in Cairo: 1919-1987* (AUC Press, 1987).

The AUC may not be on your list of places to go in Cairo, but we suggest that you pay close attention to the many activities that go on throughout the school year. You do not have to be a college student to take full advantage of all that the AUC has to offer. Especially pleasing for adolescents and teenagers are theater productions and art and photography exhibitions. In fact, the AUC sponsors some of the most dynamic photography exhibitions in town; the subject matter is usually Egypt, Islam, and the Middle East. Moreover, if young children are in tow, stop by the well-stocked bookstore for colorful picture-books of oriental tales and fables.

Where: **113 Qasr al-Aini St., Midan al-Tahrir. Tel: 794-2964.**

Metro stop: **Sadat Station.**

Activities: **It is worth watching for lectures and theater productions, listed in most monthly magazines, or call the Public Relations Office at AUC, Tel: 797-5020/1.**

Center for Adult and Continuing Education: **28 Falaki St., Bab al-Louq. Tel: 797-6872/3.**

Sony Gallery: **Entrance on al-Sheikh Rihan St., 1st Floor Main Campus. Open 9am–9pm. Closed Fridays and Saturdays. Tel: 794-6422/3/4.**

Falaki Theater/Gallery: **Falaki Campus, 2nd Floor, adjacent to Falaki Main Stage; Falaki St., Bab al-Louq. Performances and exhibitions throughout the year. Tel: 797-6373. Falaki Gallery open 12–9pm. Closed Fridays.**

AUC Bookstore: **Main Campus. Tel: 797-5377. Open 8:30am–5pm. Closed Fridays.**

Or 16 Muhammad Ibn Thaqeb St.,
Zamalek (ground floor of AUC hostel).
Tel: 797-5900, 797-5929. Open Saturday—
Monday 10am–5pm; Tuesday–Thursday
10am–6pm. Closed Fridays.

Places to eat: Across the street from AUC as you exit
from the AUC bookstore (Main Campus),
there is a choice of fast-food restaurants.

Parking: Al-Bustan Commercial Center, Bustan St.,
Bab al-Louq or in underground Omar
Makrum garage at Tahrir Square

Web site: *www.aucegypt.edu/tools/calendars.html*
for AUC calendar of events.

Ethnology Museum and the Geographical Society

If you have been to this museum, then you know you are not a tourist! The Ethnology Museum is one of the well-kept secrets of Cairo, perhaps because it is housed among government buildings and because there is no sign to guide you. Even though it takes some perseverance to get inside, it is a clean, brightly-lit museum and worth every minute of determination it might take to reach it. (We tried three times before we got all the information right and saw the museum!)

Located on Qasr al-Aini St. just half a block south of AUC's Ewart Hall and Midan al-Tahrir (and before you reach Maglis al-Sha'b St.), it is marked by a small, tree-lined parking area on the east side of the street. The large, black, steel gateway straight ahead (parallel to Qasr al-Aini St.) is the entrance. The police officers will ask the nature of your business and possibly your nationality. After you explain you wish to visit the museum, they will direct you to the guard's room where you will need to leave an ID card to receive a pass to enter. The museum is the first building on your right. Walk a short distance and turn right onto a sidewalk; there are signs next to the door that announce the Geographical Society and the Ethnology Museum.

Before you go to this museum, you might discuss with your children why people collect things and why it is important. Museums are simply someone's collection: a person or a group who have had the foresight to gather and classify things of a certain era or culture. If your family collects antique carpets or baseball cards or has saved all of great-grandmother's nineteenth-century dresses, you are engaged in the study of cultural anthropology. The Ethnology Museum applies the same focus: it is a collection of common artifacts that Egyptians use in daily life. Well-kept displays of jewelry, smoking utensils, costumes of different occupations and life, oriental musical instruments, kitchen utensils, toys, and tools. For the most part, the collection portrays life as lived in the countryside and the city in the past century.

Besides the rooms dedicated to cultural anthropology, there is a Suez Canal Room with fascinating displays of the opening of the canal and the topography of Ismailiya. There is a map room and a room with military equipment, yet quite different from the military exhibits in Abdin and the Citadel. The Africa room houses military equipment and everyday articles from southern Egypt and Siwa. A wall of shields made from animal skins and woven cane is keenly interesting. The case next to them displays iron headgear. The original thick quilted material is attached to the holes around the bottom of the helmet, protecting the soldier's ears and neck from weather and the chafing of armor. A papyrus boat made for the Nile is in the back of the room along with pottery, elephant legs, and even a calabash.

Geographical Society

Professor Mohammad Abulezz, the fourteenth president of the Geographical Society, kindly provided a tour of the lecture hall, built in 1920, which remains in its original, stunningly beautiful condition. The Geographical Society was inaugurated by the ruler of Egypt Khedive Ismail on May 19, 1875, and is one of the oldest non-governmental organizations in Egypt. Professor Abulezz states the objectives of the Society are to foster geographical knowledge and encourage research and geographical surveys and field investigations in the different regions of Egypt, as it was when Ismail Pasha founded the Society. He explains the Society aims to enhance public awareness of geography as a development-oriented discipline and believes that through the Society, geography can be rediscovered as a discipline for environmental management and utilization of space.

There are over 28,000 titles in the library. The first *Bulletin of Egyptian Geographic Society* was published in 1876, and it has continued to be published, without interruption, every year since then. The cartographic library includes rare maps of Egypt and Africa as well as contemporary maps. For example, there are maps drawn by Mahmoud al-Falaki Pasha and a map of the Nile drawn by Gordon Pasha both donated to the Geographic Society by King Fouad I.

Where: 109 Qasr al-Aini St., in the Egyptian Parliament grounds. From the street, the name of the building, Societe de Geographie d'Egypte, is visible.

Metro stop: Sadat Station.

When: Open Saturday–Wednesday 10am–3pm.
Closed on holidays. Foreigners, residents,
students: LE20; Egyptians: LE10.
Be sure to bring: ID card for everyone to leave with the
security guard.
Telephone: 794-5450.
Web site: *www.egs-online.org*
Library hours: 9:30am–2pm.
Parking: No public parking here but the Bustan Center
or Omar Makrum garage are good places to
park your car. Arriving by taxi or with a driver
is best as the area is congested.

Bayt al-Umma and Tomb of Saad Zaghloul

On Gezira Island at the end of Qasr al-Nil Bridge is a statue that might go unnoticed because of the frenzy of traffic that swirls around its base. Yet the owner of the hand that bids welcome to the millions who pass beneath him is an important figure in Egypt's modern history. The story of Saad Zaghloul, nationalist and founder of the Wafd party, is a reminder that the fight for freedom and democracy is most often a battle ending in personal sacrifice. The statue was commissioned from Egypt's most famous sculptor, Mahmoud Mukhtar, whose works can be viewed at the Mahmoud Mukhtar Museum just down the road from Saad Zaghloul's statue.

Bayt al-Umma ('House of the Nation') and the Tomb of Saad and Safiya Zaghloul are easy to find. They are situated approximately five blocks south of AUC campus. A stop at the Ethnology Museum before continuing to the Bayt al-Umma makes for an interesting morning out. Or take the Metro to the Saad Zaghloul stop, which deposits you on the exact block of the museum and tomb.

The house of Saad Zaghloul is a humble villa compared to many palaces and mansions of notables. Walking through the doors of Bayt al-Umma is like entering into a home belonging to friends or family. The impression of warmth remains, even though no one has occupied the home since 1946. The visitor has a sense that the owners have just stepped out and will return shortly. This mood is successfully attained by the worn, yet beautiful Persian and Turkish carpets that grace the dark wooden floors, and the family pictures on every wall. Upon entering the first room to the left of the entrance, the sitting room to the right was reserved for family and friends, while the next room was dedicated to receive very important personages from Egypt and overseas. The last room was Saad Zaghloul's office (also known as the Winter Room). Be sure to notice the pictures of Wafd leaders. Under the stairwell, a secret door to the elevator can be found, which is how Saad Zaghloul could escape from an unwanted guest. Beginning at the entrance again, on the right is the dining room. Spend some extra time here to admire the glassware and silverware, notice the seating in the window area, which was used to serve tea after a meal. The door to the back of the room leads to a pantry, bathroom, and elevator.

On the second floor, Safiya Zaghloul kept talking parrots on the landing and in her dressing room, which is to the immediate right. The door to the left opens to their private bathroom, while the middle door opens onto a sitting room with magnificent arabesque-style furnishings. Take time to enjoy the pictures of their family as well as those of Egyptian leaders. Immediately behind the door, is a picture of two twins, presented to Saad Zaghloul by their parents, who named the twins Saad and Safiya. Near this, another photograph of interest depicts Safiya with Egyptian women. Take your time in this room to appreciate the styles and times in Egypt over a hundred years ago. Looking out the balcony, you will stand in the footsteps Safiya and women of the Wafd cheering, *"Yah-ya, Saad!"*

Going back to the stairwell, the rooms to the right and forward the opposite end are Safiya's dressing room, the Zaghlouls' bedroom (notice the photographs of Safiya's sister's children on the wall), and Saad Zaghloul's dressing room, respectively. The door to the left is the private bathroom, which

Saad Zaghloul

Saad Zaghloul's humble beginnings were in the Delta, where he was educated in the Quranic tradition before going on to study at al-Azhar University. Well versed in the French language and legal system, Saad Zaghloul was a skillful negotiator and orator. His political career began with his cooperation with the British and support for the Khedive. He served in 1908 as minister of education, and in 1910 as minister of justice. After World War I, however, the Egyptian nationalist movement began to gain momentum. Saad Zaghloul founded the Wafd party and asked Britain to recognize his delegation at the Versailles Peace Conference. In response, the British government exiled him to Malta, which heightened nationalists' demand for independence. Although Saad Zaghloul became prime minister of Egypt in 1924, it was for only one year, and he died in August 1927 without seeing his country truly independent of Britain.

Saad Zaghloul's wife, Safiya, marched with Hoda Shaarawi in 1919 to support the Wafd party. She joined the Feminist Union and fought for the emancipation of women and women's rights.

Saad Zaghloul's Tomb

consists of several rooms: the furthest was for bathing and showering; the middle room has a bed for resting and a relaxing massage. Be sure to look for Saad and Safiya's wooden bath clogs. True to Arabic style, the *hammam* ceiling allows in sunlight not only illuminating a small room but also providing color and design to a leisurely bath, one of the few luxuries Saad Zaghloul may have allowed himself.

On Falaki St., across from Bayt al-Umma, the tomb of Saad Zaghloul and his wife, Safiya, seems out of place in the midst of heavy traffic and high-rise apartments. A garden surrounds the pharaonic-style mausoleum. Designed and built by Mustafa Fahmi in 1931, it is an imposing granite structure, following the ancient Egyptian tradition of grandeur in the burial of great leaders. After the death of Saad Zaghloul, there was great controversy as to whether the architecture of his tomb should be designed in the pharaonic style or with an emphasis on Islamic and Arab architecture. After the construction, a political debate ensued as some politicians wished this tomb to be shared with other great men, and at one point mummies from the Egyptian museum were transferred into the mausoleum. Finally, it was Zaghloul's wife, Safiya, who returned her husband to his rightful place in history by having the government pass a law that only she and her husband were to be buried in the mausoleum. For an in-depth understanding, read the article "The Politics of the Funereal: The Tomb of Saad Zaghloul" by Ralph M. Coury (see Bibliography), who presents a full account of the controversies and intrigues of the day.

The entrance faces the side of Bayt al-Umma on Falaki St. If no one is in the garden, don't let that stop you from pushing the gates open and entering. Walk around the tomb and ascend the steep stairs with Mansur St. to your back. There is a door to a guardroom on your right. If the guard is present, he will be quite happy to unlock the massive doors. Watching the huge bronze doors being pushed opened, your curiosity will heighten. The ceremonious opening of the doors lets light invade the dark tranquillity of this odd sanctuary. Four rose granite columns grace the interior, which contains a huge granite sarcophagus.

Where:	Bayt al-Umma is at the corner of Falaki St. and Saad Zaghloul St. The entrance to the Tomb of Saad Zaghloul is across the street from Bayt al-Umma. Tel: 794-5399
Metro stop:	Saad Zaghloul.
When:	Bayt al-Umma is open from 10am–5pm. Closed Mondays. During Ramadan 10am–1pm, 6:30–9pm.
Entrance Fee:	Foreigners: LE5, Egyptians: LE1, students: 50 piasters. Photography by special permit only.
How to get there:	Arriving by Metro or taxi is the simplest. Parking is impossible unless you have a driver who can maneuver the clogged streets. Walking from AUC is an easy 5 to 6–block trek, albeit noisy.
Age appropriateness:	Older children or teenagers would appreciate this site more than younger children. If your student is studying modern leaders of Egypt, this is a worthwhile trip.

Saad Zaghloul Cultural Center

The Center is to the right of the main entrance and in the basement of Bayt al-Umma; the guards are happy to direct you. Closed on Thursday (except from 5pm–8pm) and all day Friday, this center provided lessons in art, theater, and films for children. There are monthly exhibits of the children's work. Hours: 9am–3pm and 5pm–8pm. Tel: 795-6864.

MAKAN and Egyptian Center for Culture and Art

While some people see a space, a shop, or a garage, others hear music. Ahmed el-Maghrebi has transformed a common space and brought music to us. The philosophy behind this began with a concept to bring musicians together who were particularly interested in traditional Egyptian music. The Egyptian Center for Culture and Art opened its doors in 2003 and is located near the Giza pyramids on the Fayoum Road. Musicians and supporters participated in a host of workshops, events, and theater. A major success but not convenient for the public, serendipitously, Ahmed walked out of his home on Saad Zaghloul Street and turned in a direction that he normally would not go. On the corner he noticed a door that seemed to jump out at him and he decided that this was the place for music. Voila—MAKAN.

Ahmed's philosophy for the Egyptian Center for Culture and Art and MAKAN is to preserve the Egyptian musical heritage through instruments and know-how and to present these traditions to the younger generation; to present a living legacy of the music from the pharaohs to the Mamluks and to link this legacy to people; to explore music from Nubia to Alexandria as well as different genres of music like Zar, Soufi, Shaaby; to promote cultural exchange through art and music; to take traditional music and create new music through organizing workshops and exchanges. The music at MAKAN is like meeting a stranger and wanting to learn more, much more.

Where: **1 Saad Zaghloul and Mansour St., al-Mounira, Tel: 792-0878.**

When: **Tuesdays and Wednesdays at 9pm. Be sure and stay for discussion and tea after the concert.**

Tickets: **LE10–20.**

Web site: **Check schedule at** *www.egyptmusic.org* **or** *http://groups.yahoo.com/groups/wazzup-in-cairo.*

Education Museum and Document Library

Hidden away in a corner of the Ministry of Education is a gem of a museum. Perhaps not on the top twenty places to see in Cairo, nevertheless, this museum emphasizes the importance Egypt has placed on education through the centuries. Beginning with the ancient Egyptians and continuing to the 1952 Revolution, visitors are offered a comprehensive overview of the history of education.

Upon entering the museum, the staff welcomes visitors to sign the register and show identification. All exhibits are labeled in Arabic. The tour begins on the ground floor; panels separate each era.

Starting at the entrance:

Room #1: Education in ancient Egypt provides an idea of how children learned during ancient Egyptian times. On the wall to the left is an interesting chart that compares three Egyptian alphabets—Hieroglyphs, Hieratic, Demotic—and the equivalent in Arabic, Hebrew, Coptic, French, and German.

Room #2: Education in the Islamic period is explained by viewing models, dioramas, and a beautiful replica of a mosque and madrasa. Look at the map on the wall to the right. It was drawn by Sherif Telrisi in the sixth century. What do you think about it?

Room #3: Education in the nineteenth century.

Room #4: Education at the 1952 Revolution. In the first case, view

Abd al-Nasser's school certificate and grades from al-Tawfiqiya Secondary School.

Turning around and facing the entrance:

Room #5: To your right, this room is dedicated to the education of women in Egypt.

Walk up the stairs; the first floor is dedicated to representing education in the fields of technology, commerce, and agriculture.

Room #1: There are examples of items that are made by hand. The model of a man selling his product, the fez, is particularly compelling.

Room #2: Education in the field of commerce and business. Note, in the case to the right is an example of the first typewriters in Egypt.

Room #3: Education in the field of agriculture.

Room #4: University and Higher Education.

Room #5: Islamic Higher Education. This features a model of al-Azhar University and mosque.

Room #6: Visual aids used in the classroom. To the left is an exhibit about educating the blind.

Room #7: Calligraphy.

Returning to the stairway and to the right, the Document Library houses over 22,000 books about the laws that governed education in the nineteenth and twentieth centuries, as well as curricula, reports, and examination questions that have caused many a student to suffer!

Where:	Falaki St., Ministry of Education. The museum is to the right. Follow the signs, which are in English and Arabic at first, then the signs change to Arabic only. A statue of a scribe marks the entrance of the museum.
When:	9:00am–1:30pm. Closed Fridays and holidays.
Parking:	None, arrive by taxi or with a driver.
Arrangements:	Individuals are welcome at any time; however, for a school, class, or group, it is better to call ahead and arrange for a tour guide. Call 794-6338.
Entrance fee:	Free.
Tip:	The subject matter is appropriate for older children and teenagers. This would be a great trip for an Arabic language class as all labels are in Arabic. A catalogue is available in Arabic and English.

Abdin Palace

In 1863 when Khedive Ismail became ruler of Egypt and launched his modernization of Cairo, his plans included the construction of a magnificent building to house his family and serve as the new official residence for Egyptian rulers. He had hoped to have this completed in time for the opening of the Suez Canal, enabling him to welcome the world's dignitaries in a splendid, modern palace. However, Abdin Palace was not completed until 1872, replacing the Citadel, which had served as the official residence of Egyptian rulers since 1218.

Khedive Ismail purchased the land and palace of Abdin Bey (who had served as a general under Muhammad Ali Pasha) from Abdin Bey's widow. The original palace was demolished, but Ismail allowed Abdin's name to grace the new Egyptian ruler's official residence. The mausoleum of Sidi Badran, a nineteenth-century Muslim saint, was left and incorporated into the structure of the palace.

Tickets to enter the palace museum are available in a kiosk as you leave the parking area, across the street from Bab Paris, named in honor of the Empress Eugénie, a favorite guest of Khedive Ismail at the opening of the Suez Canal in 1869. After passing through security and possibly buying a catalogue, enjoy the spacious and luxuriant gardens. Abdin Palace is immense but it is still used in an official capacity, so only a section is open to the public. The cannons and the pyramid-piled cannon balls in the garden give a clue to the dominant theme of the museum, which is mainly concerned with weaponry.

The largest sections in the museum exhibit firearms; therefore, this outing will hold special fascination for anyone curious about weaponry. Room after room is filled with the memory of how people have defended themselves through the ages, the glories, and the defeats. Youth, especially boys, will flock to these displays. It is also an excellent way to learn history as some firearms—Mamluk, Ottoman, and European—date to the seventeenth century. Especially interesting are the cases containing firearms used in dueling, and Napoleon's duel case is among the exhibits; also to be seen are pinfire blunderbuss guns and a Browning automatic pistol that belonged to Mussolini. Another room of interest is the display of medals, necklaces, and sashes of European and Egyptian rulers that were presented to men who gave outstanding service to their countries.

The many gifts President Mubarak has received as president of Egypt, such as medals, photographs, and plaques, are displayed in a President and Mrs. Mubarak Gift Museum. In the Manial Palace there is the Private Museum (closed for renovation) holding gifts given to Muhammad Ali, King Farouk, and Crown Prince Muhammad Ali Tawfiq. It is interesting to see how time has influenced the types of gifts that rulers receive. Following this hall, in the silverware museum, a lavish display of silverware and chinaware educates us on how the royalty in the nineteenth century served their guests. The exhibits are presented meticulously, and are clearly marked in English and Arabic. Don't bypass the Historical Document Museum, which would be of interest to teenagers and adults.

Very young children may find this museum wearisome, although there are no stairs to prevent a baby-stroller from moving easily through the exhibits. There are tables and chairs in the garden for drinks, if smaller children need a diversion. However, during our excursion we decided the charming moments were at the end while sitting on a park bench in the beautifully kept garden.

Where: East of Midan al-Gumhuriya, the visitor's entrance is on the east wall on Mustafa Abd al-Raziq St. The surrounding streets have direction signs to the entrance. There is a large parking lot across from the entrance. Tel: 390-0325.

Metro stop: Muhammad Naguib Station.

When: Open 9am–3pm. Closed Fridays. The hours may change slightly in Ramadan.

Entrance fee: Foreigners: LE10, students LE5; Egyptians: LE2, students LE1.

Facilities: Toilets are clean. The entire museum is on one level: no stairs to maneuver baby-strollers or wheelchairs. The museum is air-conditioned.

Photography: Camera fee is LE10, video not permitted.

Midan Ramses

Ramses is the area of Cairo located around the train station, which dominates the entire northwest side of Midan Ramses. It is a busy, traffic-laden part of town. Centuries ago, the course of the river was farther to the east, and the Midan Ramses of today would have been next to the river. When the Fatimid rulers built their city *al-Qahira* in the tenth century, they built a port at this point called al-Maqs. Saladin enclosed al-Maqs within his city walls in 1276, and built a great gate at the western end of the wall through which to enter al-Maqs from the north. This gate was called Bab al-Hadid, the 'Iron Gate,' a name that is still used and refers to the area around the train station.

By the early fourteenth century, the river had shifted its course westward, leaving al-Maqs high and dry. A new port was built to the northwest at Bulaq.

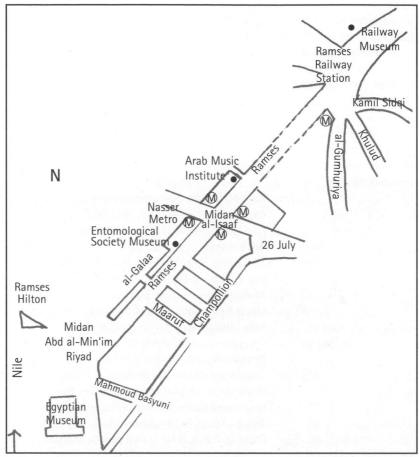

Ramses

From here, the unloaded goods were taken by land through the Bab al-Hadid and into Cairo. Bulaq was also the entry point for tourists coming to Cairo from Alexandria before the era of air travel. The Bab al-Hadid stood until 1847, when Muhammad Ali had it demolished to make way for the building of Egypt's first train station, completed in 1851.

In the middle of Midan Ramesses stands a colossal, ten-meter high granite statue of King Ramesses II. From its resting place at Mit Rahina (ancient Memphis), a convoy of trucks in 1955 painstakingly carried the ruler of the Nineteenth Dynasty to Bab al-Hadid by way of Queen Nazli Avenue, which from this time on was known as Ramses St. During King Ramesses' rule, he waged war on Palestine, Syria, and the Hittites of Anatolia but probably never fathomed that millennia later his statue would reign over one of the busiest sections of Cairo. Due to the negative effects of car emission on this antiquity, the statue is to be removed to the site of the new Grand Museum near the pyramids.

Entomological Society

This collection may not be high on the list of places to see due to its specialized contents. You may need special permission to enter, or if you are lucky, the guards may let you see the collection. However if the guards say the collection has been moved, we have been assured that the collection is definitely on the premises.

The collection of insects and birds is housed in a nineteenth-century mansion that is quite attractive in and of itself and is situated in a large garden, which adds to the unobtrusive atmosphere. Upon climbing the stairs, the first sight of the collection might seem disappointing, as the cases are dusty and the lighting is dim. Try to get past the initial desire to leave. If you stay, you will be rewarded with rooms well stuffed with birds.

The taxidermy of the birds dates to between 1909 and the 1930s. Many are mounted with prey in their claws and are set in tableaux representing their habitat. The collection of owls is outstanding and varied. Other species included are ducks, ibises, eagles, and herons.

On to the insect room, and at your fingertips you have no less than 50,000 different kinds of insects from Egypt and the Mediterranean area. If you are with a bug-crazed kid, definitely plan on lots of time to see them all. Do not overlook two out-of-the-ordinary exhibits: the life cycles of insects that live in wood, and the reproductive cycle of beetles.

This museum is for the serous-minded teenager. For younger children and others who are being introduced to taxidermy and entomology, the Hunting Museum at the Manial Palace and the Agricultural Museum would be more engaging, both of which have fascinating displays of insects and birds. There are three other good entomological collections in Egypt, one at the Faculty of Science Cairo University, one at the Faculty of Agriculture, Ain Shams University, and another in al-Azhar University.

Where: 14 Ramses St. The most prominent sign on the building is "Sadat Academy Management Service." Underneath is the sign for the Entomological Society Museum. The collection is housed on the second floor.

Metro: Nasser station; walk toward the Ramses Hilton about half a block. The museum is on the same side of the street as the Ramses

Hilton. Caution: If you must cross the street, be very, very careful. Ramses St. is one of the busiest streets in Cairo.

When: Normally the following is the correct information. However the guards may not allow you to enter without special permission. During the daytime only the bird collection can be viewed; however, in the evenings the custodian/expert opens up the bug room so both birds and bugs can be seen. Sunday–Wednesday 9am–1pm; Saturday 10am–1pm. Also on Monday and Wednesday evenings 5:30–8:00pm. Entrance free.

Facilities: Research library. In the evening, tea and snacks are available because of the classes being conducted on the lower floors. There are tables and chairs for writing.

Parking: Parking on the side of either street is a problem in the daytime. There is parking space within the compound: explain that it is the museum you want to see and the guards will probably allow you to park. In the evening there seems to be no problem of parking inside the compound. Parking cost LE5.

Other entomological collections:

Faculty of Science, Cairo University; Faculty of Agriculture, Ain Shams University; al-Azhar University.

Arab Music Institute and Abd al-Wahab Museum

'The main thing that makes man happy is to find love inside his house and respect outside it.' —Muhammad Abd al-Wahab

The newspapers and magazines prepared us for the re-opening of the Arab Music Institute, with an exhibit of instruments from the Orient and a museum commemorating Egypt's famous composer, Muhammad Abd al-Wahab. Consistent with Abd al-Wahab's philosophy, I was shown the respect and generosity that is the hallmark of Egyptian hospitality, and was kindly invited on a guided tour.

King Fuad I built the Arab Music Institute in 1923 to honor the music and musicians of the Middle East. At opening night, Muhammad Abd al-Wahab sang before King Fuad, reinvigorating the tradition of great composers, musicians, and singers performing before royalty, dignitaries, and the wealthy upper class. The Institute hosted the first Arabic Music Conference in 1932, and henceforth its reputation grew throughout the region. Neglected in the 1970s and 80s, the renewal of such a magnificent building and its history is truly a cele-

The Arab Music Institute

bration. Two statues of Abd al-Wahab remind Cairenes of this famous composer—one at the Cairo Opera House grounds, the other at Bab al-Shaariya.

Walking into the foyer is an experience. Time can be spent admiring the cool, geometrically-designed stone floor, the original chandeliers, and magnificently restored, hand-painted dome. From this point, ascend the winding staircase and within the circular hall, through the door closest to you and to the left, there is a small room to view the first movies released in Egypt; a remote control provides a choice of films. Out in the hall, turn to your left, you will come to a library with rare books, records, and tapes. Enter the hall, walking left, and through the corridor, you will see four rooms dedicated to instruments used in the Orient and the Middle East. The rooms are separated into categories of percussion, flutes, strings, and brass instruments. Return in the direction you came, as you pass the domed hallway, turn left. Comments by legendary Egyptian writers, poets, and composers are captured on the walls. Between the writing on the walls, two doors face each other. Which one will you choose?

If you choose the one to the right, you will enter a multimedia room. Egyptian computer engineers from the Opera House have compiled 60 hours of music, films, pictures, and memorabilia of Abd al-Wahab's life. Here, you can satisfy your curiosity about the man and his music. You can even hear Abd al-Wahab create his music from a small recorder that he always carried with him. But if your choice is the door to the left, you will experience the splendor of the finely designed and restored music theater. Words can hardly give justice to the tastefully done opulence of the music hall. The king and queen of Egypt sat in the boxes on either sides of the stage. Listen closely . . . you may hear a lingering melody.

Last but not least, the room at the end of the corridor is the Abd al-Wahab Museum. This room is dedicated to the Abd al-Wahab's life and his love for music. His belongings, pictures of his family, friends, and work, letters, films, awards, and medals tell an abbreviated story. We even glimpse into his home and everything is placed exactly where he left them: recorder, glasses, even his favorite turquoise telephone. Abd al-Wahab died in his rocking chair next to his favorite piano. His wife, Nahla El Kodsy, did not change the clock or the calendar at his passing . . . twelve o'clock on May 3, 1991.

Where: Ramses St. between 26th July St. and Nadl Musica St. Tel: 574-3373, 574-8149.

When: 10:30am–3pm. Closed Fridays.

Entrance fee: Foreigners LE5; Egyptians LE2.

Parking: Very difficult, it is best to take a taxi or metro.

Metro: Nasser Station.

Tip: All labels are in Arabic.

Performances: There will be musical evenings, open to the public, to celebrate and appreciate Eastern music. Tickets will be available at the Institute and Cairo Opera House.

Facilities: There are bathrooms on both floors.

Railway Museum

Are you tired of birthday parties centered on bowling or swimming? Are you looking for a fresh idea? Children will be enthralled with the interactive models and genuine train engines at the Railway Museum. There is only one entrance and exit, so feel free to let children wander throughout the two stories of exhibits.

The first railway in Egypt was built between Cairo and Alexandria in 1854. It reduced travel time from four days to several hours. Although the British had approached Muhammad Ali in 1834 to build a railway line, the scheme was not finalized. Egypt would wait nearly twenty years until Abbas I Pasha, the nephew of Muhammad Ali, agreed with the British to lay the first tracks.

The interest in establishing this museum came about in the early 1930s when Egypt hosted the International Railway Conference. The museum, claiming to be the first of its kind in the East, opened to guests and members of the conference on January 15, 1933.

Upon entering the museum, the first attractions are the two authentic locomotives to the right. The first locomotive, on the right, is sectioned through the center to demonstrate the internal working parts of an engine and how coal was used as fuel. On the left is the original royal engine of Said Pasha (who reigned from 1854 to 1866), which was a gift from the French queen Eugènie in 1862. Said Pasha used this engine to inspect his estate. Decorated with arabesques, the cab has leather sofas and brass fittings. You can climb into these marvelous engines, explore, and touch, which ensures that all visitors will begin the outing with enthusiasm. The remainder of the first floor is devoted to old and new signaling devices, with hands-on displays explaining how trains were directed manually and mechanically to different routes. The guide will demonstrate how hand levers were used to switch train tracks, each lever color coded for engineers who did not read. There are old telephones, telegraph equipment, and plenty of flashing lights, bells, and movable

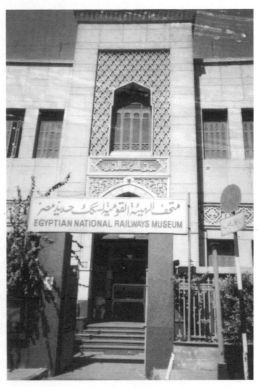

The Railway Museum

parts to keep the attention of adults and children. In addition, there are models depicting the type of bridges and railway construction used in old and new railway stations in other countries.

How did the ancient Egyptians move monuments? How did the Greeks and Romans use transportation? You will find out upstairs in the museum. Movement is the theme of these displays as well as the paraphernalia that accompanied it, such as a printing press for tickets and train schedules. Children are welcome to operate the press and come away with an understanding of the work done by human and machine rather than by computers.

Continuing to the right of the stairway, there are models of locomotives and rail cars, which help to explain the development of the railway system in Egypt. Pull the ropes under each display case and watch the movement of the train.

At the far end of the room, you will see an elaborate toy train that was owned by a rich cotton merchant, Farghali Pasha, and confiscated during the 1952 Revolution. On close inspection, notice that the landscape around the model reflects the countryside from the Muqattam Hills to Helwan. Although it has been left to deteriorate, one can imagine that it brought immense joy to young and old during its day.

After you have thoroughly investigated the museum, there is one more surprise. Outside the museum to the left, a large warehouse exhibits the first locomotive to run in Egypt in 1854. The guide will probably open the door before you ask, but if not, be sure to request him to do so. Climbing onto this old engine is, indeed, a unique experience.

Where: At the Cairo Railway Station, Midan Ramses. Facing the main station entrance, take the sidewalk to your right. Walk almost to the end of the street. There is a large sign over the entrance. Tel: 579-3793.

Metro: Mubarak Station puts you in front of the main train station.

When: 8am–2pm. Closed Mondays.

Entrance fee: Foreigners: LE10, except on Friday and holidays: LE20. Egyptians: LE2, and students: LE1. Guidebooks available free of charge. Camera charge: LE20.

Guide: A pleasant man who speaks basic English is delighted to show visitors the many exhibits.

Facilities: Bathroom available. Snacks or refreshments are not available: it is advisable to bring water. There are stairs to climb, no elevator.

Parking: None. There is heavy construction equipment and the road leading to the museum is torn up.

Sakakini Palace

Habib Sakakini Pasha built this house in 1897, and what a wonderful imagination he must have had. There are hundreds of gargoyles, flashy statues and busts, and ornate windowsills. At each corner of the house, large shells depict each season of the year. The palace resembles a Christmas tree lavishly decorated with ornaments on each corner. Sakakini's story is fittingly captured in the architectural fantasy of his palace. Gazing up at the risqué statues, one wonders if he built the palace thinking he lived in Rome rather than Cairo.

Inside the house, the floor to ceiling doors, iron work, woodwork and paneling, and elaborate murals are incredible. On the ceiling of the library, Habib Pasha has painted himself among the angels. In its heyday, it took forty servants to keep up the house and serve the family.

Habib Sakakini arrived in Cairo from Syria as a teenager and began his success by an ingenious scheme to sell starving cats to the rat-infested Suez Canal project. Khedive Ismail appreciated a man with initiative and gave Sakakini the job of finishing the Opera House before the opening ceremony of the Suez Canal. Hard work paid off and his success brought more building contracts.

In an interview with Asma el-Bakri, great granddaughter of Habib Pasha and who lived at the palace as a child, Asma told the story that Habib Pasha did not believe in automobiles and until he died in 1924, he refused to allow any member of his family residing at the Palace to own one; the only mode of transportation

Sakakini Palace

was the horse and carriage. Asma also explained that in 1953, her grandmother was the only person living in the palace and moved to Zamalek. During that time, houses and palaces were being confiscated by the government; therefore, the family decided to present their palace as a gift to the Egyptian people. The family received thanks by telegram from President Abd al-Nasser. Unfortunately, the place was left to deteriorate. It is certainly a shame. The future plans of this palace are unknown, but at present, the fate of this unique mansion is to collapse into a pile of rubble.

If you are interested in delving deeper into the history of Habib Sakakini, here are some sites to check out. In Fagella, Sakakini bought land and gave it to the Greek Orthodox Church; a church was built in 1919. In addition, he also donated land in 1896 to create an area for a Greek Catholic Cemetery, which is situated behind the Hanging Church in Old Cairo (see map on page 151). There he built a family mausoleum and chapel where to this day, on every first Saturday of the month, prayers are offered by a priest of the Greek Malachite Catholic Church. In this quiet sanctuary, could Habib Pasha have known his generous contribution would insure him peaceful remembrance?

Sakakini Palace is close to Midan Ramses but it is also easy to get there from the Islamic Museum. Before you go to the Islamic Museum, head first to Sakakini Palace; it is only five minutes away. Need information about Sakakini Palace? Call Mohamed Mahran Ahmed, manager of Sakakini Palace, at 757-3864 or 010 734-4608.

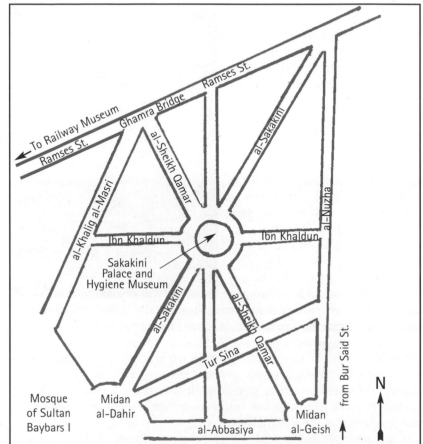

Sakakini /
Ramses Area

Where: **Take Ramses St. past Midan Ramses and turn right on al-Sheikh Qamar or al-Sakakini St. Or else drive on Port Said (Bur Said) St. past the Islamic Museum; keep on this road as it turns into al-Khalig al-Masri and then turn on Ibn Khaldun to the palace.**

Metro: **Ghamra Station; cross Ramses St. and head along al-Sheikh Qamar St.**

Mosque of Sultan Baybars I

You might pass the walls of this enormous congregational mosque on the way to Sakakini Palace. The mosque spans one hundred square meters and fills the entire midan. Only the central area around the prayer niche is still used today; the mosque has suffered horrible misuse over the past centuries. When Napoleon arrived he named it Fort Sulkowski in memory one of his aide-de-camps who was killed in Cairo (a name you can still find on old Cairo maps). Napoleon's troops set up cannons on the roof; however, the minaret that once stood over the main entrance to the mosque was gone as can be seen in the French drawing in the *Description de L'Egypte* of 1800. Later, Muhammad Ali turned the mosque into a soap factory, and the British used it as a slaughter-house and military bakery. The mosque was finally saved by a decree of King Fuad in 1920.

Baybars was a Bahri Mamluk who ruled Egypt and Syria from 1260–77. He built his mosque in Cairo between 1267 and 1269, making it the earliest Mamluk mosque built in the city. Baybars was born a Kipchak Turk in what is now Kazakhstan, and was a slave of the Ayyubid sultan al-Salih. Baybars captured Louis IX of France at the Battle of Mansura during the Crusader Wars that culminated in the siege of the Krak des Chevaliers, and also led the defeat of the Mongol army in Syria.

As sultan, Baybars was a remarkable statesman and diplomat. He formed an alliance with the Mongols to protect his empire from the Persians, and also signed commercial treaties with James of Aragon and Alfonso of Seville. He

*Mosque of
Sultan Baybars I*

established a postal service between Damascus and Cairo, which could deliver a letter in four days. The empire Baybars established lasted for 250 years.

Where: **Midan al-Dahir.**

When: **8am–10pm. Open everyday although on Friday it is crowded for prayers.**

Shubra

Shubra is the district of Cairo to the north and east of the Railroad Station: skirting Ahmad Helmi Street to the east; to the west, the Nile Corniche; to the north, the Delta by way of the Cairo-Alexandria Agricultural Road. It is one of the most densely populated parts of Cairo. The land that makes up Shubra was originally an island, which by Ayyubid times remained permanently above the water of the annual inundation. The island was called Geziret al-Fil, Elephant Island, supposedly because a ship named the Elephant has been wrecked there. By the mid-fourteenth century the Nile had shifted westward, and Geziret al-Fil became part of the east bank.

Shubra remained primarily agricultural until Muhammad Ali built his palace there in 1808. He also constructed a boulevard one hundred feet wide, lined with trees, from his palace all the way down to Azbakiya. Following the example of Muhammad Ali, other members of the royal family and the upper class built villas and summer residences at Shubra. In 1903 a tramline was built on the grand boulevard, and this area opened up to urban development. Nowadays this boulevard is a main north–south artery, Shubra Street.

National Library and Archives—Dar al-Kutub

The National Library and Archives (Dar al-Kutub) was established in 1870 by Ismail Pasha to collect and preserve valuable manuscripts. It was first housed in Prince Mostapha Fadel's Palace, and then moved to the Khedivate Library and House of Arab Antiquities, now the Museum of Islamic Art. In 1903, it was moved to its present location.

Read the works of famous Egyptian writers, stroll through cases of books donated by Egyptian families, view magnificent works of the Quran, study ancient maps—all at your fingertips. This library, with its well-lit, spacious rooms is dedicated to research. The work areas are comfortable, and the view of the Nile and Zamalek's fine palaces adds to the tranquil surroundings.

As one enters the main lobby there is a small exhibit commemorating famous Egyptians. Displayed in the lobby walking in a clockwise direction is a bust of the famous author, Abbas al-Akkad, as well as his reading glasses, his radio, and samples of his writing. A bust of Ismail Pasha is next. Paraphernalia from Tawfiq al-Hakim's wardrobe and some pieces of his writings present a visitor with an impression of his life. The poet Hafiz Ibrahim is remembered by excerpts from his work. Along the walls, there are decorated pages of the Quran from the period of Ottoman rule.

This library is for the serious student who may want to research the works of great playwrights, poets, writers, essayists, novelists, and composers of Egypt. The rooms on the fourth and fifth floors have collections of books from Egyptians such as Abbas al-Akkad, poet and writer; Abd al-Rahman al-Rafai, historian, journalist, lawyer; Taha Hussein, writer, educator, minister; Yousef Kamal, painter; Abbas Hilmi Pasha, a prince of the Muhammad Ali dynasty; and the collections from the library of Abdin Palace, the Cabinet, and much more.

Where: Nile Corniche, next to and north of the Conrad Hotel. Tel: 575-1078, 575-0886.

When: Open Saturday–Wednesday 9am–9pm. Closed Thursdays and Fridays.

Fees: Free, bring ID.

Parking: Some spaces along the street or park at the Conrad Hotel.

Tip: All bags must be checked. Have pockets to carry money and important items.

Camera: Prohibited.

Muhammad Ali Palace—Shubra Palace

In marble pav'd pavilion where a spring
Of living water from the center rose,
Whose bubbling did a genial freshness fling,
And soft voluptuous couches breathed repose,
Ali reclined, a man of war and woes.
—Lord Byron

In his book, *In the House of Muhammad Ali*, Hassan Hassan shares Lord Byron's impression of Muhammad Ali Pasha lounging in the Fountain Pavilion during the end of his life. Shubra Palace, as described by Hassan, was a favorite palace of the ruler that blended lush countryside with elegant simplicity.

Muhammad Ali Pasha built this palace along the northeastern Nile riverbank to celebrate festivals and holidays and as a guesthouse for foreign dignitaries. Being built in the northern most area of Cairo it caught the fresh, prevailing winds, all within the lush, green countryside. It took thirteen years to finish, and by 1821 thirteen buildings on 11,000 feddans of spectacular gardens were ready for Muhammad Ali Pasha's guests and his family. Only three buildings remain, the Fountain Pavilion *(al-faskiya)*, the Waterwheel Pavilion *(al-saqya)*, the Mountain House *(al-gabalaya)*.

Walk through the alabaster entrance to the Fountain Pavilion. It is a feast of beauty for the eyes and you are immediately cooled by the northern breeze passing over white marble and the gurgling waters. Almost demure in its elegance, it was created by the engineer Pascal Coste. A square pavilion with European-style painted ceilings and four terraces on each side is connected by way of a promenade, which surrounds the basin (much like a huge wading pool for children) and fountain. From each corner, as water spouts from the mouth of lions, it cascades over fish and reptiles carved from the marble, which gives the on-looker the impression of their movement. Around the fountain there are twenty-four crocodiles that support the main fountain. On each corner are rooms (locked, but someone might have the key) once used for dining, recreation, and sleeping quarters.

Walking toward the Nile, the Mountain House explains its name as it towers over the gardens and the Nile, being built like the step pyramid of Saqqara. What a view two hundred years ago! Inside, the walls and floors are alabaster and many beautiful paintings remind us of the how the gardens were thick and lush and one could sit on the veranda and see the Giza pyramids.

Where: Alex-Cairo Road on the Corniche, Shubra al-Khamieh. From the Conrad Hotel drive about six kilometers north along the Corniche; follow the Alex-Cairo Road. After Aga Khan gardens, you will begin to see a high beige cement wall. The gate, facing the Nile, is not open to the public. Continue to the first right and follow this past the church on the left and a school entrance on the right. You will come to a flyover, keep to the right and you will see a gate to the Agricultural College on the right. You can park your car here and walk to the palace. There has been some contention about having visitors walk through the college but as the gates on the Corniche are not open for now, this is the only entrance.

When: 9am–2pm. Closed Friday.

Tip: Some monuments, when not clearly open to the public, still will allow visitors. Muhammad Ali Palace is one of these monuments; though there is no clear statement that it is open to the public, upon arrival, the gatemen are welcoming. For more information and for family stories about **Shubra Palace**, read *In the House of Muhammad Ali: A Family Album 1805–1952* by Hassan Hassan (AUC Press, 2000).

Camera: No photography unless permission is granted from the Supreme Council of Antiquities.

Midan al-Ataba

The area of town known as Ataba centers on Midan al-Ataba, Midan al-Opera, and the Azbakiya Gardens. The importance of Ataba arises out of the fact that Midan al-Ataba was the central terminal for all the tramlines established in 1896. Midan al-Opera was the site of the Opera House built by Khedive Ismail, which opened on November 1, 1869 with the performance of *Rigoletto* by Verdi. Unfortunately, the Opera House burned down in 1971.

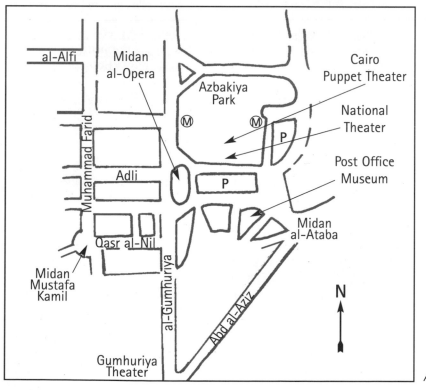

Ataba

Ibrahim Pasha at Midan al-Opera

The area that is now Azbakiya Gardens used to be one of a string of lakes parallel to the river. In 1476, the Mamluk emir Azbak, the general of Sultan Qaitbay, chose to build his palace on the edge of this lake. Wealthy and important noblemen followed him, built luxurious houses along the tree-lined banks, and referred to the area as Azbakiya, after Azbak. In the late eighteenth century, a most magnificent palace was built on the west side by Muhammad Bey al-Alfi. When the French invaded Egypt, Napoleon took this palace as his headquarters.

By the time Muhammad Ali gained control of Egypt, Cairo had become an unattractive city, unsafe from years of

What was Black Saturday?

In the early 1950s, many Egyptians were angered at the influence the British government maintained in Egypt and Sudan and the British military presence in the Suez Canal Zone. The loss of Palestine, the civil war in Greece, and the outbreak of the Korean War were a few of the reasons why the British wished to remain in control of the Suez Canal. Egyptians did not want the British on their soil, which allowed the British government to intervene in their politics. On January 25, 1952, British troops retaliated and attacked a police station in Ismailia killing scores of Egyptians. The following day, on Saturday, January 26, outraged groups from all sectors of Egyptian society marched together in demonstration to Abdin Palace. The crowds shifted to Midan al-Opera, the Europeanized area of Cairo. Up until this point, the crowds had been merely demonstrating but it took only a small incident to ignite their anger and frustration. This incident happened when the crowd spotted an Egyptian police officer sitting at a cabaret with one of the dancers. Furiously, the mob set fire to the establishment and continued until the Metro Cinema, the Turf Club, Barclay's Bank, Groppi, foreign shops, department stores, airline offices, and cars were all set ablaze. The famous Shepheard's Hotel was burned to the ground. The estimated cost of damage to property was nearly $500 million.

political instability, unhealthy due to clogged canals and lakes, and unsightly due to deteriorating houses, mosques, and public facilities. One of Muhammad Ali's vast programs to remedy these problems was to fill in the ponds and lakes that harbored mosquitoes and insects, which contributed to the unhealthy conditions in Cairo. Azbakiya was one of the lakes Muhammad Ali filled and transformed into a garden. Rejuvenated, the area became the center for social life of the elite and foreign visitors. The palace of Alfi Bey became a hotel run by Samuel Shepheard in 1849. The hotel was rebuilt several times and was eventually burned down in 1952 during the Black Saturday riots.

Little remains of al-Ataba's former glory. The burning down of the Opera House and Shepheard's Hotel, the encroachment of buildings, and the splitting in half of the gardens by the construction of 26th of July St. have all contributed to its decline. A statue of Ibrahim Pasha, the father of Khedive Ismail and acting governor of Egypt for three months in 1848, stands in the center of Midan al-Opera, an area that no longer captures the gardens' former grandeur.

Post Office Museum

This museum is one of the treasures of Cairo. Do not let the fifty-piaster entrance fee misrepresent the importance of this collection. The museum is devoted to the postal history of Egypt from pharaonic times, through the Ptolemaic period and the Romans, to the present. Postal paraphernalia such as leather mailbags, miniature statues of postal workers, and a stamp printing machine are some of the memorabilia collected in this museum. Models of steam engines, ships, feluccas, camels, and bicycles explain the movement of letters. Postal uniforms from around the world provide an opportunity to compare apparel of the mail carrier. The first post box in Egypt, as well as post boxes designated for specific destinations, let the visitor contemplate differences between the past and future of postal distribution. And of course, what would a postal museum be without stamps? Visitors will not be disappointed with the display of local stamps with pharaonic, Islamic, and Coptic designs and international stamps, memorial stamps, and public stamps used in government offices. There are commemorative stamps of King Farouk's coronation, the July Revolution, Nile Day, the October War, and much more.

The ancient Egyptians were probably the first to initiate a postal service, as documented in the Amarna room at the Egyptian Museum. Nearly 3,500 years ago, letters in the form of square clay tablets were sent as diplomatic correspondence between Pharaoh Akhenaten and rulers from empires and provinces such as Babylon, Mitanni, Assyria, Syria, and Palestine (see Egyptian Museum section, page 31, letter V).

However, the history of the postage stamp is recent compared to the letters sent in Akhenaten's reign. In Britain, the first stamp was introduced on May 6, 1840, and Khedive Ismail issued the first Egyptian stamp in 1866. Egyptian stamps were printed in Genoa up until 1961, after which Egypt acquired its first stamp printing press.

At the end of the room is a mosaic that covers most of the wall. From a distance, you would never guess that it is made of 15,000 stamps—all the same and all postmarked! Can you make out the image the stamps form? The desk and chair in front of the tapestry are those of the first postmaster in Egypt, Jacob Muzzi, an Italian. This is a good place to take a picture.

Where: Midan al-Ataba at the Central Post Office, which is next to a fire station. To buy a ticket, go through the door marked 'Main Post Office,' and purchase tickets at the commemorative stamp office, on your right. Then go out to the street and enter the door marked 'L'Organisme Nationale des Postes.' The museum is on the second floor: take a right and then another quick right turn. People are happy to help you find your way when they see your ticket. There is an elevator to the left of the stairway. Tel: 390-0151, 390-0737.

Metro: Ataba Station.

When: 9am–1pm. Closed Fridays. During Ramadan, 10–12 noon.

Entrance fee: 50 piasters. Cameras are allowed with no fee.

Stairs: The stairway is steep and circular.

Parking: There is a large parking facility behind Midan al-Opera and diagonally across from the Central Post Office, on Ataba car park. If you have a driver, it might be possible for him to wait in the road between the fire station and post office.

Tip: Sunday is a good day to see this museum since many Downtown shops are closed.

Cairo Puppet Theater

Although the surroundings are rather dilapidated, the theater is clean and air-conditioned. Puppets and props are colorful. Performances are in Arabic and

Cairo Puppet Theater

specifically for children 7 years and younger. There is enough color and animation in the show to entertain even the non-Arabic speakers. Each season there is a new show.

Where: In front of Azbakiya Park. Drive around Midan al-Opera, keeping the Central Post Office on the right; stay to the left. This is a one way street. Drive past the National Theater, taking the first left between the Ataba car park and the Ministry of Telecommunications. The Puppet Theater is at the end of the road and where the Azbakiya Park begins. Facing the park, the Puppet Theater is to the left and the Cairo Traffic Department is to the right.
The front of the building is decorated in blue and white tiled vertical spears.

Metro: Ataba Station.

When: Thursday 7:30–8:15pm,
Friday and Sunday 11:30am–1pm.

Entrance fee: Foreigners: LE10, Egyptians: LE5. Reservations are generally needed, especially if there is a group. Call: 591-0954. If you are few, it might be possible to find some empty seats. However, it is a popular theater so it would be advisable to call ahead.

Reservations and information are in Arabic.

Parking: Available at Ataba Car Park next to the Puppet Theater.

Garden City

Driving through Garden City, one might wonder about the name of this congested and overbuilt mini-city in central Cairo, but in the past this area was beautifully green with flowering trees, and its surroundings lived up to its name. The development of the area began only in 1905. Before that time, it

Grey Pillars,
Garden City

had been filled with plantations, bean fields, and orchards that supported the city's agricultural needs. Muhammad Ali's son Ibrahim built his palace, Qasr al-Dubara here, and later Khedive Ismail's mother built her palace, Qasr al-Aali, leaving a large area for their gardens. However, the end began when a group of land developers bought the plantations, gardens, and palaces in 1905, demolishing and carving unsymmetrical plots out of the land, and designing twisting roads that often ended where they began.

Since the building of the Aswan Dam in 1902, the Nile shoreline became stable, and low-lying swamps were filled in, which meant that the city's land would not be flooded annually. With the building of bridges to connect islands to the west and east banks and the development of mass transit, areas such as Garden City, Gezira, and Zamalek were urbanized at a fast pace.

It is easy to pass through Garden City with its continuous rows of high-rise buildings without realizing it. New hotels will soon overshadow the once secluded and quiet streets. Still, a quick search for the Grey Pillars might reveal a few stories of interest to teenagers.

Grey Pillars
On the corner of al-Saraya al-Kubra Street and al-Birgas Street still stands the building that was once fondly referred to as "No. 10" by many British officers. Nicknamed "No. 10" after the British prime minister's residence in London, the new Minister of State for Middle East Affairs was located at Garden City's No. 10 Tolombat Street in 1941. The name, Grey Pillars, was the codename for this secret ministry. Oliver Lyttleton, the new minister, and a host of international personalities such as Charles de Gaulle, Zionist leader Chaim Weizmann, and Lord Moyne passed through these doors. Although today the street's name has changed to Ittihad al-Muhamiyin al-Arab and the carriages that once brought allies and enemies together have been forgotten, the walls of No. 10 probably are still entrusted with arcane affairs.

At 1081 Corniche al-Nil, Cairo's first skyscraper, built in the late 1950s, is no longer unique or noticeable. Although now lost among the high towers, this Garden City building was the first in Cairo to establish the architect's desire to utilize air as living space.

One piece of the past is still obtainable and for all ages: an hour's sail on a felucca is a fine way to end any tour in the downtown area. In Garden City across from the Four Seasons Nile Plaza, at Dok-Dok felucca rides are available any time of day or evening.

Cultural Centers
American Research Center in Egypt (ARCE)
2 Midan Simon Bolivar, 1st floor. Tel: 794-8239, 796-2429. ARCE has fantastic excursions, usually within Egypt, led by Egyptologists and experts in the field. Space is limited on trips. The library is for ARCE members only. Open 8:30am–3:30pm. Closed Fridays and Saturdays. See their Web site, *www.arce.org*, for complete schedule.

Sayyida Zaynab
The part of Cairo called Sayyida Zaynab takes its name from the granddaughter of the Prophet Muhammad, who came to Egypt in the later part of the seventh century. The Mosque of Sayyida Zaynab takes up the whole southwest side of Midan Sayyida Zaynab, the center of the district. Sayyida Zaynab's mosque, which also contains her tomb, has been rebuilt and enlarged many times. The latest expansion of the building was just finished in December 1999, doubling the area available for worship inside the mosque.

Sayyida Zaynab
1. Saniya Secondary
   School
2. Bayt al-Sinnari
3. Sabil-Kuttab of
   Sultan Mustafa
4. Sayyida Zaynab
   Mosque
5. Sayyida Zaynab
   Cultural Park
6. Sarghatmish
   Mosque
7. Ibn Tulun
   Mosque
8. Gayer-Anderson
9. Sabil Umm Abbas
10. Qasr Amir Taz
11. Mustafa Kamil
    Tomb & Museum
12. Citadel
13. Al-Rafai
    Mosque
14. Sultan Hasan
    Mosque &
    Madrasa
15. Whirling
    Dervish Mevlevi
    Complex
16. Islamic Art
    Museum
17. El-Mastaba
18. Saint Samaan

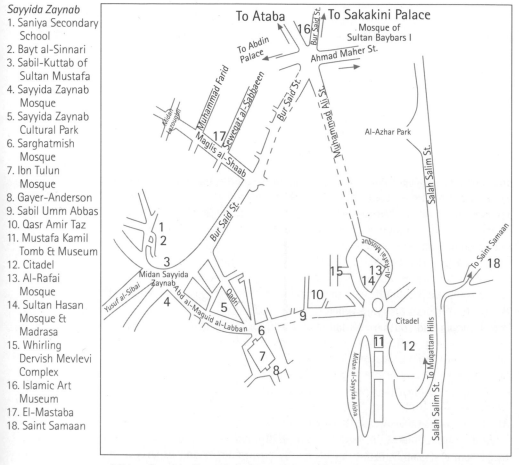

Midan Sayyida Zaynab is located just where the old Nile to Red Sea canal curved and headed north. This canal, the Khalig, was cut in late pharaonic times, and from then until the nineteenth century provided a way to go by boat from Cairo through the Delta to Lake Timsah and the Red Sea. Houses with beautiful gardens once lined the canal.

Little by little the Khalig lost its function, and in 1897 it was filled in and a north–south thoroughfare with a tramline took its place. The tram functioned up until a few years ago, when the tracks were torn up.

In Ramadan, Sayyida Zaynab is an especially busy place, as stalls selling *fawanis*, colorful lanterns, open on the streets next to the mosque. Lanterns are available in all sizes and price ranges, from tiny key chains to huge copper and glass lanterns too heavy to carry.

Across the street from Sayyida Zaynab Mosque is an Ottoman *sabil*—a public water source that was donated by a private individual to the community. Built in 1759, the *sabil* is decorated in an intricate colored marble design.

El Mastaba Center for Egyptian Folk Music

El Mastaba is an independent cultural center based in Cairo, which is dedicated to collecting and documenting Egyptian music, song and dance, and recording it. Folkloric music is passed down through generations connected by instruments, language, beliefs, and communities. For example, the music of Rango developed when peoples from Sudan and Ethiopia began to settle in northern Egypt. Muhammad Ali's army conquered Sudan in 1820. During the next fifty years, Sudanese joined the army. Slaves were brought from Ethiopia and southern Sudan to work in cotton cultivation. People from these tribes formed communities such as one found today in Ismailiya, Arayshiyyit al-Abid (the Slave Stockades) and they developed their music that has similarities to Middle Eastern culture but with its own sense of rhythm and meaning.

The Ottoman sabil of Sultan Mustafa on Midan Sayyida Zaynab

El Mastaba Center focuses on the similarities and variations of traditional music from Port Said, Ismailiya, al-Matariya, Suez, and Upper Egypt. The documentary film *Sirens* by Zakaria Ibrahim, explores the legends of the *simsimiya* and the ancient Egyptian lute, and how it is still played in Egyptian communities. One of the center's main activity is in Port Said where the main musical band (Tanbura) is located. They perform in Port Said every Wednesday (and have done for fifteen years) and present traditional and popular 'canali' songs and music.

Where: **4 Seweqat al-Sabbaeen St., off Maglis al-Shaab St., al-Sayyida Zaynab, Downtown. Drive east on Maglis al-Shaab (toward Port Said) past Midan Lazoughli, continue past Muhammad Farid Street (where there is a vegetable market). Drive toward the huge RIRI advertisement on a multi-story building. Take** the first RIGHT before the garden. (On the left of Maglis al-Shaab is the al-Hanifi Ottoman mosque.) The door of the building is metallic orange, and there is a small sign to the left of the door: Markaz al-Mastaba li-l-Musika al-Sharqiya, 4th floor.

Telephone: 392-6768, 012 322-6345.
When: 10am–4pm.
Web site: *www.elmastaba.org*
Activities: Musical events, documentary films, database for music and videos, discussion groups, work shops.

Architectural Elements of a Cairene House 14th–18th Century

Hammam–bathroom.
Haremlik–women's quarters.
Hosh–open-air courtyard, often with a fountain, windows, and doors of the house open onto the courtyard.
Malqaf–rooftop dome or wind catcher that faces the north to catch the prevailing winds.
Ma'qad–an open, triangular veranda on the first floor that overlooks the courtyard.
Mashrabiya–wooden lattice coverings for windows, used to soften the direct rays of the sun. Also, an area where women could see but not be seen.
Qa'a–a formal living room for important male guests, the floor covered in marble with a fountain in the center, cooling the room during the hot months.
Salamlik–men's quarters.

Bayt al-Sinnari

Bayt al-Sinnari has quite a history and fortunately for us, this history has been preserved so we can take a glimpse back into eighteenth-century Cairo. There are few seventeenth- and eighteenth-century private houses still in existence. Without the assistance of private and government organizations, even these are at risk of being lost. The foresight and generosity of preserving ancient sites is a gift to all who come later, as there is no better way to understand the past than to walk through the actual rooms and halls of history.

Bayt al-Sinnari is one of twenty-nine Islamic private dwellings listed in 1970 as still standing in Cairo, as compared to six hundred dwellings listed two hundred years ago. Through abandonment and progressive urban modernization, these historical treasures have been demolished and forgotten.

The original owner, Ibrahim Katkhuda al-Sinnari, built his home in the late eighteenth century on the edge of the old Fatimid city, an area now known as Monge Alley in Sayyida Zaynab. Ibrahim was a Berber who came to Cairo as Ibrahim al-Aswad and worked as a *bawwab*, or house guard. He was self-educated and became known to the ruling Mamluks as someone who could predict the future. Apparently he was a master of his art and soon was accepted by Murad Bey, one of the two ruling emirs, who became Ibrahim's patron. Ibrahim changed his name to Katkhuda al-Sinnari. Through the generosity of his patron, al-Sinnari's home was built in the area then called al-Nasriya. When Napoleon Bonaparte defeated Murad Bey at Imbaba, he requisitioned Bayt al-Sinnari and two other nearby houses to accommodate members of the Commission des sciences et des arts, the scientists and artists who accompanied the invading French army and who later, back in France, produced the magnificent *Description de l'Egypte*.

By the nineteenth century the Khalig had become excessively polluted and a haven for mosquito breeding, and in 1898 it was filled in and replaced by Port Said (Bur Said) St. The area quickly became accessible and urbanized. To make room for more modern buildings, many of the private houses were destroyed, among them the two houses next to Bayt al-Sinnari.

It is most fortunate that we are able to enjoy the splendor of this domestic structure. Islamic houses all had certain elements, adapted to environmental and cultural needs. (A description of these elements can be found in the Gayer-Anderson Museum section.) As Bayt al-Sinnari has just been renovated, there are no furnishings, but you can get a good feeling of the important features of an Islamic house. The courtyard, the covered verandah *(maq'ad)*, the reception room *(qa'a)*, and the *mashrabiya* woodwork are seen while strolling through the house. The master of the house resided in the larger of the two sides, while the smaller side was the harem. A particular feature to notice is the windcatcher *(malqaf)* that faces north to let fresh air enter the *qa'a*, while the hot air escapes through a central dome.

Until it was restored, Bayt al-Sinnari housed the Institute of Applied Arts, where students researched and studied the arts and techniques of Egyptian handicrafts. Today, this house is used to host musical events.

Where: **Off Nasriya St., next to Saniya Secondary School for Girls. Follow Monge Alley, which goes straight to the house, or take the short**

winding road along the walls
of the secondary school.
When: 10am–2pm.

Gayer-Anderson Museum

Next to the Ibn Tulun Mosque are two old houses joined together by a bridge at the second floor. A visit to this complex constitutes one of the most enjoyable outings in Cairo. The family of al-Kiritli, who originally came from Crete, built the first house in 1540 and the second house in 1631. Bayt al-Kiritliya is the proper name of the two houses, but they are popularly referred to as the Gayer-Anderson Museum. As it happens with property, owners change, and the al-Kiritli family sold the house to a man named Sulayman, who in turn sold it to the government. In 1934, Major John Gayer-Anderson, who was working in the Egyptian civil service, expressed the desire to restore an ancient building in Cairo. The government gave him guardianship of Bayt al-Kiritliya and he proceeded over the next eight years to restore the house and furnish it with Ottoman household furnishings. Major Gayer-Anderson had to return to London 1942 because of poor health, and he died there in 1945.

When you take your family to see old Islamic houses, it might be helpful to know something about the unique characteristics of their design. The architecture of the house took into account the environment and climate, and was designed to be sensitive to the culture. The thick walled exterior, often windowless or with small, high windows, kept bandits from having easy access to the interior, and as well as providing privacy to those inside. This fortified-looking exterior also kept dust, heat, and noise to a minimum. These elements are clearly recognizable at Bayt al-Sinnari and the Gayer-Anderson Museum, as well as Bayt al-Sihaymi (near Khan al-Khalili), Bayt al-Harrawi, and Bayt Zaynab Khatoun (both behind al-Azhar Mosque), and Qasr Amir Taz in Sayyida Zaynab.

Windows on the ground floor were few and barred, while on the second floor, windows were covered with *mashrabiya*, intricately carved wooden coverings that filtered the sunlight and allowed the breeze to enter while protecting the inhabitant's privacy. Homes were stone-built, with a grand, decorative entrance. A guard or *bawwab* sat just inside on a bench, watchful of intruders, announcing guests, and overseeing errands. On entering the front door a guest could not pass directly into the house nor see inside but went through an angled passageway before entering a courtyard, or *hosh*. The master of the house would receive his guest at this point. Depending on the importance of the guest, the master of the house would either remain in the courtyard or escort him to the verandah, or *maq'ad*, which was open to the courtyard and on the second floor. The floor of this roofed reception area

Left: The salamlik qa'a (reception room for men) and malqaf. Right: Courtyard entrance to verandah or qa'a, Bayt Zaynab Khatoun

was covered with *kilims* and carpets and there was low seating where coffee and tea could be served while business was conducted. This area was utilized in the summer, while a winter reception room, the first internal room of the house, was used to receive guests during the cooler months. Around the four walls of the courtyard, *mashrabiya* windows permitted women and children to watch the courtyard and the male visitors discreetly.

Houses were separated into two distinct parts, the public quarters, or *salamlik*, where the men received their guests, and the private quarters, or *haremlik*, where the family rooms were. The kitchen and servants' quarters were on the ground floor. If the family were wealthy, the house would have a bathroom *(hammam)*. In northern countries such as Syria, bathrooms had hot water that came under the floor to warm the room, and wooden clogs were worn to protect the feet from the heat. In Egypt the *hammam* might not be heated, but clogs were used to protect feet from water. These wooden slippers could be works of art, decorated with inlaid mother-of-pearl. *Hammam* ceilings were dome-shaped, and fitted with geometric colored glass to let in the light through pleasing designs.

Another important feature of an Islamic house was the formal reception room, the *qa'a*, reserved for important male guests and ceremonies such as weddings. The *qa'a* was an immense rectangular room overlooked by *mashrabiya* screens on the second floor so the women could observe the happenings below. A fountain surrounded by marble mosaic cooled the room, refreshing the atmosphere and creating tranquil sounds. Also to keep the grand reception room cool, a wind-catcher *(malqaf)* built on the roof caught the cool north breeze. Furniture was minimal and the men sat on low couches or thickly carpeted floors. Servants carried large trays of food into the *qa'a* and set them on low tables or on the floor.

What to see at the Gayer-Anderson Museum

Facing the entrance to Ibn Tulun, the large entrance on your left is the east house. Go through the passageway to the central courtyard with a fountain and find the arched recess that holds the Well of the Bats, about which many neighborhood tales have been told. As you proceed upstairs to the *maq'ad*, notice the ornamental wooden ceilings, built-in cupboards, and *mashrabiya* windows around the courtyard. Upstairs, you will see the writing room, women's quarters, and secret closet used to look down onto the reception hall without being seen. Another flight up and the roof garden, surrounded with *mashrabiya* screens, offers a good view of the minaret of Ibn Tulun.

The two houses connect on the level of the roof garden through an internal bridge, and you can enter the west house. The Byzantine Room, Queen Anne's Room, the library, and the picture gallery all hold Major Gayer-Anderson's paintings and collections. The Damascus room is a hidden gem; the ceilings and walls are covered in inlaid and gilded wood, which was brought from a demolished house in Damascus. Down the stairs in the west house, you will enter the ornate *qa'a* that you saw from above. Looking upward, imagine the curious eyes staring down through the *mashrabiya*. Before you leave the west house, turn into the small courtyard, and the first room to your right contains a collection of birthing chairs, used by women to deliver their babies.

Before you go: **If you have younger children, it is worth buying** The Legend of Lotfiya, **written by Andy Smart and illustrated by Theo Gayer-Anderson, Major Gayer-Anderson's grandson. The fable is one told about the well of Bayt al-Kiritliya, and the beautifully drawn pictures portray life during this time. Also, look for** Legends of The House of the Cretan Woman, **AUC Press, 2001.**

Where: **It is easy to combine a visit to the museum with a trip to the Ibn Tulun Mosque. Go south on Port Said St. and turn left on Qadri St., a** large street before you actually enter Midan Sayyida Zaynab. You will see the minaret of Ibn Tulun looming at the end of the street. Make a left when the street ends and then a right around the side of the mosque. The Gayer-Anderson Museum is attached to the southeast corner of the mosque, and is perhaps the place to start. Tel: 364-7822.

When: 9am–4pm. Closed Fridays during midday prayer.

Entrance fee: Foreigners: LE30, students LE15; Egyptians: LE2, students LE1.

Camera: No fee for cameras; video: LE25.

Guide: There are guides to tell you about the house. They will expect a small tip at the end of the tour.

Suggestion: Starting at the Gayer-Anderson Museum is best with children, as after touring the confined rooms, Ibn Tulun Mosque is spacious. The large open space will definitely give any one a feeling of tranquillity.

After you go: It might be fun to rent the James Bond movie *The Spy Who Loved Me*, which was filmed at the Gayer-Anderson Museum, Ibn Tulun Mosque, and the Pyramids. This area is a cultural center, so be sure to investigate.

Mosque of Ahmad Ibn Tulun

Ibn Tulun, the oldest mosque in Cairo proper, was begun in 876 and finished in 879. The mosque is considered one of the finest mosques in Cairo and is all that is left of the Tulunid princely city, which was built by Ahmad ibn Tulun. He had been sent to Egypt by the Caliph of Baghdad (the Abbasid ruler) in 868 to serve as the governor of Fustat, but within two years he set up his own ruling dynasty. The mosque is modeled after the great mosque in the city of Samarra in Iraq, where Ibn Tulun grew up. Notice the distinctive type of crenellation on top of the walls, which is just like that in Samarra. Cut out a chain of paper-dolls and notice the resemblance! This mosque is the only one in Cairo constructed of brick, rather than of stone, and therefore the structure has suffered from ground water problems.

The plan of the mosque consists of a large courtyard, surrounded by arcades.

Ibn Tulun Mosque

The arcade with the *qibla* wall, containing the niche facing Mecca, is deeper than the others, and the single minaret is on the opposite side. On the right side of the *mihrab* niche, indicating the direction of prayer, is a wooden *minbar*, or pulpit. In front of the *minbar* is a raised platform called a *dikka*, from which the Quran could be read.

The Abbasids came in 905 to restore their control over Egypt, and plundered and destroyed the city of Ibn Tulun, except for the mosque. The mosque apparently fell into disuse in 1066, and was used as a hospital. In 1296 the Mamluk sultan Lajin restored the fountain in the center of the courtyard, parts of the minaret, the stained glass and marble, the *mihrab* niche, and the wooden *minbar*.

The minaret is built of stone; its shape is square at the bottom and then cylindrical with an exterior stairway. Your children will want to climb the minaret—there are no safety railings, so make sure they are old enough! If you don't make it all the way up, part way there is a stone bridge leading to the roof of the mosque, and a fine view of the city can be seen from there. To get to the minaret, go back out the door of the mosque and turn left. You will be walking outside the wall of the mosque proper, but inside a second wall called the *ziyada*.

A fun stop when you are done with sightseeing is the Khan Misr Tulun, right across the street from the mosque entrance. This store specializes in handicrafts from the Egyptian oases and carries a variety of unusual and attractive articles. If you want to get a special gift for a little one, the store has non-toxic wooden puzzles in both ancient and modern Egyptian motifs and scenes, and spectacular ones in the shape of different Red Sea fishes. There are also lamps for the nursery, colorful clothing hooks, and Egyptian village motif puppets and dolls. Khan Misr Tulun, Tel: 365-2227.

Where: **Located between Ibn Tulun St. and Qadri St. If you are walking from Midan Sayyida Zaynab,**

Elements of a Mosque

Dikka—a raised platform from which the Quran is recited.
Mihrab—the niche in the *qibla* wall indicating the direction in which to pray.
Minbar—the pulpit from which the Friday sermon is given.
Qibla—the wall of the mosque facing the direction of Mecca.

Mosque architecture developed in order to answer the specific needs of congregational prayer. The very first mosque was in the house of the Prophet Muhammad in Medina. It was simply a courtyard with a covered portico on one side. The portico faced the direction of Mecca, called the *qibla*, the direction in which Muslims say their prayers. Later in the Umayyad Period, a *mihrab* niche was established in the *qibla* wall to mark the place of the *imam*, the prayer leader. The Prophet Muhammad preached to the congregation from a three-stepped chair, and from this developed the *minbar*, or pulpit, from which the Friday sermon is given. The accepted place for the *minbar* became the right side of the *mihrab* niche. In the early years of Islam, the call to prayer was proclaimed simply from a rooftop. The minaret *(ma'dhana)* appeared somewhat later, in the Umayyad Period. It is necessary to wash, or make ablutions, before prayer, and a tradition developed to build a *fountain* for this purpose in the mosque courtyard.

walk northeast for about 200 meters along Port Said (Bur Said) St. and turn right onto Qadri St. You will see the spiraling minaret in front of you.

When: 8am–5pm. Closed Friday's midday prayer.
Admission: Tips are appreciated for cloth slippers, which cover shoes.

Qasr Amir Taz (Amir Taz Palace)

Five steps down and you are in the medieval world of the Mamluks. This fourteenth century palace built in AD 1352 is a magnificent example of the use of space, water, and prevailing winds in a royal household. Later, the Ottomans used the palace and covered original walls with their own designs and built additions to the court. Today, due the Ministry of Culture's Historic Cairo Project and the World Heritage Center of UNESCO, you can see the palace, superbly restored, through the layers of history from Mamluk to Ottoman times.

The original owner of the palace was Amir (Prince) Taz, Saif al-Din Taz Ibn Katghag. At that time the palace grounds were 2 feddans but today due to encroachment and restoration, the palace covers 1.5 feddans. It consists of two central courtyards with architectural elements of a palace such as the *ma'qad* (an open, triangular veranda on the first floor), *salamlik* (men's quarters), *haremlik* (women's quarters), two *hammam*s (bathrooms), fountains, school, stables, *sabil*, rooms for Sufis and stores.

The high monumental entrance to the *maq'ad* is decorated with geometric designs. In the center, there is the 'coat of arms' or symbol—a cup—of Amir Taz's title, which has a loose meaning 'the man who holds the drink for the Sultan.' (His symbol can be seen throughout the house.) On the ground floor and beneath the *maq'ad* is a *qa'a* (reception room) with fountain. Continue toward the back of the room; there is an ancient waterwheel. Can you imagine the archeologists' faces when an ancient Mamluk water wheel, the only one of its kind in existence, was discovered? The extensive water system with aqueduct and cisterns throughout the palace demonstrates the use of water as a luxury: hot, cold, and warm running water, fountains for beautifying and relaxation, and using water as a cooling fan as the hot summer winds pass over. Continuing up the stairs, a *sabil*, Ali Agha Dar al-Saada was constructed in 1677 AD. This beautiful room has a marble floor and ceiling with a wide calligraphic bar of a verse from the Quran and decorated with ornamental flowers. The floors, thereafter, house a *madrasa* (school), a room for the *sheikh* (religious teacher), and Sufi rooms.

If you have strong legs, climb up to the *haramlik* and *hammam*s. In the men's and women's quarters, are two *hammam*s. Both consist of rooms for massage, cold water, warm water, and hot water rooms, and Arabic toilets. The ceilings are covered in colored glass domes.

In the first courtyard, a room next to the *qa'a* is set to exhibit jewelry. Most objects found during the excavations are on display in a Mamluk exhibit within the rooms at the end of the courtyard. During the excavations, the archeologists found various objects such as pottery, ceramics, letters, pages from books and the Quran, decorated wooden pieces, stone and marble items, and coins. Off the main portal, prints of life during the Ottoman days are exhibited. The stables are being used as rooms for art exhibits as well. Also, be sure to see the before and after restoration pictures in the room between the two courtyards. There is consideration to develop a Historic City Museum at this site.

The Palace of Amir Taz was the home for royal families up to Muhammad Ali's reign when it was utilized as storehouse for military supplies. Under

*Amir Taz
Palace*

Ismail Pasha and Abbas Hilmy it was converted into a school. After 1952, the Ministry of Education operated it as a warehouse for books. The earthquake of 1992 destroyed much of the palace. But rescue came by way of the Historic Cairo Project, which took Qasr Amir Taz into its portfolio.

> Where: Souffiya Street in the Khalifa district. From Sultan Hasan Mosque go toward Ibn Tulun Mosque on al-Salbiya Street (pass Sabil Sultan Qayetbay and Mosque of Qanibay on the left) turn right at Sabil Umm Abbas (on right), Tel: 514-2581.
>
> When: 9am–2pm.
>
> Tip: Young children might enjoy the space but be careful because there are lots of high stairs and areas with sharp drop-offs. Adolescents and teenagers are sure to love this medieval palace.
>
> Watch for: This palace is an excellent venue for musical evenings. Watch for information especially during Ramadan and in the summer.

Sayyida Zaynab Children's Cultural Park

Sayyida Zaynab Children's Cultural Park was the first park in Cairo to receive the Aga Khan Award for Architecture on September 19, 1992. The Aga Khan

Award for Architecture is presented to achievements that enhance the communities and cultures of the Muslim world through examples of re-use of areas, conservation, landscaping, community development, restoration, and design.

The Children's Park, built in the historical area near the mosques of Ibn Tulun, Sarghatmish, and Sayyida Zaynab, is situated on 12,000 square meters (1 hector) adhering to an Islamic style of garden development. Low walls and arched openings form the entrance to the park. The use of open spaces, fountains, and maze-like corridors is based on complicated geometric patterns that reflect the geometries of Ibn Tulun Mosque and other Mamluk and Ottoman monuments nearby. At the park, activities for children include film, theater, painting, and drawing opportunities, rooms with computers, and playgrounds. The park has two libraries, a reading room for children in primary schools and a library specifically for adolescents. The latter from time to time was a lending library but it is not clear if this is still the case. The park is not open for an impromptu visit, rather parents and children may attend when an event occurs. To find out this information, a trip to the park is necessary.

Where: **Between Abd al-Magid al-Labban and Qadri St., in Sayyida Zaynab (see map on page 80).**

Mustafa Kamil Tomb and Museum

Although the tomb is dedicated to Mustafa Kamil, in reality there are three other men—Muhammad Farid, Abd al-Rahman al-Rafai, Fathi Radwan, all nationalists—buried in the tomb, as well as Mustafa Kamil's mother. Abd al-Rahman al-Rafai first thought of a mausoleum for himself, and built this structure in 1949. Mustafa Kamil was moved into it in 1953, Muhammad Farid in 1954, and later Abd al-Rahman al-Rafai in 1966 at his own death. Fathi Radwan was buried here as well, in 1988.

Mustafa Kamil's mosque and tomb Entering the tomb, a bust of Mustafa Kamil is at the back of the tomb. Facing the bust, the room to

Mustafa Kamil

Mustafa Kamil lived only 34 years but his name remains synonymous with the quest for independence from the British. Born in Cairo in 1874, he studied law in France, before returning to Egypt and becoming active in nationalist politics. The Khedive Abbas sent him back to France to persuade the French government to help Egypt throw off British rule, but he failed. Although Kamil was successful in having Lord Cromer, the consul general, sent back to London, he exhausted himself organizing national rallies for Egyptian independence and, a few months after founding the Nationalist Party in 1907, died in February, 1908.

the right contains his personal belongings, such as letters, family portraits, clothing, and murals depicting events during his life. These murals tell the story of Britain's colonization of Egypt. At the far door to the right is Mustafa Kamil's writing desk. Across from this is an unusual picture: Taken in the late 1800s, the women have no veils and their dress is Western. The seated lady is Mustafa Kamil's mother, and the two girls are his sisters.

Crossing to the opposite side of the tomb, the room is divided into three offices commemorating the three noted Egyptians:

Muhammad Farid (1868–1919) was of Turkish heritage although he was born and raised in Egypt. He became a writer, lawyer, and leader in the Nationalist Party. He and Mustafa Kamil worked closely together to further Kamil in his political pursuits. A statue of him stands in Azbakiya Park, near the Puppet Theater.

Abd al-Rahman al-Rafai (1889–1966) was a journalist, lawyer, member of Parliament, and active in the National Party. He received a membership in the Higher Council for the Arts, Letters, and Sciences in 1966, and was regarded as one of Egypt's most important historians and political writers.

Fathi Radwan (1911–1988) received his law degree in 1933. He was an activist in encouraging Egyptian industry. He helped establish Misr Fatah, a group resisting British occupation and in 1944, he joined the National Party. The subject matter of his writings ranged from Talaat Harb and Gandhi, to art and music.

Where: 1 Midan Salah al-Din. Tel: 510-9943.
When: 10am–6pm. Closed Mondays.
Entrance Fee: Free. Bring an ID or passport.

Photography: No cameras are allowed inside the tomb but pictures are allowed outside.
Toilets: Available.
Tip: All labels are in Arabic. This museum is appropriate for adolescents and teenagers who might be interested in Egypt's leaders and its modern history.

Sultan Hasan Mosque

The mosque of Sultan Hasan is one of the most magnificent monuments of the Islamic world. It was constructed between 1356 and 1361 by Sultan Hasan, son of al-Nasir Muhammad, the great builder of the Citadel (see page 101). The mosque is actually a *madrasa*, or school, for Islamic law, connected to a tomb for its founder. This impressive building is situated directly across from the Citadel, and in fact, at various times was used as a fortress from which rebels fired onto the Citadel.

The enormous entrance is set off at an angle from the rest of the façade, perhaps so it could be seen from the ruler's residence up on the Citadel. Above the doorway are tiers of stalactite decoration. An enclosed passageway leads you into the enormous central courtyard with a fountain. On each of the four sides of the courtyard is a porch, or *iwan*; one for each of the four schools of Islamic law: Hanafi, Shafa'i, Malaki, and Hanbali. Each of the four corners of the building around the court had rooms for the students attached to each school. The windows of these rooms can be seen on the outside of the building. Note the chains hanging down in the porches. They once held glass mosque lamps, some of which can be seen in the Islamic Museum, which is closed as this book goes to print.

The largest porch on the southeast side contains the *qibla* wall with the prayer niche, or *mihrab*. Note the pulpit, or *minbar*, next to the niche and the *dikka*, or platform, out in front (see page 89 for "Elements of a Mosque"). Going through the door on the left side of the prayer niche, you enter into the mausoleum. The tomb is in the center of the room surrounded by a wooden screen. Sultan Hasan is not buried here, but it is said that two of his sons are. Note the wooden desk for holding and reading the Quran. Be sure to look out the windows for a view of the Citadel.

The original dome over the mausoleum was wood covered with lead; it collapsed in 1661. The minaret on the northeast corner also collapsed in 1658, leaving only the original minaret on the southeast corner. At about 81 meters high, it is one of the tallest minarets in Cairo.

Where: Midan Salah al-Din.

When: Open everyday.

Entrance Fee: Admission is free, but donations are requested. Check your shoes at the door, so don't forget to wear socks! Dress conservatively.

Parking: There is parking on the street around the midan at the east end of the pedestrian area, which runs between the mosques of Sultan Hasan and al-Rifai.

Facilities: A bathroom is located in the garden at the west end of the pedestrian area.

Whirling Dervish Mevlevi Complex

"Do not look at my outward shape
But take what is in my hand."
—Jelaluddin Rumi

If your children have witnessed the touristy flair of the Tannura on a Nile cruise or at a cultural event, take them to the Mevlevi Complex to experience the authentic environment where Sufis studied and performed their trance-like religious ritual by turning or whirling.

Renovation of this unique complex has been on going since 1979 under the Italian-Egyptian Cultural Institute. The complex includes the Yazbak Palace, the minaret, the mausoleum of Hasan Sadaqa, and the *madrasa* of Sunqur Sa'di. In 1607, Prince Sinan gave this area to the Mevlevi dervishes, a Turkish (Mevlevi) Sufi order—a mystical branch of Islam—founded by Jelaluddin Rumi of Konya. The *samakhana*, or auditorium for the whirling dervish, was built in the eighteenth century. It is a round building with a large wooden floor surrounded by wooden banisters where the sheikh and audience sat to view the whirling dervishes. The musicians would have positioned themselves on the second floor. Take the staircase to the lower floors and ask a worker to turn on the lights. You will visit a *madrasa* of Sunqur Sa'di, the monastery where the Sufis lived, an ancient well from the Fatimid period, and the mausoleum of Hasan Sadaqa, AD 1315.

Where: Near Sultan Hasan Mosque: Go past Sultan Hasan as if going to Muhammad Ali Street; turning left then right puts you on al-Mudarfar Street and facing Khalifa al-Am Hospital. The name of this street is Shari al-Suyufiyya. Park at the hospital. With your back to the hospital, walk to your right on Shari al-Suyufiyya. The entrance is through a restored door, on which is written: "Centro Italo - Egiziano per il restauro e l'archeologia." Ring bell on the left. Go up the stairs and turn to the left. There are three doors through which you enter into the reconstructed area for the whirling dervish.

When: Open 9am–4pm. Closed Fridays. Appointments for times other than these can be made by calling 510–7806.

Entrance fee: Free.

Photography: It is forbidden to take a picture of the mausoleum of Hasan Sadaqa; otherwise, photography is welcomed.

For More Information: "The Italian-Egyptian Restoration Center's Work in the Mevlevi Complex in Cairo" by Giuseppe Fanfoni from *The Restoration and Conservation of Islamic Monuments in Egypt,* edited by Jere L. Bacharach (AUC Press). For information about Jelaluddin Rumi go to the web: *www.mevlana.ws,* or the AUC Bookstore has an array of books of his poetry translated by different authors. See performances of Tannura Dancers (commonly known as the Whirling Devishes) to Sufi music: Wikalat al-Ghuri (al-Ghuri Caravansari), Sheikh Muhammad Abdu Street, off al-Azhar Street. Tel: 510–0823, 512–1735, every Saturday and Wednesday normally at 7:30pm; check times in *Al-Ahram Weekly.*

Admission: Free.

Museum of Islamic Art

The Museum of Islamic Art is closed for restoration and is scheduled to open in 2006. Some pieces have been relocated to other museums such as the seventeenth-century ceramics that are now at the Gezira Arts Center. The following information gives you an idea of its contents. The positions of objects may change when the museum reopens.

The Museum of Islamic Art occupies the lower floor of what was originally the Dar al-Kutub, the National Library, which has been relocated to a new building on the corniche in Bulaq. There are more than 80,000 objects in the museum's collection, many absolute masterpieces of Islamic art. The museum itself is not overly large, and you could stroll through it with children of all ages in about an hour. It is an excellent way to expose children to the achievements and expressions of Islamic culture without being overwhelmed or bored. Most pieces are well-labeled in Arabic and English.

Places in the museum to be sure to see with children are marked on the plan with letters, and a short description is given below. You can work your way through the museum and return to the entrance by following these letters. Suggestions for older children and teenagers are given at the end of this section. Often, you will encounter classes of art students sketching at the museum. The artist in your family may want to do so as well.

In brief, Halls 2–5 are chronological, covering the periods from Umayyad to Mamluk. Halls 6–10 have woodwork, Hall 11 metalwork, Hall 12 arms and armor, Halls 13–16 ceramics, Hall 19 manuscripts, Hall 20 Ottoman pieces, Hall 21 glass, and Hall 22 Persian pieces. Throughout the museum, Turkish carpets decorate the walls. In our experience, it is the parents more than the children who will appreciate these splendid carpets.

A: As you enter, and in Hall 8 to the right and Hall 6 to the left, are incredibly huge brass chandeliers, all Mamluk in date. The one in Hall 6, made for Amir Kaisun, weighs one ton. The inscription on it gives the name of the craftsman and says that he made it in fourteen days in the year 1330.

B: Have the guard turn off the lights in this room (he'll probably offer to do so) and you will see daylight through the beautiful stained glass windows. The fountain in the middle of the room dates to the fourteenth century; its design is executed in pieces of different colored marble.

The Islamic Museum

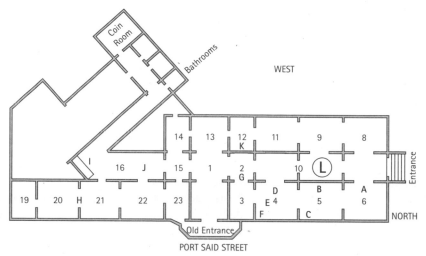

Ground floor
plan of the
Museum of
Islamic Art

PORT SAID STREET

C: Look carefully at the arabesque pattern on this thirteenth-century brass door. Can you find the animals?

D: In this room, there are two excellent examples of marble water jars (there are a few in Hall 5, as well). The water containers were placed in gardens; the large jar full of water was for people to drink from, and the trough below was filled with water for animals and birds. Today, one still sees ceramic water jars at the side of the road. Passers-by are welcome to drink from the tin cup.

E: In the right corner of this case of cast bronze pieces is a lion with a snake's tail. It was once a waterspout on a twelfth-century fountain in Cairo.

F: Against the wall in the corner is a very tall wooden door. It was one of three thousand doors that once adorned the Western Palace of the Fatimid city of al-Qahira—the area where Khan al-Khalili is now. Look up and notice the top of the door. Cut in half, the door was reused in Mamluk times. It used to be twice as tall!

In this room and the next are wonderful examples of Arabic writings, written in the Kufic script. Kufic developed in Kufa, Iraq in the second half of the eighth century. In Kufic, the width of the letters is greater than the height, so the script lends itself to oblong surfaces. Notice the examples of ornamental Kufic in which the letters end in plants and leaves. After the twelfth century, ornamental Kufic also developed intricate patterns in which the letters interweave and overlap. A form of overlapping, square Kufic was used on ceramic tiles.

G: This superb brass ewer was part of the treasure of Marwan II, the last Umayyad caliph, killed at Abu Sir in Lower Egypt in 750. Its neck is decorated like a crown; its spout is a crowing rooster. A similar but less spectacular ewer, dating to the ninth century, is in a case in the middle of Room 3.

H: Hall 21 contains the most valuable collection of enameled glass mosque lamps in the world. On the right are two raised cases, each with three lamps from the Mosque of Sultan Hasan—his full name, Nasir Hasan ibn Qalawun, is used on the labels. He had hundreds of these made for his mosque. Originally, the lamps held small containers of oil, and were suspended from the mosque ceiling by long chains attached to the handles on the body of the lamp. Above the lamp hung a glass ostrich egg that helps to balance it.

I: Coming out of Hall 21, turn left. At the end of the corridor is a carved wooden classroom of the seventeenth century from Damietta in the Delta. The niches and alcoves kept books and other supplies.

J: Walking back toward the entrance in this wide corridor (Hall 16), a long, rectangular case contains round stamps to press into cookie dough, just like those still used to decorate Ramadan cookies today. On the opposite side of the case are circular water jar filters from the Fatimid Period. These were placed in the neck of the jug to strain the water before you drank it. Look at all the different designs—peacock, fish, rabbit, and elephant. Imagine putting that kind of detail into a very ordinary, everyday object that would mostly go unseen. Stunning Iznik ceramics line the walls of this hall.

K: Continue walking back toward the entrance and then into the rooms on your left to enter Room 12. This will be most children's favorite room in the museum. In two corners of the room are chain mail tunics of the Mamluk Period. The guard will let you hold up a sleeve to see how heavy the tunics really are. Imagine walking around weighted down like that! The large guns in the case are Persian siege rifles from the sixteenth and seventeenth centuries. They were much too big for a soldier to carry, and were propped on a wall. The center case displays typical Mamluk armor: a chain mail shirt, helmet with nose guard, leg guards, and bow and arrows. Also note the shield to protect a horse's face, brass inlaid with gold and silver.

Modern-day ceramic jar for drinking-water

99

L: Look up and see the splendid wooden ceiling with three domes, which was once part of an eighteenth-century Ottoman house. The marble column in the fountain holds it up. Water was forced up the column and flowed back out the holes at the top and into the fountain below.

As we wait for the Museum to open, another opportunity to view Islamic art from countries around the Mediterranean is now available on the Internet. 'The Discover Islamic Art Museum'—*www.discoverislamicart.org*—shows Islamic heritage from the Mediterranean basin as well as art from participating museums. The site is in English, French, and Arabic as well as in the languages of participating museums.

Further Things to See for Older Children

On the north wall of Hall 6 are carved planks of wood from the Western Palace of the Fatimid city of al-Qahira. Note the scenes of hunting, dancing, and music amid the floral patterns. As you pass from Hall 6 to Hall 5, notice the enormous wooden doors from al-Azhar Mosque, made by the Fatimid caliph al-Hakim in 1010. There are delicate inlaid brass objects in Hall 5, as well as in Hall 11. In Hall 23 is a display of Abbasid medical instruments, as well as astrolabes and compasses. Find more astrolabes in a case against the west wall in Hall 11. Beautiful handmade copies of the Quran and other illustrated manuscripts are in Hall 19. If you are a coin collector make sure to walk all the way back to the coin room, turning left as you pass the washroom. The coin room also displays court medals, glass stamps and weights, and some jewelery.

The sabil of Umm Abbas, on the street leading from Ibn Tulun Mosque to the Citadel

Where: Midan Bab al-Khalq, entrance on Port Said (Bur Said) St. Purchase tickets inside the entrance. Tel: 390-1520, 390-9930.

For more information: Read *The Treasures of Islamic Art in the Museums of Cairo*, edited by Bernard O'Kane (AUC Press, 2005).

Periods of Islamic History in Egypt

Umayyad 658–750
Abbassid 750–868
Tulunid 868–905
Abbassid 905–935
Ikshid 935–969

Fatimid 969–1171
Ayyubid 1171–1250
Bahri Mamluks 1250–1382
Burgi Mamluks 1382–1517
Ottoman 1517–1805

The Citadel

You cannot miss the Citadel, as it is the highest point in Cairo. Topped by the Mosque of Muhammad Ali, the Citadel has virtually become the symbol of the city. The Citadel is built on an outcropping of the limestone Muqattam Hills, which you can see behind the Citadel in the east. The rocks between the two hills have been quarried away, and now Salah Salim St. and the autostrade run between them.

There was virtually no construction in the area of the Citadel until late in the twelfth century under the Ayyubid ruler Saladin. From that time, building at the Citadel evolved within two areas, the Northern Enclosure and the Southern Enclosure. The Northern Enclosure, surrounded by massive walls and towers, has always had a military function. The Southern Enclosure, with smaller, more irregular walls and no towers, was the ruler's residence. There were three major periods of building at the Citadel: Ayyubid in the late twelfth century and beginning of the thirteenth; Mamluk, particularly in the fourteenth century; and Ottoman (or Muhammad Ali) in the first half of the nineteenth century.

The Citadel and Muhammad Ali Mosque

101

Saladin came to Egypt with a Syrian army in 1169 to save it from the Crusaders. He became vizier to the last of the Fatimid caliphs, al-Adid, and took over when the caliph died two years later. Saladin went on to rule for 24 years, but because of battles against the Crusaders, he spent only eight years in Cairo. Saladin began the construction of the walls of the Northern Enclosure in 1176. His walls, with round projecting towers pierced with slits for archers are seen best at the rise and curve along Salah Salim St.

Saladin built his fortress in conjunction with the walls surrounding all of Cairo. The walls spanned north, enclosed the Fatimid City, al-Qahira, and then west to the river, ending with the Bab al-Hadid—the gate whose name identifies the area of the train station today. To the south, Saladin's wall enclosed Fustat, and for the first time al-Qahira became a unified, single city.

Saladin never lived in the Citadel. Al-Malik al-Kamil, Saladin's nephew, built the first royal residence there in 1218. From this time onward all the Ayyubid, Mamluk, and Ottoman rulers until Khedive Ismail resided at the Citadel, except for Sultan al-Salih Nagm al-Din, who built a fort and palace on the island of Roda.

The next great phase of building at the Citadel was under the Mamluk ruler al-Nasir Muhammad in the early fourteenth century. He assembled a vast palace, al-Ablaq (the 'Striped Palace'), which covered an enormous area of the western and southern section of the Southern Enclosure. In the eastern part of the enclosure he built a Hall of Justice, as well as his mosque. Only the mosque stands today.

Muhammad Ali was the next ruler to change the character of the Citadel. He leveled the area of Mamluk buildings in the Southern Enclosure and constructed a raised terrace for his mosque and Gawhara Palace. A decade later he built a larger palace for his family in the eastern part of the Northern Enclosure, the Harem Palace. The royal family continued to live there until Khedive Ismail moved to Abdin Palace in 1874.

The monuments and museums in the Citadel are extensive. Plan to visit more than once to see them all. At the time of writing, it is not possible to walk the walls of the Citadel, but plans are underway to restore them, and open them to the public.

Southern Enclosure
The Mosque of Muhammad Ali
The Mosque of Muhammad Ali dominates the skyline of Cairo from atop the Southern Enclosure of the Citadel. Muhammad Ali began the construction of the mosque in 1824 by tearing down the old Mamluk palaces here. Then he filled in the area, raising it up with ten meters of rubble, and created a new terrace on which to build.

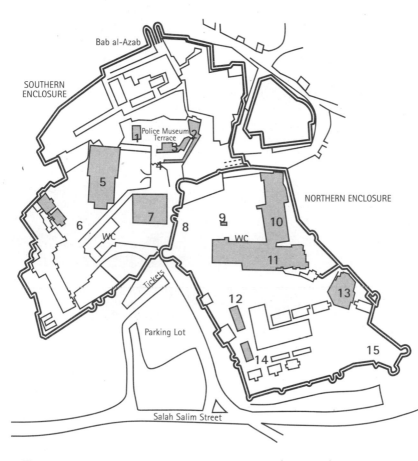

The mosque is constructed in Turkish imperial (Ottoman) style, like those in Istanbul, and Muhammad Ali consciously planned his mosque to be very large and visible. Typical of Ottoman mosques, it has a vast central dome that creates a grand, open interior. In addition, the two pencil-shaped minarets, 83 meters high and fixed at the front corners of the mosque, are Ottoman in style. Another element of Ottoman mosques followed here is the immense courtyard with central fountain, stretching in front of the entrance.

Upon entering the mosque courtyard on the north side, you will see a clock tower on the west wall, a gift from the French king, Louis Philippe, to Muhammad Ali in 1846 in exchange for the obelisk of Ramesses II taken from the front of Luxor Temple, which had been erected in the Place de la Concorde in Paris in 1833. The clock has never worked since the day it arrived.

The courtyard of the Muhammad Ali Mosque, with its clock tower

Muhammad Ali (1769–1849)

Muhammad Ali was born in Cavalla, now in northern Greece but at that time part of the Ottoman Empire. He rose through the ranks of the Ottoman army, and in 1805 was named governor, or pasha, of Egypt. Overtime, Muhammad Ali distanced himself as an Ottoman ruler and began his own dynasty. He attained unquestioned control over the country after the slaughter of the Mamluk aristocracy in 1811. His son, Ibrahim Pasha, succeeded him in 1848, and the ruling dynasty that he founded lasted until the abdication of King Farouk in 1952.

Directly inside the mosque on the right is a bronze screen surrounding the marble tomb of Muhammad Ali, who died in 1846. On the right side of the *mihrab* niche stands the original wooden *minbar*. King Farouk gave the smaller, alabaster *minbar* to the mosque in 1939. Around the dome are six large medallions with the names of God, the Prophet Muhammad, and the first four caliphs.

Gawhara Palace

Behind the mosque on the southwest side is the Gawhara Palace, built by Muhammad Ali in 1814. He and his family lived here until 1827, when the Haremlik Palace, now the Military Museum, was completed. After Muhammad Ali moved, visitors stayed at the Gawhara Palace. The Gawhara Palace seems a rather modest palace by our expectations. It was originally more extensive: an electrical fire in 1972 destroyed a large section of it.

There are two parts to the palace, but currently only one of them is open to the public. After you go down the stairs (with the mirror in front of you) go out to the left and around to the door marked Guest Palace Museum. Up a flight of stairs is the Muhammad Ali throne room. The throne room is interesting because of the throne itself: Muhammad Ali sat on the floor in oriental style and so it has no legs!

A good way to clarify the genealogy of the Egyptian royal family is to study the portraits on the walls of this room. The pictures begin with Muhammad Ali and go through King Farouk. Opposite, on the other side of the stairs from the throne room, is a bedroom. It has been furnished with pieces taken from Abdin Palace, recreating the atmosphere of a nineteenth century palace bedroom.

Mosque of al-Nasir Muhammad

This mosque, located in the courtyard between the Police Museum terrace and the entrance into the Northern Enclosure, is a good example of a Mamluk mosque. It is a quiet, cool, and restful place, and worthy of a stop.

The original mosque was constructed in 1318, but the mosque as you see it today dates from al-Nasir's rebuilding of it in 1335. Until the Mosque of Muhammad Ali was completed, this mosque served as the congregational mosque for the Citadel. Walk into the courtyard, with its arcade or covered porches, and you will see the *qibla* wall with *mihrab* niche straight ahead. Actually, there are three niches, a main one in the center and a smaller one on each side. Notice the remains of inlaid marble panels on the walls. If you are a real detective, you will notice the same type of inlaid decoration used in al-Nasir Muhammad's Striped Palace, which you can look down into from the Police Museum terrace.

The capitals on the columns are from different pharaonic and Roman temples, and Coptic churches. Not one capital is the same as another. Just inside the entrance, two basket-shaped capitals resemble the enormous latticework capital seen in the collection of the Coptic Museum. In the arcade, try to find the column of thick, red granite with the remains of palm fronds at the top. It is from an Old Kingdom royal mortuary temple.

This mosque has two minarets, each architecturally different from the other. The green-enameled finials at the top of the minarets have an unusual 'garlic' shape. As there were no microphones in those days, the voice of the muezzin had to be strong and loud. The first minaret faced the palace area and called the royalty to prayer. The second minaret was closer to the entrance of the Northern Enclosure and called the troops stationed in their barracks. The royalty and soldiers used two separate entrances.

If you have not visited other mosques in Cairo, the Mosque of al-Nasir Muhammad presents an excellent example of the difference between a Mamluk and an Ottoman (Turkish) mosque such as the Mosque of Muhammad Ali. Notice, as you enter the large courtyard with columns supporting the arcade, that there is only a dome-covered area in front of the niche on the *qibla* wall: the space created here is different from that of the Ottoman Mosque of Muhammad Ali, where the huge dome covers the entire interior.

Police Museum Terrace

As you walk down and away from the north side of the Muhammad Ali Mosque, you enter this terrace through the stone gateway, Bab al-Alam. The gateway dates to Muhammad Ali's reign but Ibrahim Pasha restored the upper half.

Al-Ablaq, the "Striped Palace"

A description of this palace written shortly after it was built says that the walls were constructed of black and yellow stone (hence the name *ablaq*, or 'striped'). This palace was modeled after the Ablaq Palace which the Mamluk ruler Baybars constructed in Damascus in 1264. Al-Nasir had stayed there and was very impressed by it. He brought stone-cutters from Damascus so that his Ablaq Palace would be built correctly. This palace was used for audiences and receptions. The walls inside were decorated with marble and gold mosaic detailed in mother-of-pearl and colored paste. The floors were of marble. The ceiling was gilt with lapis lazuli. The windows were filled with colored glass.

Between the Striped Palace and his mosque, al-Nasir Muhammad built a Great Court, or Hall of Justice, in which he sat twice a week to hear petitions and complaints. Ruins of the Great Court could still be seen until 1824 when Muhammad Ali removed it to make room for his mosque.

Military Prison

Immediately turn to your right inside the gateway, and go up a few steps into the military prison. The prison has forty cells in two rows, with an open corridor in between. The oldest part dates to the time of Khedive Ismail, and it was completed in 1882. In 1968, prisoners accused of crimes involving state security were incarcerated here. The last prisoners to be jailed here were the men arrested for the assassination of President Sadat. The prison closed in 1984 and became a museum. During the Mamluk era and before, dungeons in the towers of the Citadel walls were the prisons.

Go back out of the prison and straight ahead to the terrace. On your left is a fenced off excavation area with what remains of the al-Ablaq ('Striped')

Palace, of al-Nasir Muhammad, built in 1315. What was left of this enormous palace Muhammad Ali filled in and covered when he built the terrace for his mosque and this lower terrace for cannon embankments.

From the edge of the terrace you have a splendid view of Cairo. Walk along toward the Police Museum. Go to the farthest point of the terrace wall and look down into the enclosed road below. This is where Muhammad Ali had the Mamluk leaders slaughtered in 1811. He invited them to a celebration in Gawhara Palace, and when they rode back down toward the *midan* outside the Bab al-Azab gateway, soldiers shot them from the buildings lining the road.

The Police Museum
The Police Museum housed an artillery school during Muhammad Ali's reign. The terrace outside, with its commanding view over the city, was lined with bombardment cannons. A cannon was fired to mark the end of each day's fast during Ramadan, which is still the tradition today.

The museum itself is small, and although interesting does not take long to visit. The displays depict everything connected with police, crimes, and criminals. Before you go in, look at the building from the front. At the bottom on the left side, the stone blocks have lions carved on them: this building was constructed on top of a tower, known as the 'Lion's Tower,' built in the later thirteenth century by the Mamluk sultan Baybars.

On the walls of the center room are pictures of Egypt's ministers of the interior. Over the doors is a portrait of Muhammad Ali, and in cases on both sides of the door are weapons of the Ottoman Period. Look carefully at those on the right. The shields are turtle shells and the scabbards are baby crocodile skins!

Start in the corner room on the left and move through the rooms clockwise. The first room has weapons and illustrations of law enforcement from pharaonic and Ptolemaic Egypt. The next room is being renovated for Islamic period weapons. In a temporary display (labeled in Arabic), the story of sisters Raya and Sekeena, who murdered thirty women in early 1920s, is sure to give most people the shivers. There are also drawings of Ottoman period officials, showing different turbans and headgear. The next room centers on a scale model of the British attack on the Ismailia police station on January 25, 1952. This event sparked riots in Cairo and the next day, Black Saturday, the old Shepheard's Hotel and other foreign establishments were attacked and burnt. (See "What was Black Saturday?" on page 74.)

The rear of the building is devoted to political assassinations. In the case by the wall, there is the gun used in the attempted assassination of President Abd al-Nasser in 1954.

The next room exhibits examples of forgery and counterfeiting. There is a printing press with counterfeit bills, as well as a fake passport from the Ottoman Empire. The cane and cloak of Adham al-Sharqawi known as the Robin Hood of Egypt is in a case on the opposite wall (labeled in Arabic).

The last room displays illegally owned antiquities, confiscated by the police. There are small pharaonic and Coptic pieces, as well as beautiful silver-inlaid Ayyubid armor, and stamps and seals of the Egyptian royal family.

Note: At the time of going to press, the Police Museum was being renovated, and many of the displays had been removed.

Fire Engine Display

On the side of the prison building open to the terrace and between the cafeteria and the Police Museum is a large room with antique fire engines that were once used in Cairo. The two oldest are on the right side of the room: an engine with a hand pump from 1766, and another from 1885 with a steam engine to run the pump. On the other side of the room are two fire engines made in England in 1936, as well as a ladder on wheels. Helmets, axes, old fire extinguishers, and other equipment are against the wall.

Bab al-Qulla

Northern Enclosure

Enter the Northern Enclosure by going through the Bab al-Qulla, built originally in the thirteenth century by the Mamluk sultan Baybars. The gateway was narrow, so Muhammad Ali enlarged it so that his carriages could go through. Straight ahead, you will see the Harem Palace of Muhammad Ali built in 1827. Three separate wings—central, east, and west—make up the palace.

During the British occupation of Egypt, British troops were stationed in the Citadel, and the central wing of the Harem Palace was a military hospital. The British evacuated the Citadel in 1947, and the palace first opened as a museum in 1949. In front of the museum is an equestrian statue of Ibrahim Pasha, an exact reproduction of the statue that is in Midan al-Opera downtown.

National Military Museum

This museum is huge and entails a great deal of walking and climbing stairs. A visit to the Citadel just to see this museum might be enough for some little ones. In fact, if your day has been filled with sightseeing, youngsters might be happy just walking around and looking at the tanks and planes from the 1973 Arab–Israeli War that are outside the west wing. If you go through the museum, you see this military equipment at the end of the tour.

The floor plan of the museum is somewhat confusing, because the exhibits stretch throughout all three wings of the palace. You enter and begin on the ground floor of the central wing, and then go into the east wing, which has a mezzanine and upper floor to visit. You connect again with the central wing on the upper floor, and cross over into the west wing, which takes you downstairs and to the exit. Each of the main exhibit halls has many side rooms that may or may not be open. Ask one of the many guards stationed around, and they might open certain exhibits for you.

As you start out in the enormous downstairs hall of the *central wing*, be sure to stop and take a good look at the palace building itself, noting all the decorative details and painting. These halls give better evidence of the opulent royal lifestyle in the time of Muhammad Ali than the Gawhara Palace.

In the *east wing*, on the first floor there are uniforms from Muhammad Ali's reign up to the present, including medals, decorations, weapons, and artillery. In the *mezzanine*, exhibits depict the army in ancient Egypt from the beginning of pharaonic history to the Ptolemies. There are a number of dioramas of famous battles with taped narration available in different languages. The modern paintings that portray famous events from ancient Egypt are quite effective. The many pharaonic monuments you see are all reproductions. On the *upper floor*, the displays relate battles of the Islamic armies, including famous battles that took place in other parts of the Islamic world. There is a diorama of the Arab capture of the fortress of Babylon in Egypt. Children will be interested in the models of medieval siege weapons, such as the catapult, battering ram, and siege tower. Back on the upper floor of the *central wing*, this main hall is concerned with all the events and personages of the 1952 Revolution. The upper and lower floors of the *west wing* are completely devoted to the 1973 Arab–Israeli War.

Coming out of the Military Museum, walk completely around the long wing of the building on your left. The road on the other side leads straight, and then to the right, into the large open area of the Northern Enclosure. A sign with arrows points out the way to the Carriage Museum. There is a row of metal horse heads on the outside. The Stolen Antiquities Museum is the next building after it. There is a pleasant garden in front, and on the far side is the Mahka, an area used for outdoor musical performances. The Mosque of Sulayman Pasha is at the far northeast end of the enclosure, opposite the Carriage Museum.

Carriage Museum

During the British occupation this building served as the mess hall for troops stationed at the Citadel. Before displaying carriages in this hall, royal carriages were kept at the Museum of Royal Carriages near downtown. However, the most important carriages have now been moved to the Citadel.

The open interior displays eight carriages that belonged to the Egyptian royal family. Most impressive is the carriage in the center: Khedive Ismail rode in it at the opening of the Suez Canal in 1869. A re-creation of this scene is painted on the back wall of the museum. Mannequins of Ismail and the French Empress Eugènie sit in the carriage. Horses, grooms, footmen, and a front runner, known as a sais complete the display. The job of the sais—usually they worked in pairs—was to run in front of the carriage and clear the way by shouting, "Make way for the Pasha!" or "Mind your feet!" During the day they ran with a stick in their hand, and at night with a torch. It is said that these young men had a short life span, as they literally ran themselves to death. Notice that men riding on two of the horses control the team, rather than a driver with reins.

Against the front wall, second from the door, the children's carriage is compelling. It was made in England in 1924 for Crown Prince Farouk when he was a little boy. All of the other carriages in the room came from France. Next to the door is a picnic carriage dating from the time of Khedive Abbas II. It was used to ride in the gardens of Montaza Palace in Alexandria. In the corner to the right is the carriage used in the wedding of King Farouk and Queen Nariman in 1951. Queen Nariman was King Farouk's second wife. The marriage kiosk of Farouk and his first wife, Queen Farida, is in the Gawhara Palace.

Stolen Antiquities Museum

This museum exhibits antiquities confiscated from people trying to smuggle them out of the country. Although the museum is small, an array of objects spanning five thousand years of Egyptian history—pharaonic, Greco-Roman, Coptic, and Islamic—can be reviewed. These items are worth large sums of money, and people had attempted to secretly slip them out of Egypt to sell at auction houses and to private collectors. The museum offers an opportunity for parents to discuss with children the need to protect antiquities for future generations. Unfortunately, this museum is closed indefinitely.

Mosque of Sulayman Pasha

The Ottoman Turks conquered Egypt in 1510. In the Ottoman Empire a governor (or pasha) picked by the sultan ruled the conquered state. Sulayman was governor of Egypt from 1524 to 1534. He built this mosque in 1528 to serve the Janissaries, the elite corps of Ottoman troops who were stationed in the Northern Enclosure. A small staircase and door lead into this, complex of mosque and Quranic school. Note the Turkish style minaret, like those on the mosque of Muhammad Ali.

From the door, you walk directly into the domed prayer area. Notice the intricately painted designs on the dome and upper part of the walls; they resemble Turkish ceramics. The lower part of the wall is done in marble geometric patterns, and is Mamluk in design. Directly opposite the entrance is a

Mamluk family tombs in the Sulayman Pasha Mosque at the Citadel

111

door that leads to the school complex. Another door, opposite the *qibla* wall, leads to a small courtyard. In the northeast corner of the courtyard there is a sheikh's tomb, which apparently dates back to the Fatimid period. The door is locked, but see if the guard will let you in. Mamluk family tombs are inside. Tombs of the Ottoman period are also located inside the shrine. The tops of the tombstones are decorated with different types of turbans. Older children and teenagers might enjoy a visit to this mosque.

Where: On Salah Salim St., just north of the Sayyida Aisha overpass. There is a parking lot outside the entrance. Tel: 512-1735.

When: 8am–4pm. Closed Fridays for noon prayer.

Entrance fee: Foreigners: LE35, children LE20, under 6 free; Egyptians: LE2, under 6 free.

Facilities: Bathrooms are inside the Citadel entrance on the right side of the road leading to the Police Museum Terrace; outside on the right of the Police Museum; and outside on the right of the Military Museum. Book and photo stores are in these same three locations. There are cafeterias outside the Police and the Military Museums.

Guides: If you would like a guide, ask for one at the entrance of the Muhammad Ali Mosque. Make sure you settle on the price before beginning your tour.

Be aware: This is a popular museum for school visits. If you do not like crowds, it is a good idea to go on school holidays. Sometimes schoolchildren are curious about the origins of other visitors and they enjoy practicing their newly acquired language skills, so be prepared for some well-meaning greetings and questions in your language. However, sometimes this attention bothers younger children. Visiting the Citadel involves a great deal of walking, and on a sunny day will be very hot. Please keep this in mind if you have a very young child or an elderly person with you.

Muqattam Hills
Church of Saint Samaan

Church of Saint Samaan

Driving along Salah Salim at night, you will see a glow of light radiating over the Muqattam cliffs. These lights are from the Church of Saint Samaan. If you search for the source, the journey leads through the heart of the Zabaleen City to a narrow entry way that opens onto the holy ground of six Coptic churches and a monastery, all carved into the Muqattam mountain. The Church of Mary the Virgin and Saint Samaan the Tanner has the capacity to hold 20,000 people. Halfway through the entrance toward the cathedral, there is a plaque which relates the history and building of this area. The other churches are not small by any means, each holding from 5,000 to 10,000 people. A Polish artist spent years depicting scenes from the Bible by carving on cliffs high above the churches.

Where: Take Salah Salim and turn onto the Muqattam Road at the Citadel. At the first road turn left, take the first right, which will take you into Zabaleen City (the city of garbage collectors). The drive may be unpleasant due to the impoverishment of the population, but people are kind and friendly. Ask anyone for the way, and they will be happy to give directions.

When: It is best to visit during the week or on Saturday. Fridays and Sundays are crowded.

Entrance fee: Free. You may be asked your nationality.

Facilities: Cafeteria serves simple food; toilets are clean. There is a bookstore to purchase books about this area. Paperback books are sold in all languages that tell the story of the miracle of the Muqattam Hills: *The Biography of Saint Samaan, the Shoemaker "the Tanner"* by The Church of Saint Samaan, the Tanner in Muqattam, Cairo, Egypt.

Al-Azhar Park

Think OASIS—tall palm trees, green, water, shelter from the sweltering sun and from the glare of the desert sand—a welcome sight for any traveler. Created by the Aga Khan Trust for Culture, al-Azhar Park has quickly become an OASIS in one of the world's most populated cities, Cairo. Bound on the west by Darb al-Ahmar and on the east by Salah Salam Street, seventy-four acres of former landfill and military camps have been converted to the greenest, most spacious park in the city. More than twenty years ago, this dream began; the official opening was held in May 2005 and well worth the wait.

As you enter al-Azhar Park from Salah Salem Street, you'll find yourself with immediate choices. You are about midway and just in front of you, at your feet, lies the first of many creative fountains to be found throughout the park. As you enjoy the sound of the water bubbling from holes in the slightly indented geometric patterns on the central walkway, consider your choices—there are three major venues for dining, a theater, twelfth century walls to explore, an orchard, dozens of splashing fountains, acres of green and well-landscaped lawns, even a hill to climb!

To your right, perched on a gently rising hill, is a Fatimid-style building housing two restaurants and a gift shop. Beyond this building is the children's play area. To your left, the central walkway slopes downward to a lake, another restaurant and stunning views of the Citadel. Immediately in front of you, is the Southern Lookout (a carefully sculpted hill) topped by a gazebo. Beyond this hill, there is al-Geneina Theater and the twelfth century wall, currently under restoration.

A motorized trolley follows the pathways of the park for those who don't want to walk. But, if you crave strolling and interesting panoramas, this is the place. Go to the park about an hour before sunset and head to the right.

Tannura Dancer at al-Azhar Park

The graduated incline you will follow leads you to several excellent choices: the Citadel View Restaurant on the terrace for tea or a buffet meal, the small café, tucked into the west side of the building for snacks or ice cream. Either will afford you a magnificent view of a Cairo sunset over the historic district below. When weather permits, you'll even be able to see vague outlines of the pyramids on the horizon.

You may wish, however, to turn to the left upon entering and follow the pathways to the Lakeside Café situated on a lake with cascading fountains. This is an ideal place to take a break or arrange for a birthday party—there are several rooms available that can be booked for groups. Order a variety of mezza and enjoy the scenery and sounds.

There is a special children's area for the youngsters to enjoy. In addition to the usual park fixtures such as swings and climbing equipment, you'll find a stage and a small amphitheater. Kids love to play in this area! For a very special treat, call one of the numbers listed below to arrange for a private party here.

The major north–south walkway from the palace on the hill to the lake is divided by a terraced channel of streaming water often interrupted by a fountain. These fountains are all a delight—each different, all playing with traditional geometric design to create something modern yet reminiscent of traditional patterns and structures. Some shoot sprays of water high in the air while others bubble from small holes in a complex grid in the middle of the pathway. It is quite difficult to resist the impulse to remove your shoes and wade right in when you encounter one of those 'puddle' fountains in the pathway.

Although there are several entrances noted on the brochure for the park, only one is open at this writing. Located on Salah Salim Street, the main entrance can be reached from any part of the city. There is limited parking inside. If you arrive by taxi and don't want to limit your time, taxis do seem easy to catch on Salah Salim at all times of the day or night. You can always book a taxi to return at a set time. There are performances in the theater and special exhibitions on the grounds from time to time. Watch for listings in local papers and magazines.

Where: **Salah Salim St.**

When: **9am–12 midnight.**

Entrance fee: **Non-resident: LE10, Resident: LE5; there is also a special rate for students—inquire at the ticket office but be prepared to show your student ID; Parking in the first tier, LE3; Parking next to the Citadel View Restaurant: an additional LE3.**

Web site: *www.akdn.org/agency/aktc_hcsp_cairo.html*

Tips: **Picnicking and wading in the fountains are not permitted! There are other park rules listed on your ticket. There are well maintained and clearly marked toilet facilities throughout the park. To inquire about conference and meeting facilities: 510-7378, 510-3868, ext. 206/211. Reservations for the Citadel View: 510-9151, 510-9150.**

Khan al-Khalili
and al-Qahira

By Jayme Spencer

Khan al-Khalili

Whether you wander through the labyrinthine streets of Khan al-Khalili or go there with a specific purpose, this is one area that will always stimulate the imagination. Located in the heart of al-Qahira, the old walled city, the Khan al-Khalili is now known as the tourist bazaar, the place to go to find treasures and junk, to browse and to bargain, to have things made just for you or to buy a pharaonic replica carved in genuine ebony. But there are more than tourist wares here. Unlike many other Middle Eastern bazaars, this area has always been a place that mixed the commercial, religious, and domestic. Spending an afternoon or a morning here

Sikkit al-Kabwa in Khan al-Khalili

117

will give you great insight into the fabric of Cairo, allowing you to visit old mosques, shop for antiques or newly made items, explore alleyways, observe people, and enjoy a meal or a glass of tea.

The Khan al-Khalili, sometimes referred to as the Muski, is a relatively small pedestrian area bounded on the east by Midan al-Husayn (Husayn Square), on the south by Sharia al-Muski (Muski St.), and on the west by the portion of Sharia al-Muizz known as Sharia al-Sagha (Street of the Goldsmiths). Having no large street as a northern boundary, Khan al-Khalili fades into the warren of small side streets that meander north until meeting the old wall of the city. Over the last twenty years the small storehouses and workshops located in this area have been converted into shops.

Madrasa-Khanqah of Sultan Barquq and Egyptian Textile Museum

Hundreds of years ago, the Khan al-Khalili was a collection of small and large *khan*s or *wikala*s. The observant eye can still find traces of these commercial structures in a vaulted archway or a fragment of Arabic inscription. Built around an enclosed square or rectangle, a typical two- to three-story *khan* would have allowed stabling for the camels and donkeys of the caravans in the courtyard or ground floor and storage of merchandise and perhaps small showrooms on the first floor, while providing housing for the merchants themselves on the floor above. Just imagine the excitement and chaos of the arrival of grand caravans from the east laden with silks and spices, the bustle of unloading, counting and inventorying, stabling the animals, settling the dusty travelers. Small covered alleyways ran between *khan*s. While most are not covered these days, you will occasionally encounter an area that is.

Today, you can stroll these alleyways in the Khan al-Khalili without worrying about being overtaken by a camel caravan. The name of the area derives from an extensive *khan* built by Amir Jarkas al-Khalil in 1382. By 1511, this area had developed into a major center for commerce. Sultan al-Ghuri ordered the *khan* built by Amir al-Khalil destroyed, and initiated the construction of a new, grander *khan*. The name should have changed to Khan al-Ghuri, but for some reason the name of the original *khan* was retained. By 1581, Jean

Khan / Wikala / Caravanserai

Originally, a *khan* was a two- or three-story structure built around a square or rectangular courtyard. This commercial building provided stabling, storage, and housing for travelling merchants. On the trade routes outside the city, a *khan* was often referred to as a 'caravanserai.' By the Ottoman period (1517–1805), the term *wikala* had replaced *khan* in the Cairene vocabulary.

Palerne, a French traveler to Cairo, described the Khan al-Khalili: ". . . a great palace with a fine fountain in the center. In it were sold beautiful clothes, pearls and other gems, porcelains, and fine cottons and other goods from India and Persia."

The seventeenth and eighteenth centuries saw a decline in the commercial activity of Egypt for a variety of reasons. By the early nineteenth century, however, Khan al-Khalili had once again become an important center, catering to the foreigner as well as the local population. Travelers' accounts of this period abound with descriptions of the architecture of the area and the curiosities for sale. Ivory, hides, gum arabic, and ostrich feathers from the Sudan were sold alongside cotton and sugar from Upper Egypt. Indigo, shawls, and carpets from India and Persia competed for shop space with sheep and tobacco from Asiatic Turkey. Almost every traveler wrote about the slave market, also in this area, and recorded the purchase of some Egyptian antiquity. Numerous Western artists, captivated by the exotic Middle East, painted in detail the colorful life of the Khan al-Khalili.

The end of the twentieth century saw major changes in Khan al-Khalili. High rents and limited space pushed development to the north. Retail merchants claimed areas once used only for warehouses and workshops. Older buildings were demolished and several modern malls rose in their place. Douglas Sladen, in 1887, wrote a passage that could apply to this later time as well: "In the Muski . . . the 'caboot' or wooden roof that formerly spanned the street has been removed, and the small but attractive native shops, with their old-world superstructure, have to a great extent been replaced by large plate-glass windows and modern fronts."

To Sladen's catalog of modernisms we would have to add air-conditioning—not a bad idea in Cairo's heat! As new challenges are being met, old buildings, perceived to be wasteful of space, are being demolished or reconfigured. Recently, a restaurant that had been closed and locked for over twenty years was converted into a two-story marble-façaded mall with dozens of small shops and escalators. Late in the nineteenth century, the Comité de Conservation des Monuments de l'Art Arabe surveyed and catalogued significant buildings and/or fragments of buildings. Today, regulations govern the construction of new buildings and the structural alteration of existing ones.

In the late 1990s, a tunnel was built to carry through traffic from Midan al-Opera to Salah Salim Street in an effort to alleviate the crowded streets of this historic area. Now that the tunneling is finished and traffic runs smoothly beneath al-Azhar Street, there are proposals to close portions of al-Azhar Street and create a vehicle-free zone. Just when this might take place and exactly which areas will be affected are not known yet. Some proposals call for a complete closure from Midan al-Ataba to Salah Salim Street, while others argue for partial closure. Most plans include dismantling the elevated street above Midan al-Ataba and removing the present pedestrian bridge over al-Azhar Street. Efforts to coordinate these various plans will no doubt take several years. Choose to shop one day and sightsee another, or combine the outings and enjoy this unique commercial and historic complex to its fullest.

Where: See Central Cairo Map or Map A:7 (page 132)

Getting there:

Private car: It will be quite an adventure if you decide to drive to Khan al-Khalili. If you do decide to drive, consult a road map for the best route from your neighborhood. There is a government-run parking lot at the top of the incline of al-Azhar Street. Cost is LE1 but the lot is unshaded. The easiest way to use a private car is to have your driver (dad?) drop you and then return at a prearranged time and place for pick-up.

Taxi: Any taxi driver can find Khan al-Khalili for you easily. You can also ask for al-Muski, al-Husayn, or al-Azhar Street. Any of these terms will get you there from any place in the city, but it is best to fix the price beforehand. Coming from downtown, you can get out of the taxi on al-Azhar Street at the foot of the pedestrian bridge or in front of al-Azhar Mosque a few blocks further on. In either case, you will then have to cross over al-Azhar Street by bridge or by tunnel to reach Khan al-Khalili. When you are ready to leave the Khan, walk out to al-Azhar Street to catch a taxi. The taxis parked near the Khan tend to be more expensive, but there may be days when you prefer to take one of them. You can always bargain! You can also hire a taxi by the hour so that the driver drops you at the Khan and returns at a fixed time and place for you. Be sure to negotiate a price that includes a tip before setting out.

Bus: You will want to take the number 102 minibus (looks like ١٠٢ on the bus sign) from the station in Bab al-Louq (just a few blocks east of Midan al-Tahrir). These small buses are less crowded than the larger ones. You will get off the bus at the stop in front of al-Azhar Mosque and use the pedestrian tunnel to get to the Khan. When you are ready to leave the Khan, the bus pick-up is just in front of al-Husayn Mosque.

Foot: The walk from Midan al-Tahrir or elsewhere in town is just over two kilometers through busy, crowded streets. If you are in no hurry and enjoy seeing 'local color,' the walk will be fun. There are several routes that will take you there, so consult a map for your best one.

Paying: If you have a student card, be sure to take it with you; it will entitle you to pay half-price entrance to some of the monuments. In Khan al-Khalili, some merchants take credit cards, some take dollars, all take Egyptian pounds, but none take travelers' checks or personal checks. There are two banks in Midan al-Husayn open for cash exchanges every day including Fridays and holidays. Banque Misr opens from 8:30am–2:30pm and 3–9pm; the Faisal Islamic Bank of Egypt opens from 8:30am–2pm and 5–9pm. There is also an ATM located on Sikkit al-Badistan near the Naguib Mahfouz Café. Any of the merchants will gladly show you the way!

Shopping / Browsing

For many centuries, the Khan al-Khalili was a collection of *suq*s or bazaars, areas where artisans and merchants specializing in one type of merchandise clustered. Remnants of these *suq*s exist today but the lines have blurred. You may find a copper merchant's shop next to a carpet dealer and across from a jewelry store. Certain areas are still referred to by the dominant merchandise or craft: Suq al-Nahhasin (coppersmiths); Suq al-Sagha (goldsmiths); Suq al-Attarin (spice merchants). For the purposes of this guide, a bazaar refers to a shop that sells more than four kinds of articles. There are over 150 shops in the Khan al-Khalili that fit this description and hundreds more that specialize.

The bazaars are great places to browse and to begin your souvenir or gift hunting with comparison shopping. The bazaars have all kinds of merchandise, so are often less expensive than the shops that deal in only one kind of craft or article. Pharaonic replicas, alabaster statues, vases, beads, stamps, papyrus bookmarks, Muski glass, small brass and copper articles, finger cymbals—the list of the treasures in these shops is endless. Best to wander and compare, then to bargain and buy.

In the shops that specialize, quality is often better so prices may be higher. They may also have fixed prices. The merchant will tell you so; often signs are posted. If there is no sign, do try to bargain, especially if the prices are significantly higher than you feel the quality warrants.

The alleyways that penetrate the Khan al-Khalili are filled with shops selling antiques, brass and copperware, carpets, gold and silver jewelry, glass, ceramics, clothing, woodwork, inlaid boxes, precious stones, papyrus, to mention only a few. Some of the shops are well known; some are so tiny that only

Bargaining

Bargaining is a game; learn to play and you'll enjoy the give and take. It may take half an hour or more to seal a deal this way but the memory will be worth it. Merchants love to hear anyone trying Arabic, although most of them are quite competent in English or French. A kid attempting a few words of Arabic is a sure deal clincher! Most people will tell you to cut the quoted price by half when you make your offer. This will give you and the merchant a lot of bargaining room. No merchant will sell at a loss; if he hits rock bottom and you are still convinced that the price is too high, walk away. If he doesn't call you back, shaking his head in sorrow over his losses, then return to bargain another day. On the other hand, once you have gotten him to agree to your top price, the deal is considered done.

one customer can fit inside. It is fun to find a genial merchant and return from time to time, building mutual trust and understanding. Some of these merchants will patiently explain their trade to children. There was, for example, the jeweler who never seemed to tire of the visits of an eleven-year-old nephew, each time full of questions about certain stones: the jeweler always answered patiently and would, at times, spread out a variety of stones and explain the differences in quality and prices. The boy never bought anything but you can bet that the grateful aunt did!

Customizing

In these specialty shops it is often possible to customize orders. Gold cartouches with a name (yours or a relation's or a friend's) spelled out in hieroglyphics can be ordered in almost all the jewelry stores. Twenty-four hours and the finished cartouche can be delivered or called for. Prices vary widely as do designs and quality of work, so shop wisely. Silver cartouches are much less expensive but just as lovely and unique. All jewelry shops will execute your original designs for rings, necklaces, pins, etc. One young man drew the ring described in Tolkien's Hobbit books and had it made for himself. Some of these shops have trays of loose beads and silver pieces you can pick though. Combine two or three unique beads with an old piece of Bedouin silver and voila!—you have created a unique necklace.

Personalized brass nameplates for the office or the home door are handsome items. A large variety of styles of pots, vases, lamps, and the like in brass, copper, and white metal exist but the artisans are always willing to create your personal brass dream. Notice items waiting to be picked up at some of these shops—intricately engraved brass hard hats, beer mugs with initials or names, a brass pot shaped like a jack-o'lantern, a delicate, personalized brass camel decoration for the Christmas tree. All these items were custom ordered.

Papyrus shops all have a few styles that can be personalized with names or initials usually placed inside a cartouche. In some of these shops you can request an original painting on papyrus. Certificates of appreciation, graduation diplomas, invitations, and other types of documents can be executed on papyrus.

Caftans, shoes, belly dancing costumes, shorts, shirts, and sandals can all be made to measure in the shops selling textiles. You can pick out the fabric, braided trim, and style, then the tailor will create a unique evening outfit or a unique dress for everyday wear. Shoes can be covered to match any creation. Although the leather shops have extensive displays of belts, wallets, bags, and briefcases, you can order a favorite item copied in the leather you choose.

Outside the Khan al-Khalili proper, on the street behind al-Azhar Mosque, you can visit the bookbinder (see Map B:4) and pick out the leather and mar-

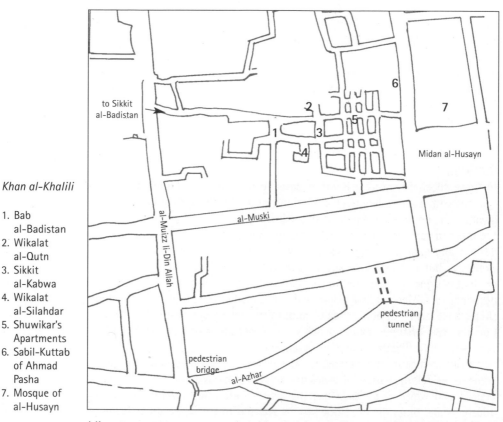

Khan al-Khalili

1. Bab al-Badistan
2. Wikalat al-Qutn
3. Sikkit al-Kabwa
4. Wikalat al-Silahdar
5. Shuwikar's Apartments
6. Sabil-Kuttab of Ahmad Pasha
7. Mosque of al-Husayn

bling to create your own sketchbook, photo album, or diary. You can have golden initials added to the spine to make it even more personal. These are great gift items and are made in a bookbinding shop that has been active for more than two hundred years. Indeed, the surrounding area is referred to as *suq al-kutub* (the book bazaar) because of the large number of bookbinders and booksellers located in the proximity of al-Azhar University. Unfortunately, the crowded conditions have forced many of the booksellers to move to other locations in the city.

In terms of what you can custom order, you are really limited only by your imagination. Chances are that if you can dream it up, you can find an artisan to create the design and make the item. Maybe you'll start a trend. A few years ago, a customer asked an artisan on the Street of the Tentmakers to stitch a wall hanging full of colorful Brazilian parrots. Today, cushions and hangings adorned with colorful parrots are routinely produced, though the first customer left Cairo long ago. Finding the right artisan or designer can lead to hours of interesting investigations and discussions. You may not find just the right person the first time you inquire, but persevere!

Index numbers

From the 1880s until the 1940s, the Comité de Conservation des Monuments de l'Art Arabe surveyed and indexed hundreds of architectural structures within al-Qahira, the walled city. Every building or fragment was given an index number, along with a description. A small green and white oval containing this index number is affixed to each structure. Look for these numbers on buildings as you wander along al-Muizz Street. In the text of this section, beside the name of each historic building, you will find the index number in parenthesis, followed by the dates of the building. How many other index numbers can you spot?

Historic Sights

Along the section of al-Muizz Street that is the transition from the coppersmith's bazaar to the goldsmith's bazaar, you will find a narrow street heading east toward al-Husayn Mosque. This is Sikkit al-Badistan, which leads you past the gates of several old *khan*s. In the span of this short, ten-minute walk, you cover more than five hundred years! The passageway you follow is one of the few still roofed as it was more than a hundred years ago. Skylights pierce the wooded timbers and provide a cool, soft light.

When you have reached the Naguib Mahfouz Café, pause and look up. Through the arch of the Bab al-Badistan (53: 1511) you can see the minaret of al-Husayn Mosque. The Bab al-Badistan is attributed to Sultan al-Ghuri and dated 1511. On the basis of its decoration, though, which differs significantly from his other two portals, it can be argued that it should instead be dated to after his reign, in the mid- or late- sixteenth century.

If you continue on Sikkit al-Badistan through this portal toward Midan al-Husayn until you reach what looks like a cross street (approximately one block), you will find the next two important structures—Wikalat al-Qutn (54: 1511) and Sikkit al-Kabwa (56: 1511).

Wikalat al-Qutn was known as Khan al-Khalili until recently. Although this present structure was built by Sultan al-Ghuri in 1511, it was constructed on the site of the original building erected by Jarkas al-Khalil in 1382. Most of the *wikala* is in ruin, but both its doorway and façade were restored in the middle of the twentieth century. The foundation inscription to al-Ghuri is still visible. Another *wikala* built by Sultan al-Ghuri is in much better shape and should be visited to get a more accurate impression of what a *khan* (or

The Islamic Calendar

The Islamic Calendar is calculated from the day of the Prophet Muhammad's departure from Mecca for Medina, and is a lunar calendar with twelve months of 30 or 29 days. The month begins when two responsible witnesses sight the first crescent of the new moon. Because it follows the lunar changes, the Islamic year differs from the western solar calendar by approximately eleven days each year. Each thirty-three years it passes through all the solar seasons, needing only a periodic adjustment. There are tables that can show you the conversions, although most Islamic countries today use both calendars. However, the actual sighting of the moon's changes can alter everything, which explains why Ramadan may not begin on the day indicated by the printed calendar, lending an air of excitement not found in the fixed calendar! The abbreviation A.H. is usually used in English to denote *Anno Hegirae* ('in the Year of the Flight'), just as A.D. refers to *Anno Domini* ('in the Year of the Lord').

In the text of this section, in parenthesis beside the name of each historic building you will find the dates of construction according to the western calendar, preceded by the index number.

wikala) actually looked like: Wikalat al-Ghuri is located near al-Azhar Mosque and is detailed below under 'Al-Ghuri Complex.'

Turn your back to Wikalat al-Qutn and walk through the vaulted passage to the next small street, Harit Khan al-Khalili. Now stop and look up at the passageway you just walked through. This is Sikkit al-Kabwa, also attributed to Sultan al-Ghuri. It bears the same inscription as Wikalat al-Qutn and was meant to enclose another structure. Instead, its vast, decorated vaulting now stands over a few modern shops built into the recesses of the portal.

Now that you are on Harit Khan al-Khalili, turn and walk away from Midan al-Husayn until you find Wikalat al-Silahdar (604: 1819) on your left. The huge gates and vaulted doorway are hard to miss when you are looking for them. The massive doors mark the entrance to a *wikala* built for Sulayman Agha al-Silahdar. The decoration of the façade reflects Ottoman tastes, but other details appear to be of the Mamluk tradition. The Ottoman foundation inscription is interesting:

> Praise and glory be to God
> May God the most high be praised
> May the glory of Sulayman Agha also increase, who is the
>   builder of this new khan
> The master worthy of compensation has given all his effort
> He has achieved the completion of this khan

I write its date in wonder. Al-Silahdar has built the new
    khan. [A.H.] 1235.

Until recently, this *wikala* was filled with storerooms and workshops, a dark, seldom visited area. Today, shopkeepers urge you forward to visit their shops. On the second story, more shops have opened in the last few years, but they are not accessible from the courtyard; stairs farther down and just to the left of Harit Khan al-Khalili lead to this level.

Backtrack to Sikkit al-Badistan and turn toward Midan al-Husayn. Just before reaching the square notice the buildings on the left. These blocks of apartments were erected in 1936 on a site owned by Shuwikar, the first wife of King Fuad. The architect used a neo-Islamic style for the living and working quarters, connecting them at the second-story level with balcony-style bridges. On the east side of the building, he incorporated the sixteenth-century façade of Wikalat al-Qutn.

As you follow Sikkit al-Badistan to Midan al-Husayn, the minarets of Sayyidna al-Husayn loom large in front of you, serving as a beacon for the midan. This late nineteenth-century mosque, built on the site of an earlier mosque, is one of the most venerated in Cairo. It houses a mausoleum reported to contain the head of Husayn, one of the sons of the Caliph 'Ali. Husayn was slain in battle in Mesopotamia (about AD 680). Although thousands come to pray and worship in the Mosque of al-Husayn daily, non-Muslims are not permitted. The large open doors afford a glance into the spacious well-lit area. Recent additions to Midan al-Husayn include three large metal columns with bulky ribbed "umbrellas" in front of the mosque. When the sun is blazing, these "umbrellas" are opened to provide shade in the midan.

One more structure you must see: the restored *sabil-kuttab* on al-Mashhad al-Husayni Street. From Sikkit al-Badistan turn left onto the street running beside Sayyidna al-Husayn and walk past the dealers in stuffed animals, amulets, and prayer beads. A few meters later on the left you will see the elaborately decorated *sabil-kuttab* of Ahmad Pasha. The lavish Ottoman colors and floral designs will give you an idea of the splendor of al-Qahira at one time. This *sabil-kuttab* is only one of the many surviving such structures scattered throughout al-Qahira. While most were built with convex or flat façades, the *sabil-kuttab* of Ahmad Pasha presents a concave grillwork front. These public drinking fountains are echoed in today's earthenware jars filled with water that you will see all over Cairo. Often a cup is chained to the stands holding the jars, signaling that any thirsty person is welcome to drink. Offering water is a mark of hospitality.

By now you are probably thirsty. Instead of water at the *sabil-kuttab*, ask anyone for Fishawi's Café and have a glass of mint tea.

Watching Artisans

There were always copper engravers, *mashrabiya* turners, bead cutters, inlayers, and others working outside shops in the Khan al-Khalili. Now, however, you must seek out these skilled artisans, as economics have pushed the workshops into lower-rent areas, and the older, traditional workshops have been converted into places of business. The glassblowers and the tentmakers practice their trades outside the Khan al-Khalili proper, and are described in detail below (see Maps A:1 and B:10). Another craft that is intriguing to watch is that of the fez (or tarboosh) maker. Once representing a thriving business, the tarboosh maker has nearly become extinct now that Egyptian men are no longer required to wear this felt hat. A mark of Ottoman allegiance, it was abolished after the 1952 Revolution and is now produced only as a curiosity. There are only two tarboosh shops left; both are just past the al-Ghuri complex on the street leading from Sharia al-Azhar to Bab Zuwayla. The process of making felt hats is an interesting one involving the use of hot forms and presses (see Map B:7).

Making tarbooshes on the street from Sharia al-Azhar to Bab Zuwayla

Listen for the tapping of metal against metal while wandering in the Khan. You may find an occasional engraver busy at work. His piece of brass or copper anchored securely in a glob of tar, he uses a variety of chisels and a small hammer to create the flowing lines of arabesque patterns or floral motifs. A small piece may take months to create, so intricate is the design work. A larger piece may have large looping lines and thus be less expensive.

If you are lucky you will also be able to watch one of the inlayers at work. His tools are glue and tweezers, fitting tiny pieces of mother-of-pearl, ebony, and wood into intricate patterns. Egyptian ivory is used extensively in these pieces (don't worry—Egyptian ivory is made from camel or donkey bone!), and the lovely arabesque patterns adorn boxes, plates, clips, etc. Once you see the real craft, you will appreciate that pattern and materials determine price. A large box with large patterns in Egyptian ivory can take little time to create; another box, smaller but covered with tiny stars in Japanese mother-of pearl, will cost more.

Watching a skilled artisan work gives you a better understanding and appreciation for prices and quality. There is something pleasing about the quality (though often irregular) of things made by hand. Only a few workshops remain in use in this area, so if you spot a craftsman at work, pay attention!

Time Out!

All that shopping, browsing, bargaining, and looking will probably make you thirsty and/or hungry. Take time out to rest and reflect on what you have seen and done. If it is a thirst you want to slake, best head for Fishawi, a tea, coffee, and waterpipe café in the heart of Khan al-Khalili. Here you can sit at one of the tiny tables crowded into the alleyway and sip mint tea while you watch tourists and Cairenes flow past. Wallet sellers and tissue hawkers will stop and try to persuade you to buy. However, you can just concentrate on the glass of fresh mint and how much of it to crush into your tea. Cold drinks and bottled water are also available (both here and at kiosks throughout the market area). In the winter, a delicious (and calorie-laden) hot drink called *sahlab* is served.

If you are hungry, you will want to seek out a place to sit and eat. There are several small restaurants along the Khan side of Midan al-Husayn. Most of them serve *kabab* and *kofta* or rice and vegetables or sandwiches. There are two places in the Khan worth singling out. One of these is the restaurant next to Bab al-Badistan, the Naguib Mahfouz Café. Here you can sit outside the café and have a drink and a sandwich or a waterpipe or go inside to more elegant surroundings. Inside, the foyer is used for casual seating and most people order mezza or sandwiches. A larger dining room offers regular dinner service from a selected menu. Whether you eat a sandwich or try the *tagen*

Spice Market

Your nose will tell you when you have found this area! As you approach the corner of Sharia al-Muski and Sharia al-Muizz, you will begin to notice a dominant, sweet scent in the air—incense. After turning the corner and heading toward Sharia al-Azhar, you will see many tiny stalls, fronted with baskets or tall canvas bags of sticks, powders, leaves, and seed pods of all sizes. This street and several other streets adjacent are referred to as *suq al-attarin*, the spice market. This market has always been a vital element of al-Qahira's economy. Pepper and other such commodities from the East have been traded to the West through Egypt for centuries. These shops also sell prescriptions: mixtures of spices to treat ailments, to help you gain weight, to keep your complexion clear. Candles are also sold here, as well as raw wax. All spices are sold by the kilogram and will be weighed on the scales that are an essential in all shops. Buy a kilo of henna or three threads of saffron, or just enjoy the exotic aromas and colorful displays. (See map A:8)

Neatly sacked wares of the spice market

bamya, the atmosphere will charm you. In the summer, this is a favorite place to escape the heat. The Naguib Mahfouz Café is a good landmark to set for meeting others in the Khan and for taking care of necessities (they have very clean toilets).

The other restaurant that is popular is Egyptian Pancakes. This establishment is located on the street leading from Khan al-Khalili to Sharia al-Azhar near the pedestrian tunnel. The seating is primarily outside. Cold drinks accompany the *fatir* of your choice. You can have sweet (jam, raisins, coconut) or salty (spicy ground meat, eggs, cheese) in any combination cooked for you in the oven. It is a treat to watch the *fatir*-maker tossing and stretching the dough until it is thin enough. He then flips it onto a marble counter, fills it with your order, folds it and pops it into the huge oven. The flaky pastry comes to the table piping hot! The waiters can bring you coffee or tea from the shop next door.

Important Note

Recently, the Egyptian government initiated an ambitious project to clean and restore important monuments in this historic area. In addition, there are some privately-funded projects also underway. As you follow the walks outlined below, you will notice many buildings draped with heavy green material, hiding scaffolding and protecting passersby from debris. Some of the areas described in the following text may not be open due to this process of cleaning and restoration. Ongoing work is probable for the next few years. As restored monuments do reopen, expect an adjustment of the fees.

Al-Qahira, the Walled City

The decision to establish a new city away from the Nile community of al-Fustat was significant. The site was chosen by the Fatimid general Gawhar al-Siqilli at the foot of the Muqattam Hills and the first walls and gates of the new city were completed by 970. Within a few years, al-Qahira was a thriving city. Today, over a thousand years later, Cairo is still a vibrant city waiting to be experienced on many levels, a city full of historic monuments, opera, fast food restaurants, shops, galleries, gardens, cinemas, and so much more. No section of the city captures the sense of vibrancy like the old walled city. Khan al-Khalili is at the heart of that city within a city. Nowhere else can you blend the sense of the historic with the modern so easily. Here you can buy a music cassette in a shop that occupies space in a four-hundred-year-old structure; here you can stroll Sharia al-Muizz, a street that has connected the north and

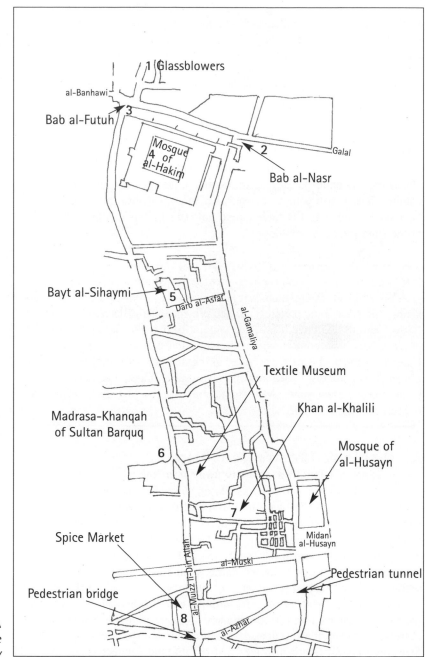

1 Glassblowers

al-Banhawi

Bab al-Futuh — 3

Mosque
4 of
al-Hakim

2

Galal

Bab al-Nasr

Bayt al-Sihaymi — 5

Darb al-Asfar

al-Gamaliya

Textile Museum

Khan al-Khalili

Madrasa-Khanqah
of Sultan Barquq

Mosque of
al-Husayn

6

7

Midan
al-Husayn

Spice Market

al-Muizz li-Din Allah

al-Muski

Pedestrian tunnel

Pedestrian bridge

8

al-Azhar

Map A
*Al-Qahira, the
Walled City*

south gates of the city for more than nine hundreds years, and watch kids play an impromptu soccer game.

It is this historic street, Sharia al-Muizz, that will serve as a major guideline for you. Following the street from just outside the northern gate of Bab al-Futuh to just beyond the southern gate of Bab Zuwayla, a number of places are worth spotlighting. This street has been referred to as "the cultural spine of historic Cairo." It would be impossible to detail all of the sights along this thoroughfare. One guidebook lists more than seventy-five mosques, *madrasas*, *bayts*, and other monuments worthy of exploration along this street alone! For convenience, we have

The north walls of al-Qahira, with one of the minarets of al-Hakim on the left and Bab al-Futuh on the right

divided al-Muizz Street into two parts. Using the pedestrian footbridge over al-Azhar Street as a natural divider, Map A covers the route from just before Bab al-Futuh to the bridge and Map B covers the route from the bridge to just beyond Bab Zuwayla. The places that are highlighted are only to whet your appetite for more. The reading list in the back of this book will lead you to works in greater depth on the area.

With all this in mind, plan several trips to Khan al-Khalili and the surrounding area and combine pleasure, culture, history, and just plain fun!

Glassblowers

The ancient art of blowing glass is a fascinating thing for all ages to watch. Finding Fatimid Cairo's last glass-blowing factory (all the rest have moved out to the edges of town) is worth the trouble. After walking about five to ten minutes beyond Bab al-Futuh through an ordinary neighborhood, you will find the street dead-ending in a medieval setting. You step off the street into a large, windowless room dominated by a huge kiln in the middle. Men sit on either side of this kiln calmly firing glass blobs on the ends of long pipes. Typical Muski glass is blown from recycled glass shards. Once the desired temperature is reached (and they know it just from sight and feel), the men remove the pipes from the fire, blow gently into them and start shaping the glass using a variety of techniques and tools. The two men work independently of each other and provide quite a show—as if by magic, these glowing blobs become vases, plates or long-necked bottles, typically a crackled green, brown, or blue color. Neither man appears to be disturbed by an audience or the snapping of cameras.

There is a showroom of articles in a nearby apartment where you can purchase the Muski glass at a fraction of its cost in Khan al-Khalili. Unfortunately, the pieces you watch being blown will not be available to purchase until the next day because they have to cool, but similar ones will be. Hassan Arabesque is another workshop on the same street. The owner has cleverly located his shop in front of a tourist site often looked for—the tomb of Shaykh Ibrahim Johann Ludwig Burckhardt (1784–1817). This small shop is stuffed with glass marvels, from beads to elaborate plates but is only a passageway to the garden with a few tombs, one of which belongs to the famed traveler. Burckhardt was the first European in modern times to travel to Abu Simbel. He studied Arabic in Syria, assumed a Muslim name (Ibrahim Ibn Abdallah) and often traveled wearing Muslim dress. He died in Cairo on October 15, 1817 without achieving his goal of crossing the Sahara and was buried in this local cemetery.

Where: See Map A:1.

When: 10am–6pm, any day except Friday and official holidays.

Entrance fee: None, but the men blowing the glass usually receive a tip—you decide what the show is worth!

Tips: In the summer, even on cool days, this work shop is very hot. Be sure to pack water bottles for every one. The neighborhood you walk through is quite poor, and the street is unpaved and often muddy: this would be a good time to discuss with the children the living conditions in such areas.

Bab al-Futuh and Bab al-Nasr (6, 7: 1087)

Two of the three remaining gates of al-Qahira—the walled city—rise grandly from the old walls in the north quarter: Bab al-Futuh ('Gate of Conquests') and Bab al-Nasr ('Gate of Victory'). (The third gate, Bab Zuwayla, is at the southern entrance to the old city.) Both of these towers are great examples of military architecture. Although rebuilt and renamed several times, both towers still carry their original names. Even the great Napoleon, whose troops occupied these two fortifications, failed to make a name change stick! It will probably be another two or three years before visitors will be permitted inside

*Bab al-Nasr
Insert: Close
scrutiny reveals
reused
pharaonic
stones in Bab
al-Futuh's walls*

the walls once again as the gates and the walls extending to the west are
under extensive restoration and reconstruction. Until that time, enjoy the
view from the street and use your imagination. From the front view of Bab
al-Futuh, you can easily imagine soldiers walking patrol along the top of the
ramparts or shooting from the narrow slits in time of battle. Originally begun
in 969, the parapets were subsequently enhanced in 1087 using many building blocks from Memphis and Saqqara. Re-use of pharoanic building materials such as columns and blocks of carved stone was common. If you stand in
the street (watch out for cars!) directly under Bab al-Futuh, and look up,

you'll see shafts into which boiling oil could be poured onto enemies (right where you are standing!).

Until the day these towers are open once again to the public, enjoy the surrounding area as you continue to walk on this ancient street connecting Bab al-Futuh to Bab Zuwayla. In early September, you'll find dozens of tables displaying pickling olives—tables of the green and blue-black varieties, lemons, chilies, carrots, and spices make for great photo opportunities. In late March and early April the area is redolent with the smell of freshly harvested onions and garlic. Often stacked in two-meter-high circles, the garlic is a sight not to be missed.

Where: **See Map A:2 and 3.**

Tip: **This is a busy street, so listen carefully for the clang of a bicycle bell or the hiss of a donkey cart driver and be prepared to step quickly to one side if necessary.**

Bayt al-Sihaymi (339: 1648–1796)

Located off Darb al-Asfar, just halfway between Bab al-Futuh and al-Husayn Mosque, the recently reopened Bayt al-Sihaymi has undergone extensive renovation and restoration. This nearly three-hundred-year-old merchant's house is actually two houses that were joined sometime in the late eighteenth century (the older house dates back to 1648). Neighborhood involvement in the restoration has led to the upgrading of Darb al-Asfar, with façades cleaned and the alleyway now closed to traffic.

Immediately upon stepping off the alleyway you will turn slightly to the right then back to the left—this indirect method of entering is common in these old houses. This leads to a magnificent courtyard complete with trees and flowers, a respite from the narrow, dusty streets you have just traversed. Just beyond this courtyard is another, larger courtyard that has been completely redone. Here, an old flourmill works once again and an old well has been re-excavated. Plans are to hold concerts, lectures, and receptions in this large, airy space. Public bathrooms, a kitchen, and a caterer's room have all been discreetly added to allow the modern to mix with the historic.

Stand in the *salamlik*, the large reception room off the first courtyard just to the left of the entrance, and gaze up and around. The cool tiles on the floor, the central water fountain, the high, decorated ceiling, the soft light filtering through the enormous *mashrabiya* window—all of these ensure maximum coolness in Cairo's heat. Stand in the domed bath and see the colored glass skylights and look at the channels that allowed water to run into the bath; the naturally curious will gain an understanding of the plumbing system utilized hundreds of

The Ottoman sabil of Sulayman Agha al-Silahdar

years ago. Don't miss the *malqaf*, an architectural device that catches the wind and channels it into the house for cooling in the summer. Climb the stairs to the *haramlik*, the women's quarters, and look down upon the courtyard through the *mashrabiya* windows and enjoy the cool breezes wafting through; admire the Syrian tiles decorating the room and cupboards.

It is hard to fathom living without the conveniences of today, but a visit to Bayt al-Sihaymi and a vivid imagination will help to fill in many of the blanks.

Where: **See Map A:5.**

When: **9am–5pm every day in winter; 9am–6pm every day in summer.**

Entrance fee: **Foreigners: LE20, children or students LE10. Egyptians: LE2, children or students LE1.**

Tip: **This is one of the few places in the area with modern toilets—make use of this stop.**

Madrasa-Khanqah of Sultan Barquq (178: 1384, 1386)

Originally a slave of Circassian origin, al-Zahir Barquq rose to become the first Sultan of the Burgi Mamluk dynasty (1382–1517). This school/monastery was built in the early years of his reign and houses the mausoleum of his daughter. The octagonal minaret towers 165 feet over the building. Recently cleaned

A door in the Madrasa–Khanqah of Sultan Barquq

of grime, the outer walls compliment the architecture of the Qalawun complex immediately to the left, a complex more than one hundred years older than Barquq's structure. Be sure to notice the massive bronze-plated doors inlaid with silver. In the central star is the name: Barquq (Arabic for 'plum'). The plan of the interior is a traditional one, a narrow passage leading to the central courtyard with an impressive ablution fountain in the center. Off this large courtyard are the *qibla* (sanctuary) *liwan* to the right and access to upstairs rooms used for Sufis and the students. Stepping inside the *qibla*, you are immediately struck by the color patterns reflected on the floor and walls from the five stucco windows inlaid with colored glass, one round window flanked by two arched ones on either side. Like the neighboring Madrasa of Qalawun, the ceiling is richly decorated and worth more than just a quick glance. Columns of porphyry support the ceiling and are possibly reused pharaonic ones. Many of Cairo's monuments utilized columns from the pharaonic period, providing an interesting transition between the ancient, medieval, and more modern times.

To the left of the *qibla liwan* is the entrance to the tomb chamber. The splendid domed room, filled with bands of inscription, stained glass, and decorative panels, houses the tomb of Sultan Barquq's daughter, Fatima. The Sultan and other members of his family are buried in the Northern Cemetery.

Where: See Map A:6.

When: 9am–6pm.

Entrance fee: Free for Egyptians. Foreigners: LE10, children or students LE5;
plus tip.

New: Textile Museum: Just opposite this complex is the handsome Muhammad Ali Sabil (402: 1828). Recently cleaned and restored, its premises now house a museum for textiles. The museum was created by installing state-of-the art lighting and ventilation systems. A collec-

tion of more than 250 pieces of weaving, carpets, looms, and design elements are on display
in the spacious interior. For an idea of how the
sabils operated visit another of Muhammad
Ali's sabils further along this ancient street,
Sabil of Tusun Pasha (401: 1820) (Map: B: 8).

Al-Azhar Mosque (97: 970–72)

*The main
entrance of
al-Azhar
Mosque*

The city of a thousand minarets claims also to be the city of the oldest university in the world. Al-Azhar was built only a few years after Gawhar al-Siqilli
finished enclosing the new city of al-Qahira in 970. This mosque was given the
status of a university in 988 by Caliph al-Aziz. It was an important mosque
then, and has remained so for a thousand years.

A visit to the mosque is an education itself. Recently given a facelift, the
northwest façade has been cleaned to reveal its intricately carved patterns.
This is known as the Barbers' Gate, because students long ago would have
their heads shaved here before entering. The entire complex of al-Azhar is a
collection of different styles and centuries, very much reflecting the ebb and
flow of architecture and politics in this ancient city. Conquering armies sought
to dominate it, strong leaders sought to restore its glory. Over the decades, al-
Azhar has added secular faculties and is today one of the largest universities
in Egypt, boasting a student population (both male and female) in the hundreds of thousands, from many countries.

The theological schools are not open to the public, but you can enter the Barbers' Gate, cover your shoes, and walk into the great courtyard. Directly in front of you is one of the oldest areas of the mosque. Cross the courtyard and step into the coolness of the pillared area containing the *mihrab*, the prayer niche. The nine rows of columns, 140 in all, create a pleasing space. Be sure to note the capitals; more than ninety of these columns are ancient, and the designs are unique.

Where: See Map B:1.

When: 9am–9pm. Do not plan a visit on Friday or during prayer times.

Entrance fee: No fees, but a tip for shoe cover.

Camera: No photography is permitted inside al-Azhar.

Tip: Women should cover heads, arms, and legs (in other words, no shorts). Often there are shawls available at the entrance but it is wiser to bring your own. Shorts are acceptable for small children only.

Bayt Zaynab Khatun and Bayt al-Harrawi (77: 1468; 446: 1731)

These two houses were restored by the French government and are worth visiting for a glimpse of domestic architecture. Zaynab Khatun's house was built in the mid-fifteenth century. The name refers to the last occupant, not to the person who built the house. It is an excellent example of Mamluk style, with later Ottoman features added. Built in 1731, the Bayt al-Harrawi, another example of an Ottoman home, is just across a small clearing recently paved over with large stones.

Also in this clearing is another restored house now being used as a gift shop—Al Khatoun. Here you'll find unusual items as the owners specialize in antiques (old movie posters, grillwork turned into candlesticks) and re-interpretation of traditional crafts. Instead of a traditionally appliquéd design, for example, you'll find wall hangings on linen with gold/silver thread embroidery and/or imaginative appliqué.

Since restoration, both houses are being used for a variety of cultural activities. Concerts, plays, and dance performances are often given in the open courtyard. Check the local papers for performance times and schedules. During Ramadan, there are nightly concerts or plays, usually beginning at 8 or 9pm.

Where: See Map B:2 and 3.

When: 9am–8pm (unless there are performances, then later).

Portal decoration of al-Salih Nagm al-Din, on the western edge of Khan al-Khalili

Entrance fee: Free for Egyptians, Foreigners: LE10 for each house, children or students LE5 for each house. Performances are free.

Newly renovated: Bayt al-Sitt Wassila, is a seventeenth century house nearby that carries the name of the last person who lived in it. Newly restored, it is not yet open to the public. The house is most important for its floral and geometric wall decorations, as well as wonderful murals and frescos.

Al-Ghuri Complex (54, 55, 64, 66, 67, 159, 189: 1504–05)

Following the street just to the left of the al-Azhar (when standing with your back to the Barbers' Gate) toward the pedestrian bridge, you will pass through a market area then find the entrance to the Wikalat al-Ghuri on your left. Step down through the high, wide portal into a rectangle of light and quiet surrounded by striped arches and *mashrabiya* shutters. You are now standing in one of the few remaining *wikala*s (at one time there were more than two hundred such structures in this area) and by far the most excellent example of these commercial establishments remaining. Slowly, as you look around, you can begin to imagine the merchants haggling, grooms scurrying to and fro, camels laden with packages coming in that same doorway, donkeys, boys, dust, laughter, arguments, heat . . . life in the time of the sultan.

Most of the upper-story rooms that once stored wares from the East or housed merchants are now allotted to artists. Many of these artists welcome visits from the public. Inquiries can be made at the entrance.

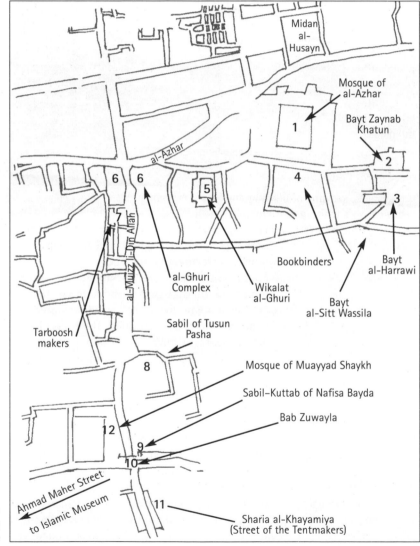

Map B
*Al-Qahira, the
Walled City*

There are several interesting buildings that were built in the early sixteenth century for Sultan al-Ghuri. The most visible are the mosque–*madrasa* and the mausoleum, both just down the street from the *wikala*, recognizable as you stand at the foot of the pedestrian overbridge on Sharia al-Azhar by their bold striped façades. In the eighteenth century, a large timber roof extended over the street linking these buildings. For the last five years, scaffolding has surrounded all the buildings in this complex but now most of that has been

The sixteenth-century mausoleum of al-Ghuri

removed. By the time of printing, the façades should be completely cleaned and renewed, soft white and off-pink stripes girdling the structures. At the street level, some new cafés now provide excellent venues for people watching!

Just opposite these two buildings is the al-Ghuri Palace, now an educational and cultural center. From time to time it houses art exhibitions and other special events; at any time, you may mount the stairs and peek into the two front rooms. The massive bronze-covered doors are beautiful. The room to the right has stained-glass windows set high on the walls and wonderful black and white marble patterned floors.

> Where: **See Map B:5 and 6.**
> When: **9am–3pm for Wikalat al-Ghuri. The artists have their own time schedule! For the Palace, you can glance inside any time you find the doors open.**
> Entrance fee: **Wikalat al-Ghuri: Free for Egyptians. Foreigners: LE6, children or students LE3. Al-Ghuri Cultural Palace: free.**

Tannura Dancers
(commonly known as the Whirling Dervishes)
Performances are at Wikalat al-Ghuri, Saturday and Wednesday, normally at 7.30pm; check times in *Al-Ahram Weekly*. Free of charge, this is great fun for

for all the family. Go a little early for a good seat; cold drinks are available. See page 95 for more details. Tel: 510-0823, 512-1735.

Sabil of Tusun Pasha (401: 1820)

Imagine life in Cairo's summer without access to a cool drink of water! For centuries, dozens of men daily brought water to the walled city and filled cisterns in homes and in public fountains. A *sabil-kuttab* is a public water dispensary in combination with a school. Upstairs, children would recite Quranic verses; downstairs, at street level, workers would hand out water from a central cistern through arched grills. The fountain/school combination was a unique Cairene structure, usually endowed by a wealthy family.

The Sabil of Tusun Pasha

This particular *sabil-kuttab* was commissioned by Sultan Muhammad Ali to commemorate the death of his son, Prince Tusun, who died in 1816 of the plague. For many years in the latter part of the 1800s, the structure was used as a school. By the early 1930s, piped water became available to most of the city and this structure was closed and nearly forgotten. Obscured by small shops until recently, the *sabil* has emerged as a major monument to be visited—the only place you can see how the cistern worked and how people were served. The six-year restoration project (1998–2004) was carried out by a team sponsored by the Egyptian Supreme Council of Antiquities and the Egyptian Antiquities Project of the American Research Center in Egypt. The space inside the old sabil has been turned into a museum. The outer room panels explain the structural interventions necessary for conservation. Several glass-covered holes in the floor allow one to see the actual cistern—an astonishing nine meters deep! This *sabil* was regularly filled to its capacity of 455,000 liters through a system of pipes running through the city.

The Turkish verses inscribed on the façade are reproduced and translated on the interior walls—the theme of water prominent. According to the director of the conservation project, this sabil, "was also a turning point in Cairo's architecture. The style of the opulent carved-marble decoration on the bowed façade was completely novel."

Where: **See Map B: 8**

When: **9am–6pm**

Entrance fee: **For Foreigners and Egyptians LE10, children or students LE5**

Tips: **Photographs are not permitted within the sabil. At the gift shop inside you will find the fascinating guidebook: Muhammad Ali Pasha and His Sabil by Agnieszka Dobrowolska and Khaled Fahmy (AUC Press, 2005).**

If you are observant you will begin to notice other *sabil-kuttab*s scattered throughout al-Qahira. Another of Muhammad Ali's *sabil*s has been turned into a textile museum just opposite the Madrasa-Khanqah of Sultan Barquq (see A: 6). One historian estimated that in 1798 there were over 300 in existence; a recent index of monuments lists only seventy extant. Their rounded forms with small arched gratings at waist height make them easy to spot. You'll see another just a short distance from here in front of Bab Zuwayla— the lovely restored *sabil-kuttab* of Nasfisa al-Bayda (see Map B: 9), another example of the baroque style of Muhammad Ali.

Bab Zuwayla (199: 1092)

Of the original sixty gates to the walled city of al-Qahira, only three remain. One of these is the imposing Bab Zuwayla, the main southern entrance. (Bab al-Futuh and Bab al-Nasr are in the northern quarter.) It is named after one of the early Fatimid units that camped just outside the gates. For centuries, caravans to Mecca and other points east set out from here. Until only 150 years ago, the doors were drawn and barred nightly. In Mamluk and Ottoman times, the recesses of Bab Zuwayla were used to display the bodies of common criminals as examples to the general population passing through. At one time the massive doors of this gate were studded with teeth and bits of cloth, offerings to Qutb al-Mitwalli, a holy saint believed to reside behind the west half of the gate. Sufferers of headaches or tooth pain still seek the help of Qutb al-Mitwalli. This has given rise to the popular name of the gate—Bab al-Mitwalli.

Now re-opened after an extensive conservation project undertaken by the Egyptian Supreme Council of Antiquities and the Egyptian Antiquities Project of the American Research Center in Egypt, Bab Zawayla offers one of the most magnificent views in the neighborhood. Be sure to notice (and read) the panels

*Left: The alley
between the
sabil of Nafisa
al-Bayda and
Bab Zuwayla
Right: Bab
Zuwayla*

installed in the entrance highlighting the historical development of the walls. Before starting up the stairs to the top of the gate, however, also take time to look at the collection of objects in the glass case next to the ticket office as well as the small museum just beside the stairs. Teeth, nails, amulets, and talismans are displayed in the first area; the small museum has well-labeled cases displaying glass, porcelain, pipes, cups, and other objects found during the restoration. After climbing the railed staircase, enjoy the panoramic view or continue your climb to the top of one of the minarets.

After your climb, take the time to really look at the massive doors of Bab Zawayla. For hundreds of years, these wooden doors hung open, witness to hangings, the annual pilgrims' departure to Mecca, thousands of everyday goings and comings, slowly deteriorating, sinking into the earth, becoming immoveable. The restoration team faced a daunting task—to remove, clean, treat, and re-hang the four-ton doors. With careful planning and specially designed equipment, just this was done and on January 30, 2002, the gates of Bab Zuwayla were opened and closed for the first time in hundreds of years. For remarkable before and after views of the gates go to: *http://www.usaid-eg.org/detail.asp?id=292.*

After investigating the doors, turn back and look at the beautiful *sabil–kuttab* on your right. Recently restored, the *sabil–kuttab* of Nafisa Bayda (see Map B:9) is another handsome example of this unique Cairene construction.

> Where: see Map B:10
> When: 9am–6pm
> Entrance fee: Everyone: LE10; students LE5. Tip if accompanied up the minaret.
> Camera: Spectacular views!

Constructing a Tent

It is hard to imagine tents made from appliqué work, but the appliqué is stitched onto panels of sturdy canvas backing. These panels are referred to as *tarq*s. A standard size, the *tarq*s are then lashed together according to the size of the desired 'tent.' It might take three *tarq*s to create the side wall of the tent and six *tarq*s for the back, with the appliqué work facing in. The *tarq* patterns blend and create a festive atmosphere on the inside of the tent. Until recently, despite modern equipment, the tents were built by a group of workmen lashing poles into the desired framework and then covering this frame with *tarq*s—with one worker atop a single ladder that he moves as if on a pair of stilts. If you ever encounter a tent being built, stop and watch the show! Unfortunately, stitched *tarq*s have become expensive, and tentmaking firms are switching to panels printed in imitation appliqué. Look closely when you spot tent panels—commonly used at weddings, funerals, and to enclose construction work—you may see beautiful appliqué examples.

Street of the Tentmakers

Here is a wonderful opportunity to observe another Cairo craft that is in danger of disappearing. Already, the focus of the Sharia al-Khayamiya (Street of the Tentmakers) has changed in the last several decades. The art of appliqué (stitching layers of cloth to create patterns) was practiced by artisans on this street to create decorative tents. These tents were used by the high-ranking military, members of the royal courts, and the government to create colorful 'rooms' in large open spaces. Falling just outside Bab Zuwayla, the street was the beginning of the road to al-Fustat. The small portion of the street named after the craft is still covered, giving a wonderfully mysterious feeling to the area. At the end of the section with the covered roof, the street takes on another name, reflecting the next grouping of artisans or merchants. Multiple names for the same street are a characteristic typical of the medieval city.

Restoration work on the covered section of the Street of the Tentmakers is taking place in stages. Once the street has been structurally restored, a museum may be housed in the upper stories. Be sure to check if a museum has opened!

Sharia al-Khayamiya is a small, narrow street lined with more than two dozen tiny stalls or shops. It is possible to watch skilled artisans, sitting cross-legged on *diwan*s in these stalls, stitch a variety of curves and lines to create flowers, arabesques, pharaonic scenes, or even donkeys and ladies with flowing dresses. Instead of the elegant tents of yesteryear, their creations adorn cushions, bedspreads, and wall hangings. The skill needed to stitch these curves and corners with only cloth, scissors, and thread is amazing to watch. There are piles of cushions and hangings in a variety of patterns and colors ready-made, but if one has the time, it is more fun to sit with an artisan and choose a pattern and colors and have a piece created just for you!

Where: See Map B:11.

When: 10am–7 or 8pm. The hours are flexible; many shops close on Sunday.

Entrance fee: No charge for looking (as the vendors often say), but be prepared to fall in love with a cushion or a wall hanging and bargain. Either will be a wonderful as well as practical souvenir of your outing.

Parking: Don't try to drive to this area. Walk from either Khan al-Khalili or Port Said Street.

Camera: Most of the artisans will not mind if you take pictures of them working, but it would be polite to ask for permission first.

Tip: Beautiful, colorful Ramadan lanterns are for sale on Ahmad Maher Street, a right hand turn as you exit Bab Zawayla heading for the Street of the Tentmakers. The best selection will be found about two weeks before the beginning of Ramadan.

Ahmad Maher Street

If you are at Bab Zawayla and Khayamiya Street why not take a walk down Ahmad Maher Street toward the Islamic Art Museum. This street is an example of a traditional Middle Eastern souk rather than touristy quarters of Khan al-Khalili bazaar. Workshops, coffee shops, *kunafa* and *fiteer* shops, metal and furniture workshops tightly squeeze the sidewalk. You can find birdcages,

Tentmakers at Sharia al-Khayamiya

ostrich feather dusters, barbecues grills, and an herbalist. There are tomb-stone cutters and marble and alabaster workshops. Peek into the *fawanees* workshops and watch the crafting of these Ramadan lights. Be sure to stop and try a *fiteer* (Egyptian pancake often filled with sugar or cheese) at Hagg's café.

Ramadan Lanterns

Two weeks before Ramadan, *fawanees* (Ramadan lanterns, singular: *fanous*) made out of recycled tin and glass, can be bought from most corners. They are the symbol of the thirty days of fasting, representing the festive nights and the light of the holy month. The Fatimids introduced the lanterns in their Ramadan celebrations. There are beautiful, handmade *fawanees* that stand three meters tall as well as little plastic ones, made in China, that play the *azan* (call to prayer).

Old Cairo

The fascination of Old Cairo is that it provides visual history of Cairo's growth
pattern and evolution. Within a relatively
small area, your visit begins at the walls of
the Roman-Byzantine fortress, through the
vault where Jesus and the Virgin Mary hid
from Roman soldiers, to Coptic churches and
a Jewish synagogue, on to al-Fustat where
the Umayyad armies camped bringing Islam
to Egypt and finally, within the tranquility of
Amr ibn al-As Mosque. Let your imagination
wander. At al-Fustat, look northward, and
reflect on conquering successors. Form a
mental image of life and try to imagine the
expressions of spirituality through the many
layers of history. This is the place to begin on
the path of Cairo's one thousand four hundred year history.

When the Arabs entered Egypt in 640, they
besieged a fortress in the area now called
Old Cairo. This fortress, whose present structure dates to the fourth century, was called
Babylon of Egypt. The Roman emperor
Trajan, who garrisoned a Roman legion
there, built the fort in AD 100.

The walls of
Babylon

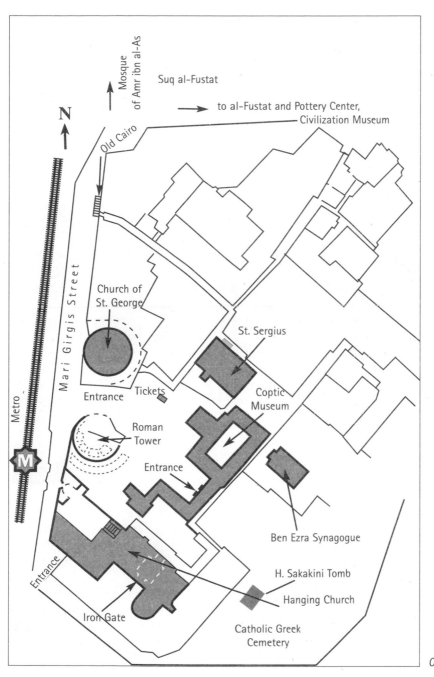

Old Cairo

*One of the
narrow alleys
of Old Cairo*

The walls of Babylon were virtually intact at the end of the nineteenth century, but only parts remain today. The original fort was quadrilateral and enclosed an area about two hundred meters wide and four hundred meters long. The walls of the fort were eleven meters high and almost three meters thick. There were projecting fortifications—or bastions—on three sides of the fort, while on the fourth, the west side, next to the river, were two round, reinforced towers about thirty meters in diameter and sixteen meters high. Direct access to the river was between these towers, and a pontoon bridge spanned the river from the fortress to the island of Roda.

Entering the fortress in Old Cairo today, you walk between the two towers. The Greek Orthodox Church of St. George is built on top of the northern tower, while the southern tower, partially broken away, has been restored. You can look down into the southern tower, for the modern ground level is six to ten meters higher than when the fortress was built. Notice how the walls were constructed of alternating layers of limestone and fired brick, giving them a striped appearance.

The true entrance to the fortress of Babylon was on the south side, guarded by four bastions. It was this gate, the Iron Gate, that was opened when Babylon surrendered to Amr ibn al-As and his army in early April 640, after a siege of seven months. Today, al-Kanisa al-Muallaqa, the Hanging

Church, sits atop this gateway across two of the bastions. Although there is an ongoing debate as to when the Hanging Church was built, it was most probably constructed after the surrender to the Arabs, when the fortress was no longer of military importance. Other churches were erected inside the fortress; the oldest of these, St. Sergius, is also included in our itinerary.

One possible explanation why the fortress was called Babylon is that in the sixth century BC, when Egypt was part of the Persian Empire, Babylonian captives were either imprisoned in or forced to build a fortress in this vicinity. Perhaps, then, the later Roman fortress was given the same name.

Where: Old Cairo is easy to find. From Salah Salim St., turn south onto Sidi Hasan al-Anwar St. Drive as far as you can go, and just after passing the Mosque of Amr ibn al-As on your left, a barricade at the corner of Old Cairo ends further car movement. Park your car on the street to the left, and then walk along the wall of Old Cairo, and down Mari Girgis St., which is closed to traffic. Around the corner on the left, steps lead down and through the wall into the lanes of Old Cairo, but we suggest you continue along the main street, visiting the Coptic Museum first, and then coming back to this point.

Metro: The station to use is Mari Girgis, which is directly in front of the entrance to the Coptic Museum.

Amr ibn al-As Mosque

After the Arab conquest importance shifted to their new settlement, al-Fustat, just to the northeast of Babylon. The name al-Fustat probably derives from the Latin word *fossatum*, meaning 'entrenched camp.' The mosque of Amr ibn al-As was built in 642 as the congregational mosque for al-Fustat. Its original plan was a simple rectangle, like the house of the Prophet Muhammad in Madina (see "Elements of a Mosque," page 89). As the city grew, the mosque was enlarged. The size of the mosque was doubled in 673 and minarets added to the corners. As al-Fustat had become a thriving economic and administrative center, the mosque had to be doubled again in 698. Many enlargements and modifications followed. The structure of the mosque as you see it today mainly dates from 1798, with modern restoration. Several pillars from the original structure still remain in the far left corner of the mosque.

The doorman at the entrance welcomes visitors and will provide an *abiya* (long cloak) for women. Please remove your shoes and deposit them with a doorman who will collect a nominal fee upon returning the shoes. There are guides or you can wander alone through the massive congregational mosque. Take your time and enjoy the tranquility of this beautiful space. On Fridays at noon prayers, the mosque receives up to 3,000 worshipers, so plan your visit around this time.

Coptic Museum

The Coptic Museum is straight ahead as you enter the Fortress of Babylon between the round towers (The Greek Orthodox Church of St. George is on the tower to the left). Marcus Samaika Pasha (1864–1944) built the first wing in 1910, choosing this site for its proximity to ancient churches and the Christian cemetery. A second wing was added in 1947. Complete renovations of the museum began in 2004 and reopening two years later, the museum exhibits some of the most important pieces of art, architectural sculpture, and writings in Christian history and in the world.

The museum is organized by themes. Displayed on the wall of each room is an overview and history in Arabic, English, and French. Entering the museum, go left and tour the downstairs rooms counterclockwise. In the last room, Room 9, there is a stairway (and elevator) to the second floor. Go clockwise through the rooms on the upper floor until the last room, Room 17, where you enter a walkway down to the Old Wing. Room 26 is the last room in the Old Wing, and you exit out into a courtyard where there is an exhibition of pieces from the early churches of Old Cairo.

Upon entering the museum, the reception room has a large ground plan on the right-hand wall. As well, all the rooms and displays in the museum are marked and labeled clearly.

Coptic Museum, Lower Floor
Room 1: Reception
Room 2: Masterpieces of Coptic Art
Room 3: Sculpture from Ahnas al-Medineh
Room 4: Tombstones
Rooms 5, 6, inner courtyard: Pieces from the Monastery of St. Jeremiah at Saqqara
Rooms 7, 8, 9: Pieces from the Monastery of St. Apollo at Baouit

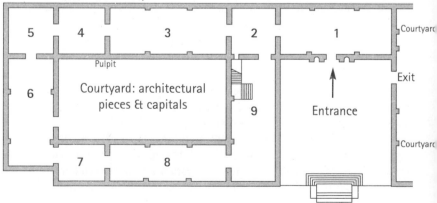

The tour begins in Room 2: Masterpieces of Coptic Art. The room's center-piece is a textile depicting a dancing horse on one side and a musician on the other. The remaining part of the textile is at the Louvre Museum in Paris. Scholars identify this textile as Coptic art as it was used in a Christian burial.

The stone pieces in Room 3 illustrate how classical deities and myths are reflected in early Coptic art. You can find Heracles holding his club, Europa and the Bull, Leda and the Swan, Pan, and Orpheus with his lyre. In Room 4, different Coptic tombstones show the development of the form of the Christian cross, and its relationship to the ancient Egyptian ankh sign, the symbol of eternal life.

The pieces in Rooms 5 and 6 and the inner courtyard all come from the Monastery of St. Jeremiah at Saqqara, which was founded in 470 and abandoned by 960. It was a large complex, including four churches. Note in particular the stone ambon, or pulpit, against the wall in the inner courtyard. It was originally placed against the wall in a refectory courtyard, and the two columns supported a vault over the pulpit to provide shade. Take time to examine the intricate floral designs on the capitals displayed in this courtyard; some still have the remains of red paint. Room 6 displays original icons from these churches; the first of which is known at the 'Egyptian Mona Lisa' as the eyes follow the on-looker.

The Ankh

On the wall on your right in Room 7 is a painted niche depicting three saints which dates from the seventh to ninth centuries. St. Apollo is the figure in the center. On your right on the wall in Room 8 is a painted niche dating from the sixth and seventh centuries. Christ in Ascension is in the upper part of the niche, and below the Twelve Apostles and two local saints flanks the Virgin Mary and infant. The upper figure of Christ is seated within a circle called a mandorla. There are wheels under it, along with four other round enclosures with wheel rims, eyes, and the four creatures of the Apocalypse: man, lion, ox, and eagle. This is the vision described in Ezekiel 10:9–14.

In the middle of Room 9 is a large marble column, the upper part of a cap-ital. It is in the shape of a basket and carved with a wickerwork pattern. The capital dates to the sixth century and derives from a type known in Constantinople. The fact that it is hollowed out with a spout on one side sug-gests that the capital was reused, perhaps as a baptistery. On the wall to the right is a fragment of painted plaster with the ancient equivalent of a car-toon. It depicts mice and a cat acting as humans. The ancient Egyptians also drew cartoons like this on papyrus. Now, take the stairs or the elevator to the first floor.

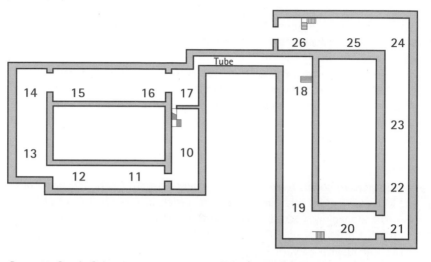

Coptic
Museum,
Upper Floor
and Old Wing

Room 10: Coptic Culture
Room 11: Religious Themes
Room 12: Liturgical Vestments
Room 13, 14: Textiles
Room 15: Naga Hammadi Texts
Room 16: Writing
Room 17: Book of Psalms

Tube (walkway): Pieces from Kellia
Room 18: Nilotic Scenes
Room 19: Daily Life Pieces
Rooms 20, 21, 22: Icons
Room 23: Metal Objects
Rooms 24, 25: Ceramics and Glass
Room 26: Large Wooden Inlaid Pieces

At the top of the stairs in a case on the right in Room 10 is a cast bronze eagle. The eagle was the symbol of the Roman Empire, and this piece would have been placed on top of a tall pole or standard. The eagle was discovered during clearance for the construction of the Coptic Museum, and came from the original old Roman fort. It is probably the oldest piece in the museum.

In the first, large glass case in Room 11, look at object B, an ivory comb with a depiction of the rise of Lazarus. Beyond this case on the left wall is part of a painting depicting Abraham's sacrifice of his son. Further along on the left, is a wall painting of Adam and Eve in the Garden of Eden before (on the left) and after (on the right) the Fall from Paradise. The painting is from Umm al-Burigat in the Fayoum and dates to the eleventh century. Note their large eyes and prominent pupils, typical of late Roman and Byzantine art. Do you see the serpent?

In the second case from the left as you enter Room 13 is a circular textile decoration from the fourth century depicting Heracles taming the lion. You can also see other classical motifs and designs in these textiles, such as nymphs, centaurs, and dolphins. These textiles were made from linen and wool, and colored with dyes from various plants. The textiles have been pre-served for us because they were used as wrappings for the dead.

Naga Hammadi Gnostic Texts

In 1945, a collection of thirteen manuscripts was discovered in a jar in an old tomb near Naga Hammadi, in Upper Egypt. They were written in the late fourth century and were translations into Coptic from texts orig-inally written in Greek. These writings belong to an early Christian move-ment called Gnosticism, which emphasized knowing oneself and discover-ing the divine 'light' within. Gnostics rejected institutionalized religion, and were considered heretics by the established church. Recently another Gnostic text, the only known copy of the Gospel of Judas was identified. There are plans to add it to the collection of the Coptic Museum.

The last display case in Room 16 contains different materials that were used as writing surfaces: pottery fragments, bone, wood, flakes of limestone. Archaeologists call these ostraca (singular, ostracon). The ancient Egyptians wrote on ostraca as well. Ostraca are the ancient equivalents of note pads and scrap paper. Room 17 contains a fourth century Book of Psalms. The glass partition allows the onlooker a moment to pause to focus on this ancient relic.

The 'tube' is the entrance into the old wing, which has been closed for decades—a true treat for long-term residents and locals. Pieces from the her-mitage site of Kellia in the western Delta line the corridor. As you turn and enter Room 18, you will be awestruck by the magnificent ceilings from old houses in Cairo that have been preserved and installed in the museum. It is hard to lower your eyes and appreciate the museum pieces on display!

Turning left into Room 20, the icons begin. As you enter Room 21, on the left is a cloth icon of the seventh century that was a type of souvenir bought by visitors to Palestine. At the left end of Room 23 there is a collection of pottery from Fustat, the city site which spread just to the east and north of Babylon. In Rooms 24 and 25 are ceramic and glass pieces from the site of Abu Mena near Alexandria. Note in a case at the right end of 25, water jug strainers, object N (more can be seen in the Gezira Arts Center in Zamalek), and decorative cookie stamps, object L.

The first piece you encounter in Room 26 is a fancy, wooden, inlaid carriage of the Ottoman Period. It was put on long poles that were suspended between two camels. Wealthy women used this type of carriage for traveling. The inlay is bone, ivory, and mother-of-pearl, and the windows are mashrabiya.

At this point, exit into the courtyard of the Museum, which is just inside the Iron Gate, the southern gateway into the Fortress of Babylon. On the east side of the courtyard is a special exhibit of pieces from the oldest churches in Old Cairo. Here, there is also an exhibition hall, manuscript room, and a library.

Metro: **Mari Girgis.**

Telephone: **363-9742.**

Enterance Fee: **Foreigners LE40; others, to be announced.**

More information: **Read** *The Treasures of Coptic Art in the Museums of Cairo* **by Gawdat Gabra (AUC Press, 2006).**

Facilities: **There are sitting areas throughout the museum. There is a bathroom on the left as you enter the Hanging Church. Immediately to the right of the admission kiosk is a small bookstore. You will encounter stairways throughout the museum and churches.**

Web site: *www.copticmuseum.gov.eg*

The Hanging Church, Old Cairo

The Hanging Church (al-Muallaqa)

Enter The Hanging Church from the street, Mari Girgis St., south of the Roman tower entrance. A long flight of stairs leads up to the church. Admission is free.

This church was probably first built in the seventh century, although the earliest written reference to it dates from the ninth century. As the church is built on top of the two bastions flanking the main gate of the fortress, it would not have been built until after the surrender of the fort to the Arabs. The Hanging Church has been rebuilt and restored many times throughout the years; the latest restoration was in 2003.

The plan of the church is that of a three-part basilica. Its central nave is separated from the aisles on each side by white marble columns. Near the front of the nave is a marble *ambon*, or pulpit, generally dated to the thirteenth century, although it may well be older. Fifteen small pillars support the pulpit: fourteen symbolize the Twelve Disciples and Saints Luke and Mark, who were not of the Twelve Disciples; the pillar that stands in front represents Jesus Christ. The sanctuary area, called the *haikal*, is divided into three parts and closed off by an ivory-inlaid ebony screen dating to the thirteenth century. The central part of the *haikal* is dedicated to the Virgin Mary, the southern part to St. John the Baptist, and the northern part to St. George.

A door in the south wall of the southern aisle leads to the 'Little Church,' which occupies the inside of the eastern bastion of the Iron Gate, the southern entrance to the fortress of Babylon. This small church is perhaps the original Hanging Church, or the earliest part of it that remains. You can look out the windows here and see the bastions of the fort.

Church of St. Sergius

Returning to Mari Girgis St., walk north, passing the Roman towers of Babylon and entrance to the Coptic Museum. Just beyond the entrance to the Greek Orthodox Church of St. George, descend the stairs on the right, which lead onto the cobblestone lanes of Old Cairo. Wear good walking shoes, as the lanes are of uneven cobblestones, and can be slippery. This passageway leads to the Church of St. Sergius and the Ben Ezra Synagogue. Admission to both is free. Turning to your right at all crossings, you come to the Church of St. Sergius. Go down the steps into the church. Notice the difference in ground level: you are stepping down into another time!

The Church of St. Sergius, actually the Church of Saints Sergius and Bacchus, is known in Arabic as Abu Sarga. It is the oldest church inside the walls of Old Cairo, and Romans garrisoned in the fort may have built it. The church has two rows of columns inside dating to the third or fourth century, but the oldest written reference to it is dated much later, in the ninth century.

Below the northern part of the sanctuary is the crypt, probably an earlier church built over the spot where the Virgin Mary, Joseph, and the infant Jesus are said to have stayed during their flight into Egypt. Stepping into the northern sanctuary, or *haikal*, you can look down the closed-off steps. These stairs lead into the crypt about six meters below the level of the church. For decades, the crypt filled with ground water but after restoration, new marble floors replace the water. The columns are a part of the original structure.

Inside Abu Sarga, you can easily see the basic plan of a Coptic church. The nave, or central part, has an aisle on each side separated from it by columns. The sanctuary is in the east, and is tripartite, or divided into three sections, and is closed off from view by an inlaid wooden screen; the central section contains the altar. The churches in this area are functioning and have regular services—therefore, it is important to remember to be respectfully silent for those who have come to pray.

Out of the church and back on the path, continue southeast and turn right to reach the entrance to the Ben Ezra Synagogue.

> Web site: *www.coptic.org*—**Egypt Coptic Orthodox directory of churchs, organizations, youth groups, and Coptic literary resources.**

Ben Ezra Synagogue

The Ben Ezra Synagogue as it stands now was constructed in 1892, and completely restored in 1989–94. The 1892 structure replaced the structure dated to the mid-eleventh century. The building has two stories; the gallery for women is on the second floor. As in a church, the sanctuary is at the east end. The central part of the synagogue is dominated by a platform for reading the Torah. West of the platform, closer to the door is a 'bench' marking a holy spot associated with Moses. This synagogue is perhaps most famous as the site where the Geniza documents were discovered. The Geniza documents provide much detail of the life of the Jewish community in al-Fustat from the eleventh to the thirteenth centuries.

The Geniza Documents

The word *geniza* refers to a storehouse or repository for discarded writings. These are documents that in the Jewish tradition cannot be thrown away because they may contain the name of God, so they are put into a special chamber called a *geniza*. The *geniza* in the Ben Ezra Synagogue was reached through a trapdoor in the second floor women's gallery. When it was cleared, it contained more than 200,000 documents dating back to the eleventh to thirteenth centuries. These were not only religious documents but also legal papers and letters. Most of the documents are now in the collection of Cambridge University.

Al-Fustat

Drive east on the road along the north side of Old Cairo. Just as the road curves to the right, the entrance to al-Fustat is on the left. You will find it easily because it is right by the Islamic-style stucco domes of the al-Fustat Ceramic Center. To the right is the same style building for artists who work in traditional crafts. Go through the entrance and find your way to the first floor by way of the stairs to the right. You will have an excellent view of the ancient ruins of Fustat.

In the tenth and eleventh centuries, royalty and the upper classes lived in the Fatimid city of al-Qahira, while others lived in al-Fustat. In 1046, a Persian traveler wrote that al-Fustat from a distance resembled a mountain. Houses were as tall as fourteen stories, and up to three hundred people could live in a single building. Plague and drought decimated the population of al-Fustat between 1066 and 1072. However, the final blow to the city came in 1168 when a decision was made to burn it rather than let it fall into the hands of the Crusader army, which was led by King Amalric of Jerusalem. After the inhabitants fled, twenty thousand pots of naphtha and ten thousand torches were used to set the city on fire. History states that al-Fustat burnt for fifty-four days.

> Where: **Off Ain al-Sira St., just east of Old Cairo.**
> Metro: **Mar Girgis.**
> When: **8:30am–3:15pm every day except Thursday and Friday.**
> Suggested reading: *The Building Crafts of Cairo* by **Agnieszka Dobrowolska (AUC Press, 2005), a beautifully illustrated, informative book on traditional crafts.**

National Museum of Egyptian Civilization

Keep an eye out for updates and news about the development of this museum. Ain al-Sira is the site for the new Civilization Museum. The vision for this museum as well as the Nubian Museum in Aswan began in 1983. The Nubian Museum was built but there was a delay while plans for the Civilization Museum were drawn up to be constructed at the Opera House parking lot in Zamalek. Fortunately, the Minister of Culture was able to restart the enthusiasm for the project when he suggested the museum be created at Ain al-Sira. The center of this site has ties throughout the history of Cairo. The fortress of Babylon, Old Cairo, and al-Fustat represent Roman, Christian, and Islamic histories, respectively, as Cairo developed. Also, the site is close to Maadi and Helwan, which were the sites of pre-historic civilizations. To the north is the Citadel, to the south ancient Christian churches and Ben-Ezra Synagogue. Thirty-two feddans spread between these historical points in which the museum will be built along with gardens, cinemas, and a shopping mall.

The museum itself will house artifacts around main five themes: the Nile, religion, writing, crafts and arts, and society. The Royal Mummies will find a new, state-of-the-art resting place. The plans call for an auditorium, educational center, and temporary exhibition halls. The training of staff has already begun. Look for the opening in April 2008.

Where: Between Old Cairo and al-Fustat.

Metro: Mar Girgis.

Suq al-Fustat

Suq al-Fustat has had its share of ups and downs. The public participated in the opening of its cool-arched stone halls with over fifty shops in early 2001. Architect Mona Zakaria and her team have renewed the area's old quarters by preserving the unique architecture of homes that line the surrounding streets. This initiative saved the original atmosphere of the area, as well as introducing the community outreach programs to the neighborhood children through art and apprenticeship opportunities. Take a stroll through the breezy halls. There may be a treasure or two to be found. Watch for monthly cultural activities and exhibitions at this venue.

Fustat Ceramic Center and Said il Sadi Museum

The Fustat Ceramic Center is a maze of ateliers dedicated to the revival of the art of ceramics. With its domed roof and arches, the architecture is reminiscent of Hassan Fathi's style of distinction. Dedicated to Said Sadr, the original founder of the site for potters more than forty years ago, is the Said il Sadi Museum, which displays a collection of ceramics representing the works of

The remains of al-Fustat

many Egyptian artists. Children of all ages will find it interesting to watch artists create their art.

Where: Ain al-Sira St., off of Salah Salim St. from the south or turn right at Suq al-Fustat and continue around the bend. (Just past the center is al-Fustat).

When: 10am–4pm. Closed Fridays.

Facilities: Wheelchair access and clean toilets.

Roda Island

The Nile once spread much farther to the east than it does today, but Roda Island is seemingly as ancient as the Nile that swept past its banks. In pharaonic times, the island was probably used as a ferry stage between Memphis and Heliopolis. The Roman fortress of Babylon (see Old Cairo) was across from the most southern tip of Roda Island: during the inundation of the Nile, to the east, a floating bridge of thirty-six boats connected the island with Babylon; in late spring and early summer the riverbed between the two often dried completely. The Romans recognized the logistic importance of the island and fortified the area with walls. Subsequent rulers acknowledged the strategic importance of the island and refined the area for encampment and pleasure.

In 640, the Arab general Amr ibn al-As arrived in Egypt and built the first mosque in Africa next to the city of Babylon, across from Roda Island on the eastern shore. After the Arabs took the fortress, they destroyed parts of the walls on Roda, and by 673 they had built a naval dockyard here. In the ninth century, under the Abbasids, the Nilometer was erected on the very southern tip of Roda, and shortly thereafter Ahmad ibn Tulun, having broken away from the Abbasid caliphate in Baghdad to form his own dynasty, rebuilt the walls of Roda and housed his harem there.

Next to the Nilometer on the west, Badr al-Gamali (the military commander who built the great gates of al-Qahira; see the section on Khan al-Khalili) constructed the Mosque of the Miqyas (*miqyas* in Arabic means 'Nilometer') in 1092. This mosque stood until 1830, when it was destroyed by the explosion of a powder arsenal built next to it. The Fatimid caliph al-Amir constructed a house and pavilion for his favorite mistress on the northern end of the island; he was assassinated in 1130 as he rode back from her home.

Sultan al-Salih Nagm al-Din, the grandnephew of Saladin and the last Ayyubid ruler, ordered a fortress and palace erected on the island in 1240. When it was finished he lived there, rather than at the Citadel. He also built barracks at Roda for a thousand of his elite troops who then became known as the Bahri ('river') Mamluks. The Bahri Mamluks seized control of Egypt in 1250, and they tore down al-Salih's palace, pillaging it for marble and granite building stone. A small part of the palace still remained on the east side of the Nilometer in 1798 when the French expedition came to Egypt; drawings and a description of it are given in the *Description d'Egypte*.

Later, in the 1830s, Ibrahim Pasha had the northern half of the island turned into a botanical forest. The Monasterli Palace was built on the southern end of Roda in 1851, partially covering the site of the Mosque of the Miqyas. Then, close to the northern end, Prince Muhammad Ali Tawfiq Pasha built his grand residence, today known as the Manial Palace. Since the mid-twentieth century, however, the vast private and public gardens have disappeared and Roda Island has become filled with high-rise housing.

Across from the island of Roda on the east side stands the great hexagonal intake tower for the

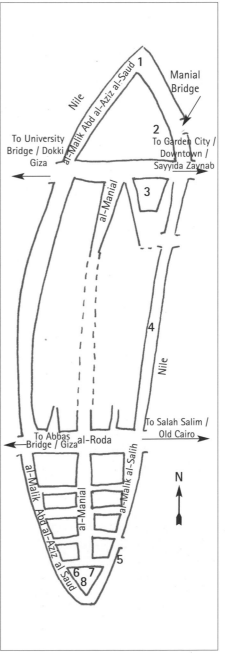

Roda Island

1. Hyatt Hotel
2. Qasr al-Aini Museum
3. Manial Palace
4. Across Nile: Magra al-Oyoun Wall Aqueduct
5. Walking bridge
6. Monasterli Palace
7. Umm Kulthum Museum
8. Nilometer

Who Were the Mamluks?

The word 'Mamluk' literally means 'owned': the Mamluks were slaves from the Turkish tribes of Central Asia, bought as young boys and raised and trained in all aspects of warfare and horsemanship. They then became the bodyguards of the sultan, to whom they were fiercely loyal. A freed Mamluk could become an important official, or amir, and own Mamluks of his own. It was only a step then for a powerful Mamluk to become sultan himself.

Following the collapse of the Ayyubids in 1250, the Mamluks ruled an empire consisting of Egypt and Syro-Palestine for roughly 250 years. Mamluk rule in Egypt is divided into two periods, the Bahri Mamluks, who ruled from 1250 to 1382, and the Burgi Mamluks, who ruled from 1382 to 1517. Bahri ('river') refers to the Mamluks stationed on the Island of Roda, and Burgi ('fortress') refers to those garrisoned at the Citadel.

aqueduct built in Mamluk times. This area is called Fumm al-Khalig, which means 'mouth of the canal.' The tower was originally built at the edge of the Nile, but the river has shifted slightly westward since then, and the Corniche road now separates the two. Almost 25 meters high, the tower has a well at the center from which Nile water was raised by six *saqya*s, or waterwheels, turned by oxen that were herded up to the tower by a ramp on the east side. The water then ran by gravity along the aqueduct east and then north to the

Magra al-Oyoun Aqueduct

Citadel. Near the Citadel, two more *saqya* towers lifted the water up to a tunnel, which ran through the rock under and into the Citadel. This aqueduct functioned as the water source for the Citadel until the city water system was developed in 1872. More than three hundred arches make up the aqueduct wall, Magra al-Oyoun, which means 'water course of the springs.' The westernmost part of the aqueduct, and the tower, are inscribed with the name of Sultan al-Ghuri, who erected this section in 1507, while the part of the aqueduct running to the north dates earlier to 1311, in the reign of Sultan Muhammad al-Nasir. Now there are six large gaps in the aqueduct made by roads and railway lines, and the section approaching the Citadel is gone completely. In March 2000, the Supreme Council for Antiquities announced a three-year plan to restore the tower and aqueduct. When completed, mechanical waterwheels will lift water up in the tower, and the aqueduct will allow water to flow again to the Citadel.

The tower stands at the south end of Midan Fumm al-Khalig, the point at which the old Khalig canal left the Nile and headed east (see further discussion in the section on Sayyida Zaynab). Each year before the Nile flood, a dike was built closing off the canal while it was cleaned out. When the floodwaters reached 16 cubits in the Nilometer on Roda, the dike was cut in a great celebration known as the Festival of the Opening of the Canal.

As this book goes to press, Magra al-Oyoun, the aqueduct wall, is nearly restored. The project patched the damages, strengthened the foundation, and drained the ground water. During the restoration, the fourth, fifth, and sixth waterwheels were discovered, complete with clay scoops to lift water from the well.

Manial Palace

> This palace was built by Prince Muhammad Ali, son of the late Khedive Tawfiq, to revive the Islamic arts and to honor them. The architecture of the building and its decoration were conceived by his highness, it was executed by Muallim Muhammad Afifi, and it was finished in 1348 [AH].

Just before passing under the arched entrance of the limestone-walled Manial Palace, you will notice the above inscription in Arabic. With this introduction, your journey begins into a beautiful nineteenth-century palace and grounds. Manial Palace was begun in 1901 by Prince Muhammad Ali Tawfiq Pasha (1875–1955) and completed around 1929 (1348 by the Islamic calendar). At that time there was a revival of interest in Islamic architecture and arts due to the rise in nationalistic interests. As a response to this movement, the planners applied the architecture of the Mamluks, Moors, and Ottomans.

Walk through the entrance and reception area to purchase your tickets from a small kiosk on the left, then retrace your steps to the reception area, where the royal family received their guests. Guests who were expected were guided through the garden to Prince Muhammad Ali Tawfiq's house; otherwise, they were probably given tea and dismissed. Whatever the wait, one can imagine the time spent was not uncomfortable. Considering waiting rooms of today, this reception room is opulent. Iznik tiles—turquoise tiles from Iznik, Turkey, with floral designs—cover the walls, which are framed with Arabic writing, stained-glass windows and a rich wooden ceiling with Turkish decoration provided a pleasing aesthetic for the waiting visitor.

There is a map of the Manial Palace across from the ticket booth. Facing the map, a private mosque and a clock tower resembling North African minarets are on the right. The mosque, built around 1933, is decorated with Moroccan and Turkish designs. before setting foot in the mosque, the attendant may ask you to remove your shoes, and women should not enter if dressed in shorts or sleeveless clothing.

Farther along on the right is the Hunting Museum, which was not a part of the original palace, but an addition built by the antiquities authority in 1963. This museum is well lit and clean, and for younger children it is a good introduction to entomology and taxidermy. The long room holds King Farouk's hunting trophies. A keen huntsman, King Farouk was extravagant in his enjoyment of the hunt. Gazelles line the walls, stuffed lions, crocodiles, leopards, and birds represent only a few of his trophies. The butterfly and bug collections are outstanding and well displayed; however, be sure to ask the guard to turn on the lights in the display case to see the vivid blue colors of the butterfly wings. For those who like creepy crawling things, there are enough snakes, scorpions, and beetles to keep a child's interest.

Following the same path back to the map, angle to the right, and wander through a garden planted with rare trees and plants that were brought to the Manial Palace specifically to enhance this garden. Among the rare tropical plants are cacti from Mexico that Prince Muhammad Ali Tawfiq transported to Egypt during his world travels. The gardens have survived the palace's interim incarnation as a hotel, swimming pool, and touristic site, which have torn into much of the rare foliage. Thankfully, a recent government decree returns the

Rulers of the Muhammad Ali Dynasty

Muhammad Ali Pasha, ruled 1805–48
Ibrahim Pasha, son of Muhammad Ali, r. 1848
Abbas Hilmi I Pasha, grandson of Muhammad Ali, r. 1848–54 (murdered)
Said Pasha, son of Muhammad Ali, r. 1854–63
Khedive Ismail, son of Ibrahim, r. 1863–79
Khedive Tawfiq, son of Ismail, r. 1879–92
Khedive Abbas Hilmi II, son of Tawfiq, r. 1892–1914 (deposed by the British)
Sultan Hussein Kamil, son of Ismail, r. 1914–17
King Ahmad Fuad I, son of Ismail, r. 1917–36
King Farouk, son of Fuad, r. 1936–52 (deposed and exiled after revolution)
King Ahmad Fuad II, son of Farouk, r. 1952–53 (exiled after revolution)

grounds and buildings to the public, following the explicit instructions of Prince Muhammad Ali Tawfiq.

Deep inside the garden, the living quarters are worth exploring. The age and interest level of children and teens will determine the amount of time devoted. Designed in imitation of the Alhambra in Spain, the living quarters have an immediate effect of tranquility upon the visitor. A fountain is centered in a marble floor, and turquoise ceramics from Iznik and Kutahaya cover the walls, all to cool the house as well as beautify it. All the rooms are furnished with authentic pieces. Notice the slots in the headboards of the bed used to rest the Quran.

Not far from the living quarters is the throne room, possibly built under the assumption that Prince Muhammad Ali Tawfiq might one day rule Egypt. Unfortunately, the throne room is closed due to a collapsed ceiling, but it is under restoration. Here, the powerful men of Egypt met to discuss state matters, and their pictures adorn the throne room walls. Outside again, turn left and walk past the living quarters to the fourteen-room private museum, which was closed at the time this book went to press but will hopefully reopen soon.

Prince Muhammad Ali Tawfiq built the private museum to keep his and his family's collections from their travels, as well as the gifts given to him by dignitaries, leaders, and royalty the world over. Depending on your children's interest, you can walk quickly or stroll through these rooms. The first room holds examples of Arabic calligraphy and beautifully hand-illustrated Qurans. Persian carpets and Turkish prayer rugs, porcelain and silver treasures, and more paintings of the royal family are but a few of the items that grace the halls. An engaging display of clothing for men and women worn during the nineteenth century is particularly noteworthy. Overall, this museum provides us with a brief understanding of the magnitude of wealth and luxury that once bedecked the Manial Palace.

View more gifts presented to Egypt at Abdin Palace and the Geology Museum. At Abdin Palace, there is the President and Mrs. Mubarak Gift Museum. At the Geology Museum, Richard Nixon presented the Egyptian people a moon rock brought to earth by Apollo XVII.

Where: On Roda Island, between University Bridge and Manial Bridge on al-Saray St. Tel: 368-7495.

When: 9am–5pm every day. Ramadan 9am–3pm.

Entrance fee: Foreigners: LE20, residents LE10 (show ID), students LE10; Egyptians LE2, students LE1. No camera fee; video fee: LE100.

Parking: School buses are allowed to park in front of

the entrance, but private cars may not. Coming off of University Bridge, past the roundabout, there is a small street on the right used for parking.

Facilities: Toilets available. There are stairways in the entrance to the house and inside it; otherwise everything is on ground level.

The Nilometer, Monasterli Palace, and Umm Kulthum Museum

On the southern tip of Roda Island is an area that should be reserved for days when one is need of serenity. Guaranteed to soothe the ruffled soul and calm the younger generation, this outing will be a favorite for the peacefulness of the area; if you and your family are so inclined, there are also interesting historic monuments to discover.

Nilometers were used in pharaonic Egypt to record the level of the Nile flood. The height of the flood would forecast the agricultural harvest of the coming year. By recording the height of the river during the flood, the ancient Egyptians could predict if the crops would be plentiful, or if there would be famine. Records of Nile heights date all the way back to the First Dynasty, or about 3100 BC.

On Roda Island stands a nilometer constructed by Caliph al-Mutawwakil in AD 861. Quranic verses in Kufic script are written under the rim of the conical-

The Nilometer and the Monasterli Palace, Roda

shaped roof, which was added during King Farouk's reign. The words speak of the importance of water to life, and about food and harvest. A pillar standing within this deep well is lined by segments to indicate 22 cubits (a cubit is based on the distance between the elbow and the tip of the middle finger). A stone stairway winds to the bottom of the shaft. Children should probably not be allowed to attempt the descent to the bottom, as there is no banister to stop a fall. At the bottom of the well, at three different levels, are three tunnels that open to the Nile allowing the water to enter. As the water would rise, the rulers, farmers, and merchants could read the fate of the population and the economics of the country: higher taxes in a good season with high waters or higher prices in a bad season, indicated by a low Nile.

Before dams were established in Upper Egypt, the Nile began to flood in the middle of July, bringing rain-swollen waters from the Ethiopian highlands. During July, August, and September, the Nile overflowed its banks, irrigating the land and leaving behind silt that fertilized it. As the ancient Egyptians and Romans recognized that the Nile waters were responsible for abundance or starvation, so did the Arabs, and the tradition of measuring the height of the Nile continued.

Next to the Nilometer and amid mature trees, the Monasterli Palace rests like a secret on a tongue. A delightful walkway and terrace guarded by an outgrowth of trees and singing birds separates the palace walls from the Nile. At this point, one might need to resist the inclination to climb over the fence and sit on a branch to dangle one's feet in the water. The palace was constructed in 1851 for Ahmad al-Monasterli, the advisor to Abbas Hilmi Pasha. The eastern section sits on the ruins of the Mosque of the Miqyas. Monasterli Palace has been renovated to its original grandeur and is now the home to the International Center for Music. Through the winter months, Cairenes have the opportunity to attend performances of world famous musicians in an intimate and ornamental music room. Intermissions are particularly pleasant on the grand balcony overlooking the Nile. Do take your children to enjoy this majestic evening of outstanding music, elegant surroundings, and Ottoman history.

Adjacent to the main palace is an Ottoman-style building that commemorates Egypt's most beloved singer, Umm Kulthum. The high ceilings and stained-glass windows frame the memorabilia of a singer who moved the hearts of millions during the time when Egyptians and Arabs raced toward national independence. The Umm Kulthum Museum exhibits not only personal paraphernalia but also presents an audio-visual library of the great diva's performances. Tastefully done, the museum offers a whiff of the life and times of the great Umm Kulthum.

Umm Kulthum was born in a Delta village into a peasant family. Her father was too poor to send both her and her brother to school, so her brother alone received an education. Yet her brother would return every day and share his knowledge with his sister. Umm Kulthum's voracious appetite to learn and her demand for excellence developed alongside an innately brilliant voice. To many Egyptians and Arabs, Umm Kulthum's voice and interpretation of religious and classical poetry are held in reverence as solemnly as the Nile that winds its course through the desert sands of Egypt.

Where: There are several roads that lead to the Nilometer, but because of no-left-turns when crossing from the Corniche on the Garden City side, the approach is rather difficult. The easiest route to take is to cross Abbas Bridge from Giza and immediately turn right at the end of the bridge onto al-Malik Abd al-Aziz al-Saud, which is the road along the Nile. If you miss that turn, any of the subsequent right-hand roads lead to the Nilometer. Take the road to the very end of the island. Entrance is on the east side.

Telephone: 363-1467, 363-1537.

When: Nilometer: 10am–5pm every day. Ramadan 10am–2pm. Umm Kulthum Museum: 10am–6pm every day.

Entrance fee: Nilometer: tourist LE6, residents LE3 (bring ID); Egyptians LE2, students LE1.

Parking: Parking space is along the street.

Footbridge: A footbridge that connects Roda Island to the Corniche can be used to walk to Old Cairo and to the Peking floating restaurant.

International Center for Music:

Performances begin in October and continue through June. Tickets are LE50 and can be purchased at entrance to the Nilometer or the Cairo Opera House.

Qasr al-Aini Medical Museum

Inside the busy medical center of Cairo University is this first-of-its-kind museum that tells the history of medicine in Egypt. Dr. Mohammed al-Menawi developed the idea, and the museum was inaugurated on March 8, 1998.

The gallery exhibits paintings depicting hospital scenes in early-nineteenth century Cairo and photographs of doctors and scholars who made headway in the medical field. There are rare books and an encyclopedia with biographies about the professors and doctors. There is an antique chair apparatus for weighing patients. Two antique, wooden pharmacies that stored medicines are also on display, as are the medical tools of Clot Bey, a French forensic physician who came to Egypt at the request of Muhammad Ali in 1825.

Qasr al-Aini is named after Shihabeddin Ahmad Ben Zeineddin al-Aini al-Qahiri al-Hanifi, who in the middle of the fifteenth century built a palace on the Nile on Roda Island that subsequently was used by the rulers of Egypt. From Mamluk times, the palace was turned into a guesthouse for emissaries and royalty, and later it was a military barracks. In 1837, the School of Medicine, previously in Abu Zaabal, was transferred to Qasr al-Aini. Clot Bey was director of Qasr al-Aini and worked with Theodore Bilharz (the man who identified the parasite causing schistosomiasis). Both were dismissed when Muhammad Ali died. The school went into a decline and Khedive Said Pasha brought Clot Bey back to Egypt as the director of the medical school at Qasr al-Aini, but he became ill and had to return to France. When Khedive Ismail ruled Egypt, the position of director and the instructors were British. From this point Qasr al-Aini has a long history of high and low points as a medical school.

This museum will not interest many children, yet it may hold an interest for the older students intrigued with medicine or the history of medicine in Egypt. In the first corridor all the labels are in Arabic, but in the inner room the labels are in Arabic and English.

> Where: **On Roda Island, across from Manial Palace, in the Convention Center of the Faculty of Medicine. Enter through the main gate of the Cairo University Medical Center and turn left at the first road (Bank Misr is on the right). Walk half a block and the Convention Center is on the right. The museum is immediately to the left as you enter the building.**
>
> When: **10am–2:30pm. Closed Fridays.**
>
> Entrance fee: **Free.**

Gezira and Zamalek

The island of Gezira was not an important area of Cairo—mostly uninhabited and accessible only by boat—until later in the nineteenth century. Among the many engineering works carried out under Khedive Ismail was a project to protect the island from being flooded every year. This was finally achieved in 1866. Just before the opening of the Suez Canal in 1869, Ismail built a U-shaped palace on the northern part of the island to house guests arriving for the celebrations. This palace has since become the jewel of the Marriott Hotel chain. Around the palace were gardens with a race course and polo field. In the late nineteenth century these gardens became the elite Khedival Sporting Club, which is now the Gezira Club. To the west of the palace, an aquarium for royalty is still in existence today: the Fish Gardens opened to the public in 1902.

Gezira

The imaginary line that delineates Gezira and Zamalek often changes according to who is defining the area. The southern part of the island, with its hotels, the Opera House, museums, sporting clubs, and gardens, is most frequently referred to as Gezira. The area from the Gezira Sporting Club to the most northern point of the island is referred to as Zamalek.

In the future, Gezira will be home to two more museums: The Revolution Museum will be located on the premises of the Revolution Command Council near the Gezira Sheraton, and the National Theater Museum will be on the premises of the Supreme Cultural Council, near al-Hanager Art Center.

Midan Saad Zaghloul

At the end of Qasr al-Nil Bridge, built in 1879, two lions stand on either side like guards as Saad Zaghloul, the famous Egyptian nationalist opens his hand in welcome to all. This statue was erected from the resources of the artist, Mahmoud Mukhtar, and the Egyptian people who were willing to give even a few piasters each to commemorate the man who led the way to Egyptian independence.

Midan Saad Zaghloul, being a prominent landmark, is a good place to start to discover Gezira and Zamalek.

Riyadi Gardens

This is a pleasant garden to have tea and wander around looking at all the statues. As a matter of fact the gardens are distinctive due to the quantity of statues: six busts of Latin American liberators and leaders—Bernardo O'Higgins, founder of the Republic of Chile; Santander, hero of independence and founder of Columbia; Eloy Alfaro, from the Republic of Ecuador; Jose Marti Perez, national hero of Cuba; Ramon Castilla, hero of Peru; Dr. Arauifu Arins, from the Republic of Panama. The four statues of famous Egyptians are Ahmad Shawqi (facing the gate), writer and poet; General Abd al-Moniem Riyad, hero in the 1967 War. Toward the back of the garden: Hafez Ibrahim, writer and poet; and Talaat Harb, a leader in Egypt's economic independence.

> Where: **Saad Zaghloul Square, facing west (back to Qasr al-Nil Bridge), the garden gates are on the left.**
> When: **8:30am–10pm**
> Entrance fees: **Foreigners: LE2; Egyptians: 50 piasters.**

Andalusia Gardens

At Midan Saad Zaghloul and facing the Opera House, the Andalusia Gardens are on the right, along the Nile. They are protected by a wall of thick green foliage. Because of the heavy traffic in this area, the gardens can be missed easily. The gardens, designed before 1935 by

The Andalusia Gardens

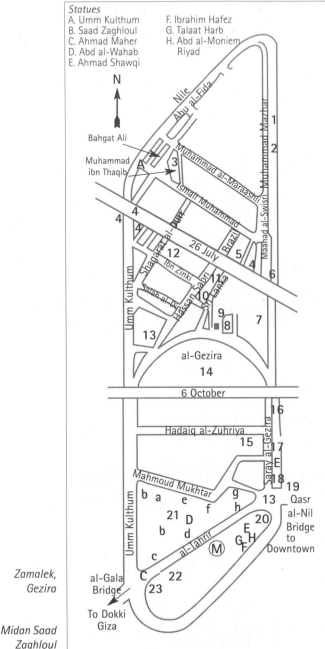

Statues
A. Umm Kulthum
B. Saad Zaghloul
C. Ahmad Maher
D. Abd al-Wahab
E. Ahmad Shawqi
F. Ibrahim Hafez
G. Talaat Harb
H. Abd al-Moniem Riyad

N

Nile
Abu al-Fida
Bahgat Ali
Muhammad ibn Thaqib
Muhammad al-Maraashli
Ismail Muhammad
Muhammad Mazhar
Muhammad al-Swisri
Maahad al-Swisri
Shagarat al-Durr
26 July
Ibn Zinki
Brazil
Safah al-Din
Hassan Sabri
Umm Kulthum
al-Gezira
6 October
Hadaiq al-Zuhriya
Saray al-Gezira
Mahmoud Mukhtar
Umm Kulthum
al-Tahrir
al-Gala Bridge
Zamalek, Gezira
Midan Saad Zaghloul
To Dokki Giza
Qasr al-Nil Bridge to Downtown

1. Safir Hotel
2. Greater Cairo Public Library
3. AUC Hostel and Bookstore
4. El-Sawy Cultural Wheel
5. Diwan Bookstore
6. Akhnaton Center of Arts
7. Cairo Marriott Hotel
8. Gezira Arts Center
9. Italian Cultural Center
10. Ministry of Culture
11. RITSEC
12. Egyptian Center for International Cultural Cooperation
13. Fish Garden & Aquariums
14. Gezira Sporting Club
15. Cairo Tower
16. Pharaonic Garden / Nile Needle
17. Arab Garden
18. Andalusia Gardens
19. Gezira Nile Gardens
20. Riyadi Gardens
21. Opera House Complex
    a. Hanager Art Center
    b. Administration Building
    c. Planetarium (closed)
    d. Main / Small Halls
    e. Mosque
    f. Museum of Modern Art
    g. Palace of the Arts
    h. Music Library
22. Mahmoud Mukhtar Museum
23. Cairo Sporting Club

In the Pharaonic Gardens: an unfinished granite lion from the east gate of the Great Temple at Tanis, time of Ramesses II

Mahmoud Zulficar Bey, were originally a private roller-skating garden for the royal family. Soon afterward, the royal family donated the garden to the people of Cairo. The garden is divided into three parts: the Andalusian, Arab, and Pharaonic.

During the early years, the Andalusia Gardens were a popular spot for family outings and star-gazing lovers, but as the numbers increased, the gardens became spoiled. Recently, the gardens are open to the public from 8:30am to 5pm at LE10 per person. The fine mosaic walks, Spanish tiles, and botanical delights confirm that the gardeners have revived the gardens to their past beauty and elegance.

Walking north along the sidewalk, you will come across the Arab Garden and then the Pharaonic Garden. Both are open to the public for a nominal fee.

Nile Needle

If your child wants to see an obelisk, you have three choices in Cairo—the Gezira obelisk, the one near the EgyptAir terminal, or the one in Matariya (see Heliopolis section). The Gezira obelisk stands in the Pharaonic Gardens on the river, just east of the Gezira Sporting

The Nile Needle obelisk, originally from Tanis

177

Club. Originally, King Ramesses II of the Nineteenth Dynasty erected this obelisk in front of a temple to the god Ptah at Per-Ramesses, the Ramesside (New Kingdom) capital in the Delta. If you look up at the tip of the obelisk, you might be able to make out the figure of the god Ptah on the two sides now facing east and west. The god is seated and the king kneels before him with offerings. On the side facing north is the god Re, and on the south, Atum.

Later, in the Twenty-first Dynasty, the obelisk was removed to Tanis, a city slightly farther northeast. There it was raised, along with other obelisks, to line the processional road to the temple of the god Amun. It was one of twenty-three obelisks found at Tanis by excavators, and its original base is still there.

The obelisk is slightly over 14 meters high, and like all ancient Egyptian obelisks, cut out of a solid piece of Aswan granite. Running down each side is a vertical inscription boasting of the victories of Ramesses II over his enemies. Also on display are smaller stone pieces from Tanis.

> **Where:** On Saray al-Gezira, the street on the east side of the Gezira Sporting Club, just north of the 6th October Bridge. The park entrance is at the north; turn right as soon as you can under the bridge on-ramp.
>
> **When:** 10am–late evenings every day.
>
> **Entrance fee:** 50 piasters for all.
>
> **Facilities:** There is a pleasant café inside the garden.

Gezira Nile Gardens

Take a few minutes for a lovely stroll next to the Nile, which is the only place in Cairo that the sidewalk is level with the water. There are no honking cars or spewing fumes to divert your attention from the boats and lapping water. On summer evenings, musical performances are organized by the Opera House.

> **Where:** Saad Zaghloul Square, facing west (back to Qasr al-Nil bridge), the entrance is on the right, next to Andalusia Gardens, across from the Opera House.
>
> **When:** 9am–12 midnight.
>
> **Entrance fees:** Foreigners: LE2; Egyptians: 50 piasters.

Mahmoud Mukhtar Museum

Mahmoud Mukhtar came from humble beginnings with an inherent talent that culminated in depicting nationalist themes through sculpture. Born in 1891, Mahmoud Mukhtar grew up by the banks of the Nile, molding mud and baking his creations in the sun or in bread ovens. Imagining the forms and shapes of heroes and creatures in folk tales told by the village storyteller, he began his career as a sculptor. He recalled: "When I was a child, there had been no sculpture and no sculptor in my country for more than seventeen hundred years. The images that appeared among the ruins and sands at the edge of the desert were considered to be accursed and evil idols—no one should come near."

He studied at a Quranic school, learning to read, write, and recite the Quran. He proved himself a

Mahmoud Mukhtar's "Egypt's Awakening"

worthy student and was able to attend the School of Fine Arts, where he met Mr. Laplagne, the French director of the school and professor of sculpture. Mr Laplagne's influence on Mukhtar was critical as he changed from an unknown artist to a nationally recognized sculptor. Winning a scholarship to Paris, he studied art at the Ecole des Beaux Arts. His bohemian life in Paris and his freedom of expression there influenced the nonconformist style of his sculptures.

Mukhtar was an artist ahead of his time. He established the Imagination Society in 1928, which introduced new art trends and advanced modern Egyptian art. Mukhtar died at the young age of forty-three.

Most of Mukhtar's works are housed in this museum, but examples of his sculpture can be seen beyond its walls: "Egypt's Awakening" is situated in front of Cairo University; the statue of Saad Zaghloul faces Qasr al-Nil Bridge on Gezira Island, and in Alexandria a similar statue faces the sea; and "The Nile Bride" is in the collection of the Museum of Modern Art, in the Cairo Opera compound.

Cross over the bridge and leave noisy Cairo to the present day. You will step into the pharaonic-style museum, designed by architect Ramses Wissa Wassef, and you will enter into a very different time of Egyptian history. The first sculpture is a form of a naked Isis that is a mixture of Greek and pharaonic styles. Each subsequent room provides a well-lit, uncluttered space to appreciate Mukhtar's themes of nationalism, revolution, and romanticism expressed through a mixture of ancient Egyptian and modern art styles. His work echoes

Saad Zaghloul's passion for Egypt's independence and the leader's commitment to Egyptians' struggle for freedom from the British occupation. Yet, Mukhtar never forgot his childhood in rural Egypt. He used materials of stone, marble, bronze, and basalt to depict village women such as "Returning from the Canal," "Intimacy," "Secret Keeper," and "Sorrow," respectively. Do not miss "Khamsin" (sandstorm), one of Mukhtar's most famous sculptures, which depicts the battle between man and the elements.

Where: Tahrir Street, across from the Cairo Opera House. Facing the street, Cairo Sporting Club is on the left and Riyadi Gardens on the right. Tel: 735-2519.

When: 10am–1:30pm and 5–9pm. Closed on Monday.

Entrance fees: Foreigners and residents LE5; Egyptians LE2. If available, a catalogue costs LE20.

Facilities: Bathrooms are clean. There is no ramp between the first and second floors. Take time to walk around the garden. There is plenty of space to sit and contemplate the stunning and diverse works by Egypt's great sculptor, Mahmoud Mukhtar.

Parking: None.

Cairo Opera House

Khedive Ismail commissioned the first Opera House to be erected next to the Azbakiya Gardens in 1869. The opening performance of Verdi's *Rigoletto* celebrated the completion of the Suez Canal. For more than a century, only the best and most prestigious international opera and ballet companies performed for cultivated and elegant audiences. The Opera House was an exact copy of La Scala of Milan and stood for over eighty years before being damaged during the Black Saturday riots in 1952. Restored, the Opera House finally met its fate in 1971 when it burned down in mysterious circumstances. Cairenes waited almost twenty years before the Opera House found a new home.

Fittingly, the new Opera House was constructed on what had once been Khedive Ismail's magnificent gardens that had been part of the Gezira Palace. Built in partnership with Japan, and completed in 1988, the new Opera House is a welcome sight from any angle. The gardens and architecture restore tranquillity—with graceful curves and eye-pleasing angles—to a crowded island.

There is always something going on at the Opera House, at the Main Hall,

Cairo Opera House

the Small Hall, or the Open Air Theater. But do you know all that this center has to offer? Whether your favorite music is classical, Arabic, modern, or jazz, the Cairo Opera House has performances for all preferences and ages. There are the Cairo Opera Company, the Cairo Ballet, and the Cairo Symphony, as well as a Children's Choir, to name but a few. Then there are the many outstanding programs brought in from around the world to enjoy. The bargain is that, unlike most cosmopolitan cities where opera tickets are sold at a premium and excellent seating is never available, here in Cairo the best seat in the Main Hall is available and affordable.

The complex also contains galleries, libraries, museums, a mosque, several cafeterias, and serene gardens that are well suited for contemplation or to pass an hour. The landscaping of the grounds themselves is of interest. There is a petrified rock garden next to the Music Library, and look for the statues of Umm Kulthum and Muhammad Abd al-Wahab, both famous Egyptian singers.

The events at the Cairo Opera House complex present diverse opportunities for learning. The following is an introduction, hopefully, to encourage you and your family to take full advantage of these excellent facilities.

Where: On Gezira Island, with Midan Saad Zaghloul to the east, Mahmoud Mukhtar Street to the north, and al-Tahrir Street to the south. Umm Kulthum Street runs along the west side, but this street is blocked to through

181

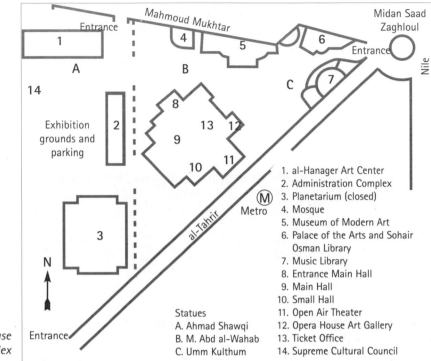

Opera House
Complex

1. al-Hanager Art Center
2. Administration Complex
3. Planetarium (closed)
4. Mosque
5. Museum of Modern Art
6. Palace of the Arts and Sohair Osman Library
7. Music Library
8. Entrance Main Hall
9. Main Hall
10. Small Hall
11. Open Air Theater
12. Opera House Art Gallery
13. Ticket Office
14. Supreme Cultural Council

Statues
A. Ahmad Shawqi
B. M. Abd al-Wahab
C. Umm Kulthum

traffic. If you are driving, the entrances are on al-Tahrir Street going west and on Mahmoud Mukhtar Street going east.

Tickets: To buy tickets at the Opera House, walk through the gates, and inquire of the guards, who will point the way. The ticket windows are open 9am–3pm and 4–9pm.

In addition, tickets are sold downtown at the Gumhuriya Theater. Tel: 739-8114, 739-8132 (main and small hall).

Schedule of events: Programs for each month are available at the main entrance to the Main Hall.

Web site: www.cairooperahouse.org

Outreach program-music lecture series:

The Opera House has initiated an innovative project that brings music to university students. Outstanding Egyptian musicians contribute their time and expertise to a series of peformances at the Faculty of Art in Zamalek, Minya, Beni Sweif, and Asyut.

Dress code: Note that there is a dress code for men in the Main hall: jacket and tie must be worn, and this rule is almost always enforced.

More performances: Often, performances are held at the Gumhuriya Theater, located downtown on al-Gumhuriya Street; tickets for these performances may be purchased at the Opera House or at the Gumhuriya Theater itself.

Artistic creative center: Modern Dance School, Theater, Cinema. Tel: 736-3446.

Parking and metro: There is ample parking in the parking lot, but if you live near a Metro line, take the Shubra–Giza line to Opera Station: there is an exit near the Opera grounds.

Cafeteria: Open every day 10am–10pm.

Opera House Museum

This collection is exhibited in the Main Hall, so you can see it if you are attending a performance there. During intermission, it is worth strolling through the three rooms dedicated to the performances staged over the last 130 years at the old and new Opera House. Evening gowns worn over one hundred years ago silently recall an elegant time when going to the opera was a formal affair. Take a peak at the keys of the piano and see what you think. Is it a piano, organ, or both?

When: Open during performances as well as throughout the day during the same hours as the ticket office.

Entrance fee: During performance, entrance is free. At other times, foreigners LE5, Egyptians and residents LE2.

Cairo Opera House Art Gallery

When you nip in to purchase tickets for a performance, the doors to this gallery are almost always open. Though the publicity leaves much to be desired, stop by: the exhibitions are like finding a message from a long-ago friend, surprising and pleasing. Local and foreign artists and photographers exhibit within this two-floor gallery. Particularly worth watching for are the exhibits of Arabic calligraphy: the texts are inspiring and the curving lines are beautiful.

Where: **Next to the ticket office.**
When: **10am–3pm and 4–8:30pm.**
Telephone: **739-8131.**

Museum of Modern Art

Three floors of contemporary Egyptian art fill this museum. The concept of having a museum of modern art dates back to the 1920s. Artists such as Yusuf Kamel, Mahmoud Khalil, Mahmoud Mukhtar, and Raghib Ayyad proposed a museum of modern art for Cairo. Moved from one place to another, the collection finally found its home within the Opera grounds in 1991.

Take your time in entering the Main Hall, look around and orient yourself. It is worth these few minutes as the museum is vast and although it is spacious and beautifully lit, the senses seem to be overwhelmed by the richness of figures, colors, shades, and lines. Throughout the museum is a wealth of paintings, drawings, sculptures, and installations. On the ground floor the displays have been chosen to represent an artist famous in the history of Egyptian modern art. The major pieces are Mahmoud Said's *The City* (1937) and Mahmoud Mukhtar's *Bride of the Nile* (1929). The diversity of Egyptian modern art over the span of a century brings together such artists as Gazbia Sirry, her neo-expressionist works (1960s); Mohamed Sabri's *Bab Zwuela* (1981); Mohammed Rizk, Untitled (1975); and a favorite, Said al Sadr's *Back from the Market* (1985).

The first floor, balconies, and corners highlight works by nine pioneers of modern Egyptian art from the period of 1906–1931: Ahmed Sabri, Muhammad Nagui, Mahmoud Said, Raghib Ayyad, Muhammad Hassan, Yusuf Kamel, Ahmed Lofty, George Sabbagh, and Aly al-Ahwany.

The second floor—balconies and corners—highlight works that are considered influential in thought and interpretation from the period of 1933–1950s. Margaret Nakhla's *Stock Exchange* (1940) is captivating. See pieces by Gazbia Sirry, Mustafa al-Razzaz, Ahmad Nawar, Kamal al-Serrag, Saleh Reda, and many others. Artists Saad al-Khadem and Effat Nagui, who have donated their homes and works to the Egyptian people, also have pieces here.

Continuing through the second floor, the art focuses on the works of contemporary artists. Off the main corridors, there are special rooms for exhibitions and galleries. Also, there is a room for lectures and cultural activities. There is so much to see and so many images, that it takes several hours to take in this museum.

A bookstore on the first floor includes books about Egypt in English and

Arabic. At times, this museum hosts exhibitions of famous artists. There is an elevator to the left of the entrance, and there are bathrooms on the second floor at the rear of the building. At the corners of each floor one can sit and rest before continuing on to the next floor, or have a coffee at the café on the first floor.

When: **10am–2pm and 6–10:30pm. Closed Fridays.**

Entrance fees: **Foreigners: LE10, residents LE5, students LE5; Egyptians: LE1, students 50 piasters.**

Camera: **No camera or video allowed.**

Hint: **Needs lots of time if you love modern art.**

Palace of the Arts and Sohair Osman Library

This space for temporary exhibitions such as the annual Youth Salon is a maze-like place with many stairways and levels. Wandering from level to level, it is a challenge to see all the exhibits. In the rear of the building the Sohair Osman Library specializes in books on art and architecture, and includes a CD-ROM library that includes CDs featuring museums around the world. The library is open to all, but is not a lending library, so all research and reading are on the premises.

When: **10am–2pm and 5–9pm. Closed Friday.**

Tip: **Bring ID to leave with librarian.**

Facilities: **Gift store and cafeteria at entrance.**

Telephone: **736-8796, 736-7628.**

Music Library

At the eastern end of the complex, the Music Library is one of a kind in the Middle East. Open to everyone, this is an excellent library for research in the field of music, including audio and video performances from the Main Hall of the Opera House.

When: **10am–9pm daily.**

Telephone: **739-9131**

Hanager Art Center

Across from the parking lot on the street side, you will find the Hanager Art Center. Throughout the year, the Hanager Center provides visitors with a constant flow of exhibits and performances. There is also a snack bar where you can discuss the latest program in Cairo over a cup of tea or coffee. If you are early for a performance this is a great place to stop.

When: **10am–9pm daily.**

Telephone: **735-6861.**

Cairo Tower

At least once in your life, a trip to the top of the Cairo Tower is a necessity. The view of Cairo is superb, and seeing the city in 360 degrees puts Cairo in perspective. Try to go on a clear day, which may be harder than one might think. A windy day is the best because most of the pollution will have blown away.

Cairo Tower and the Pharaonic Gardens: a falcon god protects Ramesses II

The Cairo Tower, with its wicker basketry and lotus flower design, and 187 meters high, is visible from many parts of Cairo. It was officially opened on April 11, 1961. There is a snack bar and restaurant on the level below the observation deck. Certainly, a trip to the top is not for people afraid of heights, or for the claustrophobic. The elevator takes no more than eight people at a time. In case of a power outage, there is a back-up generator, as well as the stairway.

The Cairo Tower is a monument with an intriguing history. Arthur Goldschmidt, Jr. describes how the Cairo Tower became a modern-day icon, in *Modern Egypt: The Formation of a Nation-State:*

> Even though books written during the 1950s do not mention Nasir's foreign backers, later works reveal that the CIA (especially Kermit Roosevelt, who had helped to overthrow Musaddiq in Iran) facilitated Nasir's takeover. One concrete form of U.S. aid was a suitcase containing $3 million that Roosevelt had ordered to be delivered to one of Nasir's aides. Although he was sensitive to any imputation of taking bribes, Nasir decided to keep the money but not to reward those who had demonstrated in his support. Instead, he built a decorative tower, topped by a revolving restaurant and a blinking antenna, officially named the Cairo Tower.

Where: Hadaiq al-Zuhriya St. Turn left off of Saray al-Gezira before the 6th of October Bridge. The street is one-way from east to west. Tel: 736-5112.

When: 9am–1am daily.

Entrance fee: Foreigners LE50; Egyptians LE15; students LE15. children under 6 are free.

Camera: Free, video LE100.

Facilities: Cafeteria and revolving restaurant. Bathrooms
are off the stairway leading to the top level.
Tel: 738-3790, 736-5112.

Zamalek

By the first half of the twentieth century, Zamalek had developed into a prime
residential area for expatriates and wealthy Egyptians. In 1912, the Abu al-Ela
Bridge, with a tramline, spanned from Bulaq to Zamalek. Today, you can see
the leftovers from this era: the villas and mansions are as beautiful as you will
see anywhere in the world, although they are now suffocating in the urban
growth. Once, the quaint narrow streets served the population, now the
streets are often impassable, clogged with too many cars. Visiting Zamalek can
be a delightful experience, but be aware that in the afternoon between two
and four the schools disperse and traffic becomes a gridlock. For a personal
recollection of Zamalek in the twentieth century, read *Zamalek: The Changing
Life of a Cairo Elite, 1850–1945* by Chafika Hamamsy (AUC Press, 2004).

Gezira Arts Center

Prince Amr Ibrahim's palace is one of the architectural delights of Cairo. Prince
Amr, a cousin of King Farouk, built this fine villa in 1920, and it has since been
occupied by a number of unusual tenants. After the revolution in 1952, Colonel
Abd al-Nasser used the palace as his office, then the Egyptian Communist
Party took it over as their headquarters until 1971, when it became home to
the Muhammad Mahmoud Khalil Museum. Now that the Khalil Museum has
moved back to its original home in Giza, the palace is the home to an impressive collection of Islamic ceramics, while the basement has several halls for
temporary art exhibtions, and musical evenings are held in the garden.

There could not be a more appropriate setting for such unique pieces of
ceramics than this splendid example of Islamic revival architecture. Even if
ceramics are not on your list of favorites, the palace is worth a visit. The
mashrabiya, stained-glass windows, mosaic floors, and Turkish tiles adorning
the fireplaces are breathtaking. The reception hall on the ground floor is often
the venue for lectures and musical evenings. The room to the right highlights
Fatimid ceramics. The luster technique of the Fatimid period was two-fold.
The first phase was a process called fumigation, which involved baking the
ceramics at low temperatures with much smoke—this produced beige, yel-
lowish-brown colors. The second stage of the technique used metal oxides,
characterized by olive metallic colors, on a background of turquoise or cream.
The decline in lusterware came about when al-Fustat was destroyed by fire
(see al-Fustat). During Fatimid rule, al-Fustat was the center for ceramics,

The Gezira Arts Center

but after the great fire many of the potters moved to Syria and Persia, where remnants of these luster techniques have been traced.

The room to the left at the back displays Umayyad, Ayyubid, and Mamluk ceramic pieces. During the late thirteenth and fourteenth centuries, the characteristic of the Mamluk potter's technique was glazing over blue with black inscriptions and decorations. The next room to the front of the building displays Turkish ceramics.

Upstairs, the exhibit is of ceramic pieces from Iran, Syria, Andalusia, Tunisia, Iraq, and Morocco. Don't miss the upstairs lounge and bathroom. Syrian ceramics dating from the tenth century are displayed in the lounge, which has stained-glass windows and an elegant sofa. In the bathroom, the sunken bathtub and basin are made of alabaster. There are several seventeenth-century Turkisk ceramics on display in the lobby, which were relocated from the Islamic Museum.

Downstairs in the basement are the four galleries that house temporary exhibitions of modern art, each named after an influential twentieth-century Egyptian artist: the Ahmad Sabry Gallery, the Raghib Ayyad Gallery, the Hussein Fawzy Gallery, and the Kamal Khalifa Gallery. The Art and Garden Museum is seen by strolling through the gardens behind the center. Sculptures abound. The garden is also used for theater productions and cinema night.

Where: **Al-Gezira St., across from the Gezira Club, near the Marriott parking lot. Tel: 736-8672, 737-3298.**

When: 9am–2:30pm and 5–10pm in winter, 6–10pm in summer. Closed Fridays. The hours change during Ramadan.

Entrance fee: Tourists LE25, residents and students LE12; Egyptians LE5, students LE1.

Web site: www.icm.gov.eg/E_island_art_center.html

Monthly programs: There is a monthly program of films, lectures, musical evenings, and poetry readings. The schedule is available at the Center, or watch the listings for events.

Book to buy: The Museum of Islamic Ceramics, by the Ministry of Culture. The introduction by Abd al-Raouf Yusuf gives an excellent overview of the history, techniques, and decorations of Islamic pottery and ceramics.

Facilities: Clean bathrooms. No refreshments are available. There are benches to rest on in the garden while viewing sculptures in the Art and Garden Museum.

Diwan Bookstore

A bookstore for everyone, Diwan Bookstore has opened its doors and welcomes the public to browse, read, eat, drink, and still find a good buy to enjoy at home. A good selection of books can be found in Arabic, English, and French. Children's books are abundant as well as a selection of CDs, and Arabic and English videos. Story telling, book launches, as well as old Egyptian films are a few more specialties introduced by the innovative owners. Put your name on their mailing list to receive their newsletter.

Where: **159, 26th of July Street, Zamalek. Tel: 736-2096.**

When: **9am–11:30pm every day.**

e-mail: info@diwanegypt.com

Cultural Centers
Italian Cultural Institute

3 Sheikh al-Marsafi St., behind the Marriott Hotel, Zamalek. Tel: 735-8791. A popular center that offers lectures, films, language courses, and art exhibitions.

Netherlands Institute

1 Dr. Mahmoud Azmi St., Zamalek. Tel: 738-2522. This institute offers lectures

that might be of interest to mature teenagers. Lecture schedules can be found in the listings. There is also an Egyptology library that offers membership.

Greater Cairo Public Library

This palace was once the home of Khedive Ismail's granddaughter, Princess Samiha Kamel. Upon her death, the princess bequeathed her palace to the Egyptian people. In 1995, this magnificent palace opened as a public library. The interior ceilings, winding staircase, and windows overlooking the garden and Nile are all worth seeing. The atmosphere is conducive to reading, with well-ventilated, quiet, and comfortable rooms. Although the palace was not meant to display thousands of books, the library contains to date 165,000 volumes of books and reference materials, and 860 periodicals. In addition, there is Internet access, audio-visual services, CD-ROM, and documents on microfiche. Books are in Arabic, English, French, and German. On the underground floor, the main library contains general references, social sciences and humanities, a children's library, cafeteria, and conference hall. The ground floor contains the library catalogue and internet services, and is the main entrance to the library. On the second floor is the periodicals hall, fine arts library, pure science library, applied science and technology library, microfilm and CD-ROM library. In addition, a map room has accessible maps that chart the growth of Cairo from 1480 to 1992. The Egypt and Cairo research center is on the third floor and the audio-visual library is in the tower.

Where: **15 Muhammad Mazhar St.**
Tel: 736-2271, 736-2278.
When: **9am–5pm. Closed Fridays and official holidays.**
Entrance fee: **Free. Bring an ID or passport to leave with the security guard; you will receive a pass to enter.**
Cultural programs: **Lectures, seminars, conferences, research groups, and theatrical performances.**
Facilities: **Bathrooms on each floor, small cafeteria, elevator.**

Egyptian Center for International Cultural Cooperation

Art exhibitions by students, foreigners, and Egyptians make this an interesting stop for teenagers interested in the arts. Tours and trips, lectures, concerts, and musical performances are an attraction of this center. Regular and intensive Arabic language courses are also offered. To be informed, put your name on their mailing list and they will send invitations to any upcoming event.

Where: 11 Shagarat al-Durr St., Zamalek.
Tel: 736-5419.
When: 10am–2pm and 4–9pm. Closed Thursdays and Fridays. During Ramadan, 10am–2pm and 7–9pm.

Akhnaton Center of Arts

Contemporary art exhibits are displayed every two weeks at the Akhnaton Center of Arts. This is another splendid villa and garden to enjoy while encountering works of art and sculptures by Egyptian, foreign, and student artists. Inside the villa, the winding marble staircase and stained-glass windows are noteworthy. At times there are lectures and musical evenings. Keep an eye on the newspapers and magazines for change of exhibits.

Where: 1 Maahad al-Swisri St. (aka Aziz Abaza St.), Zamalek. Tel: 797-5900, 797-5929.
When: 10am–1:30pm and 5:30–9pm. Sometimes closed when changing exhibits.

RITSEC

Regional Information Technology and Software Engineering Center is a non-government organization that provides technical, professional, and developmental services in the area of information technology. Their programs focus on utilization of information and communication technologies in the areas of training and education with youth, culture and environmental preservation, and professional skill development. One such program is the Arab Child Initiative, which supports the development of Egyptian and Arab children. There are workshops in IT training for Arabic speakers under the age of twenty. Within this initiative, "Little Horus" was established as the first Arab Web site for children. Another program is the Global Campus Initiative, which delivers post-graduate academic programs over the Internet. And a distance learning network, "LearnNet" that established a regional network for distance learning. Call for more information about their classes and programs.

Where: 11A Hassan Sabry Street, Zamalek.
Tel: 339-1300, 735-2665; Fax: 736-2139.
Web site: www.ritsec.com.eg

AUC Bookstore

A well-stocked assortment of books for children, adolescents, and teens is found here, as well as general fiction and non-fiction.

Where: **16 Muhammad ibn Thaqib St., Zamalek.
Tel: 339-7045.**
When: **10am–5pm, Saturday-Monday; 10am–6pm
Tuesday-Thursday. Closed Fridays.**

Fish Garden and Aquariums

Once a part of Khedive Ismail's vast garden that extended over the entire island, this land has been preserved to offer a center of natural beauty to this crowded area. Tall palm trees adorn the grass-covered hill, inviting a stroll through the shady park. In the past, there were added treats such as a grotto with aquariums of African fish, turtles, eels, and tiny alligators. The tanks are set beneath the hill, which conceals huge caves in the center of the park. The park has been completely renewed, and we again are treated to cool caverns and lots of fish, turtles, and other creatures. There is even a family of bats! New circular paths, open spaces, and the grottos have been restored providing a very pleasant area for a solitary walk or a tête-à-tête.

Where: **Umm Kulthum St., along the Nile.**
When: **8:30am–4:30pm.**
Entrance fee: **30 piasters.**
Telephone: **735-1606.**

El-Sawy Cultural Wheel

"When there is a will, there is a way," the saying goes, and Mohamed Abdel-Moneim El-Sawy is one person who has proved this saying true. Under Fifteenth of May flyover in Zamalek there was a space used as a dump but when he looked at it, he saw a space for cultural events, where music and art could flourish. His father, Abdel-Moneim El-Sawy, novelist and journalist, served as his inspiration: to spread knowledge and wisdom, and to value "the word." Mohamed El-Sawy's vision was to take his father's belief and begin a cultural center that operated like a waterwheel—sakia. Sakiat al-Sawy was born.

The cultural center is made up of halls and gardens that support his vision of promoting "the word": The Wisdom Hall, The Word Hall, The River Hall, and al-Sakia Gardens. The Wisdom Hall is air-conditioned and contains a theater and library. The Word Hall has a smaller theater and hosts exhibitions; the garden is another venue for exhibits and small productions. The River Hall, and newest addition, is a space that runs along the Nile and under the flyover.

Al-Sawy Cultural Wheel supports youth's talents, provides entertainment, workshops, and training in the arts, and is just a wonderful venue to take in a show. Be sure to check the newspapers and magazines for a schedule of their activities, pick up the monthly calendar from the center, or visit their Web site: *www.culturewheel.com.*

Where: **Under the Fifteenth of May Bridge, Zamalek.**
Tel: 736–6178, 735–4505

Facilities: **Library, Internet café, small cafeteria. Membership is by application, which allows the member discounts on tickets, monthly schedule by e-mail, and to participate in competitions for prizes. There is no smoking in all halls and gardens.**

Parking: **None.**

Agouza, Mohandiseen, and Dokki

The west side of the Nile, up until the 1920s, was predominantly agricultural land. Settlements such as Imbaba, Dokki, and Giza were rural villages, there before the arrival Amr ibn al-As in AD 640. These areas remained isolated until the control of Nile flooding by dams in Upper Egypt and the construction of bridges from the east side of the Nile. Before the 1940s, some residential palaces clung to this side of the Nile; otherwise, vast acreages of fields and plantations spread all the way to the Pyramids. However, since 1950, these areas have developed into high-density, apartment-dwelling communities, consuming villas, gardens, and agricultural land.

Agouza
Agouza is a relatively small area of Cairo sandwiched between Imbaba and Mohandiseen, with the Nile on the east side. Families would enjoy several interesting attractions in this area.

British Council
The British Council has the reputation for providing exceptional language programs in Arabic and English. There are exhibitions and lectures on a regular basis. A well-stocked library is open from 10am to 8pm, on Fridays and Saturdays from 1pm to 8pm. Library fees: Annual membership: LE200, British Council students LE30. There are no special rates for children. Bring a passport-sized picture and if you are an expatriate include a copy of your residence visa.

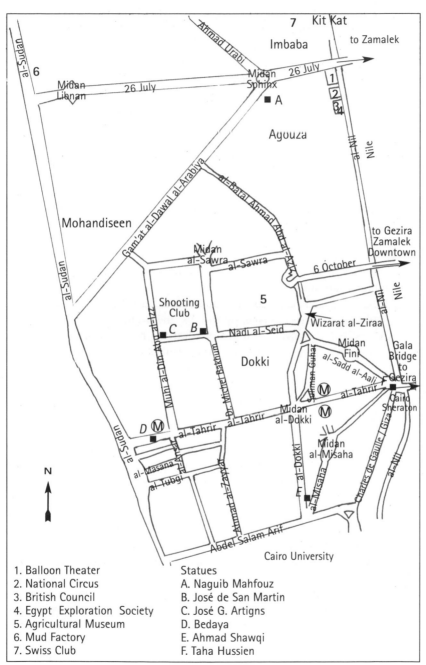

1. Balloon Theater
2. National Circus
3. British Council
4. Egypt Exploration Society
5. Agricultural Museum
6. Mud Factory
7. Swiss Club

Statues
A. Naguib Mahfouz
B. José de San Martin
C. José G. Artigns
D. Bedaya
E. Ahmad Shawqi
F. Taha Hussien

*Agouza,
Mohandiseen,
and Dokki*

> Where: 192 al-Nil St., Agouza. Tel: 303-1514,
> 347-6118, 344-8445.
> Parking is difficult.
> In Heliopolis: 4 al-Minia St., off Nazih Khalifa St.
> Tel: 452-3395/7.

The Egypt Exploration Society
Lectures, courses, and trips throughout the year.

> Where: The office is in the British Council.
> Tel: 301-8319.
> When: Office closed Fridays and Saturdays, but
> courses and tours are held over weekends.
> Web site: www.ees.ac.uk

Balloon Theater
The children's theater presents programs throughout the year in Arabic.
Sometimes a folkloric troupe performs.

> Where: Located in Agouza, across the street from the
> Nile, by the 26 July Bridge.
> When: To find out what the performance is,
> and the times, call: 347-1718, 304-3186.
> Entrance fee: Tickets sell for LE40, 30, and 10. The box
> office opens daily at 10am.
> Parking: Difficult.

National Circus
Barnum and Bailey move over! The National Circus is in town and is a must to see. However, the best part about it is that the performers are all Egyptian. Under the big top, the excitement mounts with each act. There are jugglers, acrobats, tightrope walkers, trapeze artists, trained dogs, magicians, knife-throwers, and more. Two incredibly agile children are fearlessly thrown and twirled about high in the air, and for the finale, twelve ferocious lions and tigers and a brave tamer have the crowd holding their breath. The show is a little over two hours but the acts are such fun that no one notices the time.

This is truly a family outing. As a matter of fact, the crowd is made up entirely of moms, dads, and children who did not even notice a foreign face in their midst. Popcorn and concessions are available but are not constantly being paraded up and down the isles. One of the evening's highlights is to have a picture taken with a young tiger, but that might take a bit of courage!

Where: In Agouza, next to the Balloon Theater, across the street from the Nile. Tel: 347-0612.

When: 9pm–12:30am in summer and 8pm–11pm in winter, every night except Wednesday. Closed for summer exams.

Entrance fee: Tickets are LE20, 30, 40, 50; the more expensive seats are ringside.

Camera: No camera fee, video not allowed.

Facilities: There are ramps for baby strollers and wheelchairs.

Parking: Difficult. The simplest solution is to take a taxi. If you do go by taxi, the Arabic for circus is *sirk*.

Summer extravaganza: Every summer, the National Circus invites world-class acts from the most famous circuses in Europe and Asia. A fun night for all the family, at a reasonable price!

Swiss Club Cairo

If you want to participate in the many activities and events that the Swiss Club hosts, you don't have to be a member. There is a fee for members and non-members but the prices are extremely reasonable. Hidden away is a lovely large garden and nineteenth century mansion that has been converted into an exhibition hall. The activities for youth and adults are numerous, all held in a delightful environment among friendly people. The Swiss Club has a creative flair with their event offerings, from Avocado Festival to Bedouin Exhibition (with a clay oven to bake bread) to international art exhibitions. Also there are classical concerts, open-air cinema, international buffets, and summer school for German-speakers. You and your children can find many wonderful activities to keep busy.

Where: Villa Pax, al-Gihad Street, off Sudan Street, Kit Kat Square. Tel. and Fax: 314-2811, 315-1455, 010 300-9695.

Web site: *www.swiss-club-cairo.com*

Mohandiseen

In 1945, to satisfy the demands of an expanding Cairo, seven thousand feddans in the Giza Governorate were subdivided and sold to professional cooperatives that were established on an occupational basis—doctors, engineers, teachers—and which in turn sold plots to their members. Mohandiseen is the common abbreviation for *Madinat al-Mohandiseen*, 'Engineers' City'. This suburb of concrete is congested with restaurants, up-scale stores, boutiques, and private art galleries, and boasts two major athletics clubs, the Shooting Club and Zamalek Club.

The Pottery Workshop, alias the Mud Factory

The entrance of this atelier is almost indistinguishable from the buildings that squeeze around it. A narrow alley gives no clue that behind the walls are skilled artisans who create exquisite pottery—practical items as well as works of art.

Samir al-Gindi opened his workshop over twenty years ago, mixing traditional and modern techniques to produce functional and stylized pieces. Drawing from a rich Islamic and folkloric heritage, the artisans produce revealing figurines that tell of Egyptian culture, and craft vases, lamps, and candle holders using arabesque and Mamluk designs, and Kufi writings on platters, plates, and pots. The Fatimid technique of perforation that was used to decorate water bottle filters (which can be viewed at the Islamic Museum and the Gezira Arts Center) is practiced here to create unique ceramics.

The artisans and potters are welcoming and pleased to have visitors watch them create. Pottery lessons and a visit to the pottery factory can be arranged.

Where: **Not easily seen from the street: there is no sign, so watch the street numbers carefully. 261 al-Sudan St. Tel: 347-3445, 344-7032.**

When: **10am–7pm.**

Dokki

Dokki is mainly a residential district. The Agricultural Museum is the only museum in this area of Cairo.

Entrance to the Agricultural Museum, Dokki

Agricultural Museum

The Agricultural Museum, opened in 1938, consists of five buildings that house different aspects of the Ministry of Agriculture's complex of collections, all within pleasant gardens. Unfortunately, only three of the five museums are open, but these display everything you could want to know about agriculture in Egypt from pharaonic times to the mid-1900s. The garden area is enormous by Cairo standards, with areas for strolling and resting.

After passing through the turnstile, the entrance to the Museum of Natural History is the first build-

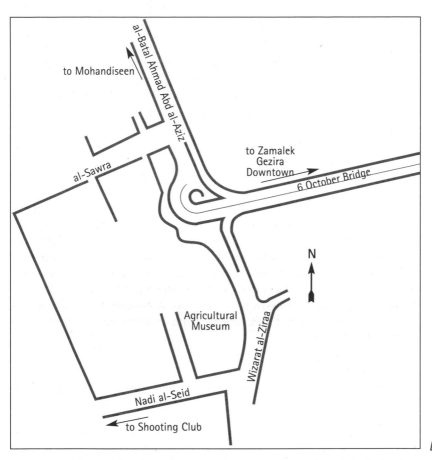

Dokki

ing on the right and the second building in the row is the Scientific Collection Museum; the last building is the Arab Pavilion. On the opposite side, there is the newly built Museum of Ancient Egyptian Agriculture, with gardens groomed in pharaonic style. The museum is open only to schools or college groups who arrange their visit in advance.

On the same side and heading back in the direction of the entrance is an office building, followed by the Cotton Museum. To our great disappointment, the doors of the Cotton Museum were locked: it is permanently closed unless special permission is obtained from the director of the Agricultural Museum.

To appreciate these museums completely, it is best to begin with an open mind. The experience is funky and dusty, as you encounter everything concerning agriculture in Egypt and more. Yet it is an excursion well worth the effort, as the exhibits are as amusing as they are informative.

Museum of Natural History

The guards who greet you at the Museum of Natural History might be the sons of previous generations of guards, judging by their uniforms. The displays and exhibits are badly in need of dusting and refurbishing, but disregard the desire to clean; there is a great deal to take pleasure in and learn from. The exhibits on the ground floor are of an ethnological nature, depicting life in an Egyptian village. Models of workers, the crafts, jewelry, traditional clothing, and musical instruments attempt to recreate what one might find in any village throughout Egypt.

Toward the back of the building is a grand stairway. At the top there is a giant, grinning hippopotamus, whose open mouth, full of teeth, is wide enough to put your head into. There are all sorts of stuffed animals on this floor: lions, crocodiles, and rhinoceros, to name a few; cases of insects and butterflies, and rows of birds, bats, ferrets, hedgehogs. Off to the sides are closed doors, and a guide will open them for a small tip. Behind one door is a room dedicated to camels. Inside another you can learn where silk comes from, how yarn is made from wool, and everything you ever wanted to know about the egg and the chicken (or visa versa). A museum worth visiting not only for the education but also for the depth in which each subject is presented, plus it is fun.

Scientific Collection Museum

It is easy to imagine a university professor and his students diligently collecting and arranging these collections many decades ago. Unfortunately, the museum feels and looks like no one has taken an interest in the collection since then. It is poorly lit and dusty, which is a pity because the displays are comprehensive, and meticulously thought out and prepared. There is not a step omitted in the explanation of the production of corn, wheat, and rice—everything you wanted to know about Egypt's agricultural production. From the types of grain planted to how grain is milled, the models show the farming process on Egyptian land. There are models of a ship that moved from village to village milling the grain, the windmills in Alexandria, and a self-explanatory flourmill. Upstairs there are products of agriculture, examples of canned produce, perfumes, and spices. A detailed explanation of summer and winter annual flowers, and fruits grown in Egypt is most enlightening.

Arab Pavilion

The first point of information you need to know is that this part of the Agricultural Museum is closed on Thursday, Friday, and Monday. The so-named Arab Pavilion opened its doors in 1961 to commemorate Egypt's union with

Syria (1958–1961). Walk through the doors and you are in a time capsule giving you a glimpse of what life was like in the Syrian countryside and agricultural communities circa 1950s. The first exhibit is a model of the Rastan Dam on the Orontes River between Homs and Hama. From this point the exhibits are as much an ethnological tour as they are agricultural. You will see traditional Syrian objects and costumes that document Syria's rich heritage—traditional dress for all occasions, jewelry, utensils, ceramics, and musical instruments. There are also cases that have examples of every fruit, vegetable, and grain that Syria produced.

Museum of Ancient Egyptian Agriculture

(The museum can only be visited by groups with advance permission, and an English or Arabic speaking guide is provided. Set up a visit by contacting the office of the director of the Agricultural Museum at 760-8682 or fax: 760-7881.) On display on the first floor of this museum is evidence of every type of plant utilized by the ancient Egyptians, and on the second floor, evidence for every animal, bird, reptile, fish, or insect. The exhibit is very thorough and extremely well done. For example, there are ancient emmer wheat seeds from 5000 BC tools, which were used to plant and harvest and thresh, an ancient granary, and ancient pieces of bread. Upstairs are skeletons from all the animals known to the ancient Egyptians and as well as mummies from many of them. For lovers of flora and fauna, as well as Egyptology students, this is an absolutely fascinating collection.

Where: **Entrance next to 6th of October Bridge and the Ministry of Agriculture on Nadi al-Seid St. Tel: 337-2933, 361-6785.**

When: **9am–1:30pm. Closed Mondays.**

Entrance fee: **10 piasters. Cameras allowed with no fee.**

Web Site: **www.agri.gov.eg**

Facilities: **There is a bathroom but it is not inviting. There are no drinks or snacks, so bring your own. A bottle of water is necessary in the summer months. First floor entrances have a few stairs, and the only access to the second floor in all the buildings is by two flights of stairs.**

Tip: **This museum is a popular field trip for many schools. Thus the buildings tend to echo with the noise. Often the children want to practice their language skills, which might become annoying, but they mean no harm.**

Cultural Centers

Cervantes Institute
20 Boulos Hanna St., Dokki. Tel: 360-1746, 337-0845, 337-1962. The Spanish-speaking community is an active part of Cairo's social scene. At this center, there are exhibitions, lectures, films, a library, and language courses through-out the year. Open 8:30am–3:30pm. Closed Fridays and Saturdays.

Jordanian Cultural Center
24 Gamal Salim St., off Mussaddaq St., Dokki. Tel: 749-5660. Open 9am–3pm. Closed Fridays.

Russian Cultural Center
127 Tahrir St., Dokki. Tel: 760-6371. There are concerts, films, chess lessons, ballet lessons, computer courses, piano lessons, and music classes offered. Open 10am–3pm and 5–9pm. Closed Fridays and Saturdays.

South Korean Cultural Center
South Korean Embassy, 3 Boulos Hanna St., Dokki. Tel: 761-1234/7. Open 9am–12 noon and 1–3pm. Closed Fridays amd Saturdays.

United Arab Emirates Cultural Center
9 Kambiz St., off Musaddaq St., Dokki. Tel: 749-9669. Open 8:30am–2pm. On Thursday, the closing time is 1pm. Closed Fridays.

Giza

The assumption is made that when one goes to Giza one is on the way to the Pyramids. Rather, Giza is a vast metropolis with an area that ranges from the Cairo Sheraton to Cairo University to the Pyramids of Giza. In the early twentieth century, one could stand on the bank of the Nile and see the Pyramids, which, of course, is impossible today.

The village of Giza was founded in the fourth century BC. Giza was a natural stopover for travelers between Memphis and Heliopolis via Roda Island. When the Arabs under the leadership of Amr ibn al-As invaded Egypt in AD 640, Amr settled two Arab tribes in the area, but isolated by the inundation of the Nile and inaccessibility from the east bank, the area remained low in population until Khedive Ismail became Egypt's ruler. Wanting to impress his European guests, especially the Empress Eugènie, during their visit to open the Suez Canal, Khedive Ismail retained the famous French landscaper, Barillet-Deschamps, to construct an elevated, tree-lined road from the west bank of the Nile to the Pyramids.

Along with a new palace on Gezira Island built for Empress Eugènie to reside in during her visit, Khedive Ismail ordered a bridge built to connect the two banks of the Nile. Ismail contracted the French company Fives-Lille to build two bridges, one a 400-meter iron swingbridge, between the two shores via Gezira Island. The bridges, Qasr al-Nil Bridge on the east and Galaa Bridge on the west, were not completed in time for Empress Eugènie's arrival, and she and her entourage crossed the Nile by way of a floating boat-bridge.

The Mena House was originally a royal lodge for Khedive Ismail and his guests, which he used during the hunting seasons. Before the road was built to the Pyramids, the way there was often muddy and rough. Travelers had to

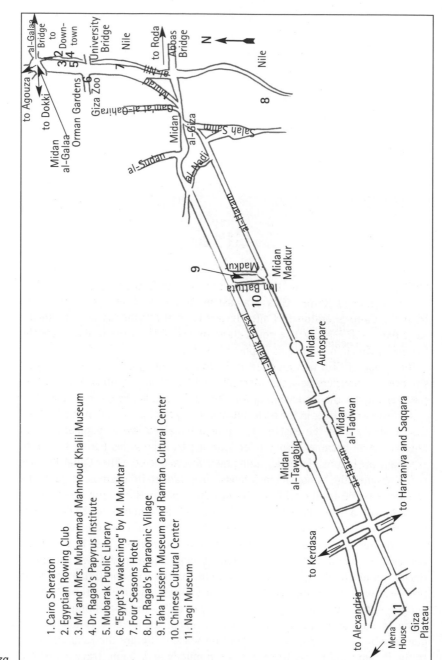

1. Cairo Sheraton
2. Egyptian Rowing Club
3. Mr. and Mrs. Muhammad Mahmoud Khalil Museum
4. Dr. Ragab's Papyrus Institute
5. Mubarak Public Library
6. "Egypt's Awakening" by M. Mukhtar
7. Four Seasons Hotel
8. Dr. Ragab's Pharaonic Village
9. Taha Hussein Museum and Ramtan Cultural Center
10. Chinese Cultural Center
11. Nagi Museum

Giza

begin the trip early in the morning if they wished to return to Cairo by evening. A traveler wrote during Muhammad Ali's reign:

> The trip was not without some difficulty. The Nile had to be crossed by a ferry; donkeys were the only means of conveyance; and the traveller must often go some miles out of his way to avoid a canal or a tract of land under water, or he must be carried over on a man's shoulders.

When Khedive Ismail became too involved with affairs of the state and could not enjoy the royal lodge, he sold it to Mr. and Mrs. Fredrick Head, who built a second floor. They also renamed it Mena House after Mena, the first king of Egypt. Following the death of Mr. Head, the Mena House was sold to another English couple, Mr. and Mrs. Locke-King.

Fabulously wealthy, the Locke-Kings decided to convert the house into a luxurious hotel. They enlarged the house, added balconies to each room, which was unheard of for a hotel, and installed mosaics and carved wooden doors. The hotel was far superior in elegance to most hotels of its time. The Locke-Kings eventually returned to England. During the First World War, the Mena House became a hospital, after which it was converted again into a deluxe hotel. For over one hundred years, the world's royalty and leaders, the rich and famous, have enjoyed the Giza Pyramids and Egypt from the balconies of the Mena House.

Mr. and Mrs. Muhammad Mahmoud Khalil Museum

Choose a weekend morning and promise yourself to take the family to this museum: when you have been there once, you will want to return often. There are many fun restaurants nearby to lure children with the suggestion of ending the excursion with food. A gift to the Egyptian people, this art collection representing realist, romantic, impressionist, and post-impressionist art is the finest in the Middle East. In fact, to see art of this quality one would otherwise need to buy an airline ticket to Paris or Rome.

The Mr. and Mrs. Muhammad Mahmoud Khalil Museum

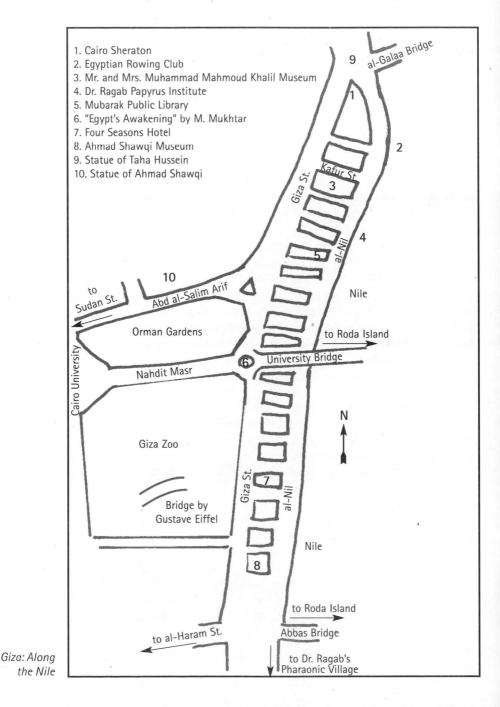

1. Cairo Sheraton
2. Egyptian Rowing Club
3. Mr. and Mrs. Muhammad Mahmoud Khalil Museum
4. Dr. Ragab Papyrus Institute
5. Mubarak Public Library
6. "Egypt's Awakening" by M. Mukhtar
7. Four Seasons Hotel
8. Ahmad Shawqi Museum
9. Statue of Taha Hussein
10. Statue of Ahmad Shawqi

9

al-Galaa Bridge

1

2

Giza St.

Kafur St.

3

al-Nil

4

5

Nile

10

to
Sudan St.

Abd al-Salim Arif

Orman Gardens

to Roda Island

University Bridge

6

Cairo University

Nahdit Masr

N

Giza Zoo

Giza St.

7

al-Nil

Bridge by
Gustave Eiffel

Nile

8

to Roda Island

to al-Haram St.

Abbas Bridge

to Dr. Ragab's
Pharaonic Village

In this magnificent nineteenth-century villa, which has an interesting history of its own, paintings by Monet, Renoir, Gauguin, Degas, Pissaro, Sisley, and Rousseau are but a few of the important pieces of European art. The diverse and rich collection of paintings, ceramics, sculptures, jade carvings, and objets d'art are spread throughout the three floors, following no particular order. Every wall of every room is lined with paintings or satisfyingly filled with the precious collection. Mahmoud Khalil and his wife prided themselves on having the finest collection of nineteenth-century impressionist paintings in the Middle East. Among the great paintings that can be viewed are Renoir's *The Young Woman Wearing the White Tulle Tie*, Sisley's *The Seine at the Beginning of the Day*, Pissaro's *A Game of Cricket in Bedford Park*, Degas's *Portrait of a Young Woman*, and Toulouse Lautrec's *The Singing Lesson*. On the first floor (second floor to Americans), viewing rooms feature Van Gogh's *Rhythm and the Poppy Flower*, painted in 1886, and Gauguin's *La Vie et la Mort*: here you can sit and contemplate two of the museum's most stunning works.

A signed replica of *The Thinker* is among a large collection of sculptures by Rodin, including *Eve*, *The Kiss*, and *The Head of Victor Hugo*. There are at least five paintings by Monet—*London, Westminster Abbey, and the Obelisk of Cleopatra* is particularly compelling. On what is labeled the second floor (third floor to Americans), you will be enticed by memories of springtime when viewing Latour's *Fleurs*. Other important works in this collection include a large selection of paintings by Corot, Millet, Daumier, Ricard, Diaz de la Pena, and Delacroix.

Being an eclectic collector as well as passionate in acquiring works of art, Mahmoud Khalil purchased superb Chinese and Japanese porcelain vases and objects, as well as Ottoman ceramic pieces. There is an exquisite jade collection. For his devotion to the arts, Khalil received the French title of Correspondant de l'Académie des Beaux Arts and the Grand Cordon de la Légion d'Honneur, while the Italians awarded him the Grand Cross of Maurice & Lazarre. During the Second World War, many European dealers were eager to sell treasured paintings, and Mahmoud Khalil was able to expand his collection substantially.

The fabulously restored villa provides an elegant backdrop to display the Khalils' collection. Walking through all three floors is an experience, all the while imagining what it would be like to own such a house. How could you decide which room would be your bedroom? Built by Egypt's prominent Jewish banker-industrialist, Raphael Menahem Suares, in the late nineteenth century, the villa was sold to Prince Omar Halim, a descendent of Muhammad Ali. In the early years of the twentieth century, Mahmoud Khalil and his French wife, Emilienne Hector Luce, moved in. Khalil was a senior member of the Wafd party and president of the senate, which gave him a high position in Egypt's social hierarchy. Mahmoud Khalil died in Paris in 1953, and soon afterward Emilienne left the villa and collection to the Egyptian people in her will. In the 1970s, President Sadat took over the villa as his private residence, and the collection was moved to what is now the Gezira Arts Center, but it was later returned to the villa, which was reopened as the Muhammad Mahmoud Khalil Museum.

Where: On the corner of Giza St. and Kafur St., next to the State Council (Maglis al-Dawla). Tel: 336-2358/76.

When: 10am–5:30pm. Closed Mondays.

Entrance fee: Foreigners LE25; residents LE12 (with ID); Egyptians LE5; students (with ID) are half price, except Egyptian students LE1. Tickets are good to enter Horizon One exhibition hall.

Horizon One: International exhibitions rotate in this exhibition hall throughout the year. If you go to the museum, be sure to stop at Horizon One to see if there is an exhibition. Because the exhibitions are not publicized well, you can come upon the most fascinating international art and object displays. Unfortunately, there is rarely any printed information available to explain the exhibit. Closed Fridays.

Facilities: Ramps and elevators within the premises. Bookstore with titles in Arabic, English, and French. The library is closed to the public. The cafeteria above the bookstore is a restful place to enjoy a refreshing tea or soft drink.

Web site: *www.mkhalilmuseum.gov.eg*

Egyptian Rowing Club

In the Cairo dawn, before crowded buses clamor across the four-lane bridge connecting Garden City and Roda Island with Giza, the morning light uncovers rowers in pencil-thin boats sweeping their long sculling oars in unison, creasing the Nile waters in silence.

You don't have to be in Oxford or Boston to learn how to crew. Rowing is an individual or group sport, and anyone in your family can take it up in Cairo. Early morning is the most satisfactory time to row because of the absence of water traffic and wind. In the mornings and late afternoon, coaches are on the premises of the Egyptian Rowing Club (established in 1935) and quite eager to assist.

Where: 115 Corniche al-Nil, just south of the Cairo Sheraton. Tel: 748-9639, 335-9029.

When: The club is open in the summer 6am–midnight, winter 6am–10pm; rowing from dawn to dusk.

Entrance fee: Club membership for foreigners: $100 for 3 months, plus $50 to participate in rowing. A day-visitor (Egyptian or foreign) with a member pays LE1, but no guests are admitted on Fridays or national holidays. There are various membership options provided to companies, colleges, and community groups.

Tip: It is helpful to speak Arabic when applying for membership, or take an Arabic speaker with you.

Other sports: Sailing, water skiing, fishing.

Cyperus Papyrus

In the tenth century, there was no more papyrus in Egypt. Previously used for making paper, rope, baskets, and boats, papyrus disappeared when Egyptians began to use other products to manufacture these essentials. Within the last thirty years, the reintroduction of papyrus to Egypt from the Sudan has mainly benefited tourism.

Cyperus papyrus grows in still, marshy areas. The reeds used to make the paper grow from a vast, horizontally spreading root system. The time of harvest is from June to September, when the plants are three to four meters tall. Stalks are cut and the umbel, or top portion, is removed. The outer skin is peeled off and the thinly cut strips are soaked in water. After being cut into shorter lengths, the strips are laid in a crisscross pattern and pressed with a heavy weight, which expels the water. The finished product can be written or drawn on.

Dr. Ragab Papyrus Institute

An extensive selection of paintings on authentic papyrus is available here. Also, books on Egypt (including children's books) are for sale. And a great hit with kids are the make-your-own-papyrus kits. The Dr. Ragab Papyrus Institute shares with Gold's Gym a houseboat that has been converted to look like an

Egyptian temple. The address is 121 Sharia al-Nil, between the Cairo Sheraton and University Bridge. The institute is open every day, 9am–9pm.

Mubarak Public Library

Is there a better bargain in the city for sublime solitude, comfortable surroundings, and a good book? With its air-conditioned, spaciously well-lit environment, the Mubarak Public Library is the place to be. The flowering gardens and appropriately placed park benches lure one to open a book and drift into the day. On the other hand, if you are more comfortable reading with a cup of tea, the quiet cafeteria is the spot. Another special attraction this library has is the brightly illuminated exhibition hall. The exhibits have not failed to be worthwhile.

The variety of general, reference, and children's books grows yearly. To find a book, consult the computer catalog, or there is a librarian on every floor to assist if needed. Books are in Arabic, English, French, and German, with Arabic and English titles in the majority. Current newspapers and magazines are available.

French architect Georges Parcq designed this brick art deco house and the French chancellery on the Corniche, as well as many houses in Garden City and downtown Cairo. Mubarak Public Library's original owner was a foreign bank, Credit Foncier Bank of Egypt, nationalized in the late 1950s. After this, the house became government property. Under Nasser's government, when many Cairo villas became headquarters or offices, or were allocated to loyal officers as living accommodations, Abd al-Hakim Amer, Egypt's army chief of staff, moved into Villa Credit Foncier. After the loss of the Sinai to Israel in 1967, however, Nasser put Amer under house arrest, and he died soon afterward. Madame Amer was allowed to remain with her family in the house until her death, when the house reverted to the government. The Bertelsmann Foundation of Germany restored the villa, and on 21 March 1995, Villa Credit Foncier became the Mubarak Public Library.

Where: 15 Tahawiya St., at the corner of Corniche al-Nil and Tahawiya. Tel: 336-0291.

When: 11am–7pm. Closed Tuesdays.

Entrance fee: Yearly membership LE10 for anyone under 21 years, LE30 for adults, LE20 for students of any age. To be a member you must be a resident or an Egyptian. Bring passport and proof of residency or Egyptian ID and two photographs.

Lending: Check out up to five books for two weeks.

Facilities: Cafeteria, elevators, toilets, and computerized library.

Exhibitions: The library has a spacious area for exhibits. Watch the papers for unique photo and painting exhibitions.

Giza Zoo

The Giza Zoo is a controversy. Those concerned with animal welfare insist that the environment at the zoo is wretched and that it should be closed. But what about the people who go to the zoo? One does not know who is more in need of a clean and open environment to romp and play—the animals or the public. The zoo is the only respite for many of the poor inhabitants of the city, providing entertainment, space, shade, and a bit of education in watching the animals. A family of six can go to the zoo for less than LE2. This is probably the best bargain in all of Cairo.

Before the Giza Zoo and the Orman Gardens existed, the entire area was Khedive Ismail's Harem Gardens. The landscaping fell to the famous French landscaper, Barrillet-Deschamps. Originally, the garden covered 21 hectares, including Khedive Ismail's harem residence (later used between 1889 and 1902 as the Egyptian Museum before it moved to its present location). In the 1870s, most of this land, which spanned the area from the Nile to where the Cairo University stands today, faced public auction to pay the debts that Khedive Ismail had incurred internationally. Ismail planted his zoological garden, known as the 'garden of delights,' with plants from Africa, South America, and Asia. An African banyan tree planted in 1871 still stands, to the delight of many picnickers. The Giza Zoo was founded in 1891, and remained under the directorship of the British until the revolution of 1952.

The zoo is a maze of sidewalks winding around an assortment of enclosures containing animals from all over the world. You can see a 300–year-old giant tortoise from the Galapagos Islands, and bears from the Himalayas—the zoo has an amazing assortment of animals, reptiles, and birds. There are some animals that the keepers allow people to feed, such as an African elephant. The keeper supplies the onlookers with plenty of carrot and potato slices to keep this elephant happy. Look for the gravity-anchored suspension bridge designed by Gustave Eiffel.

Have you ever come face to face with a hippopotamus? If not, here is your chance. At the Giza Zoo you put the greens right in the enormous mouth of the hippo. You might be lucky and hold a baby chimpanzee or wrap a harmless snake around your neck. Fridays and holidays are crowded, but usually the remainder of the week is quiet. See the lions and tigers before 12:30pm because the trainers close the doors to feed them in the afternoon.

Where: There are several entrances, one on each street. The main entrances are on the corner of Charles de Gaulle (Giza) St. and Nahdat Misr St. and on Charles de Gaulle St. across from the Four Seasons Hotel. There is another entrance on Gamaat al-Qahira St. Tel: 570-1552.

Web site: www.agri.gov.eg

When: 9am–4pm.

Entrance fee: 30 piasters. Take change to tip the animal keepers so you can feed some of the animals.

Parking: Parking along the curb of the streets.

The Orman Gardens

Across the street from the zoo is a botanical garden that is bursting with flowers, majestic trees, and plenty of space to throw or kick a ball. The Orman Gardens, cut from Khedive Ismail's Harem Garden, are under protection from builders, and thankfully saved for Cairenes. A walk through this delightful park is not to be missed, especially if you live nearby and yearn for greenery. An abundant array of shrubs, flowers, and trees from South America, Africa, and India shape this special garden.

Where: The entrance is across from Giza Zoo on Nahdat Misr St. Tel: 748-3452.

When: 9am–4pm.

Entrance fee: 50 piasters.

Flower Festival

The springtime flower festival is an annual gathering of plant and garden shops. This is a great time to buy houseplants or just browse. You might find bargains, and you will definitely see exotic plants and interesting displays. The children can enjoy browsing as much as adults, especially if you have a budding horticulturist in your midst!

Where: Orman Gardens

When: 9am–5pm. Dates vary: usually 2 or 3 weeks in late March to early April.

Ahmad Shawqi Museum

On the Nile in Giza is the second of two houses that Egypt's poet laureate called home (the first was in Matariya), and where poets, playwrights, musicians, singers, political leaders, and dignitaries met. Ahmad Shawqi's Turkish

The Ahmad Shawqi Museum

Bois de Boulogne

Bois de Boulogne, remember when the world
Was our oyster? At dark, my lady and I
would rush off to you at night. We'd stay
There with no one to hear us—my lady's words
Lute music with passion. We roamed your spaces,
The wind motionless; the birds, the whole world, asleep.
We spent the night watched by a solitary star.
We stopped at every spot, lingered in every angle.
Giddy with gazing into each other's eyes our love
Was a new born baby, our bosoms its cradle. The branches
Bowed their heads in adoration. The star stared
At us like a steadfast eye in the sky. At parting
Our bond dissolved. Now a sea separates us.
Beyond lies desert upon desert. My night's now
Here in the East, hers there in the West.
How content with her company must her night be!

—**Ahmad Shawqi**

Translated by Desmond O'Grady
(From *Ten Modern Arab Poets*, by Desmond O'Grady, Dublin: Daedalus, 1992.
Reproduced courtesy of the translator.)

grandfather came to Egypt in the entourage of Muhammad Ali and rose to occupy eminent positions, but by the time Shawqi was born in Cairo in 1868, the poet's father had already squandered the family estate. His grandmother took care of him from infancy and sponsored his education. Shawqi moved rapidly through school before studying law in Egypt and France. In 1894 Khedive Abbas Hilmi II admitted him to court as the official poet. Exiled to Spain in 1915 by the British, Shawqi returned to Cairo in 1919, and built his new home by the waters of the Nile. He adored the pyramids as much as the river, and from this site the pyramids were in constant view—almost impossible to imagine today.

Ahmad Shawqi's house is now a museum commemorating his life's work as poet laureate and highly regarded nationalist. In the garden is a copy of a bronze statue of the poet in Rome by the Egyptian sculptor Gamal al-Sigini. The ground floor consists of Shawqi's library, reading rooms, reception hall, and music room where the legendary Muhammad Abd al-Wahab sang. Upstairs the bedrooms and study allow the visitor to visualize the poet's home life. A Center for Criticism and Creativity features a conference and lecture room that encourages writers and artists to discuss and analyze artistic works through organized symposiums.

> Where: **6 Ahmad Shawqi St., on the corner of Corniche al-Nil. Tel: 572-9479, 568-0115.**
> When: **9am–5pm. Closed Mondays. Ramadan, 10:30am–1:30pm.**
> Entrance fee: **Foreigners LE3; Egyptians 50 piasters.**

Dr. Ragab's Pharaonic Village

If you want to see the entire history of Egypt in less than three hours, visit Dr. Ragab's Pharaonic Village. Dr. Hassan Ragab rediscovered the art of papyrus making in 1967, and originally established a papyrus plantation here on Jacob Island, but then, dedicated to educating the youth of Egypt and visitors, he began to transform the island into a living museum in 1974, planting 5,000 trees to provide a natural barrier from modern Cairo. He met with Egyptologists to learn of the history and lifestyle of the ancient Egyptians, and ten years later, in 1984, he opened the Pharaonic Village as an educational (as well as recreational) resource for Cairenes and foreigners. There is no doubt that after a compact and comprehensive visit, your family will have a deeper understanding of the history of this country.

The tour begins in the viewing boat, which departs every thirty minutes—you have time to look through the Hellenistic Museum and browse in the bazaar while waiting. As you board your boat and ride through the Canal of

Mythology, you will travel back in time and hear the stories of the ancient Egyptian gods. Each statue has a legend to convey. Next, one hundred actors and actresses perform daily to reenact ancient Egyptian life. In the outdoor scenes the young men and women recapture the art of weaving and sculpting, the making of wine, pottery, papyrus paper, and perfume, and the techniques of farming. At a temple, you disembark from the boat to walk through a nobleman's house and then compare it to a peasant's house.

The Boat Museum is next. Here, models illustrate the materials used to build boats. Most fishing boats were constructed from papyrus. The ancient Egyptians also used acacia wood to build vessels that sailed the Nile as cargo ships, transporting granite blocks, say, or a 600-ton obelisk from Aswan. Rope was used—no nails—to lash wood or papyrus together in the construction of boats.

Afterward, it might be fun to have a picture taken of yourself dressed in an ancient Egyptian costume—it will be ready upon departure. There is a shady cafeteria here where you can rest, or you can continue to the pyramid and sphinx models, which show the monuments in construction.

There is also a walk-through replica of King Tutankhamun's tomb with all its treasures, as seen when Howard Carter first entered the tomb in 1922. Artisans reproduced each piece of the Tutankhamun treasure with meticulous attention to authenticity. Dedicated to understanding the daily life of an ancient Egyptian, the Museum of Art and Beliefs, which essentially is a museum of ethnology, exhibits musical instruments, cosmetics and jewelry, and food and drink, enhancing our understanding of another time and people. The Museum of Mummification explains the principles of mummification, the products used, and the length of time needed for this process.

A trip through Egypt's history would not be complete without reviewing the spread of Islam and the Arab contribution to the history of Egypt: the Islamic Museum covers the history of Islam, Islamic arts and crafts, the Arab world's military and scientific leaders, and the life of the Prophet Muhammad. A Coptic Museum, a Museum of Modern History, Alexandria, Napoleon's Expedition Museum, and the Abd al-Nasser Museum are but a few more places to learn about Egypt's unique history. If your family is tired, there is a playground and a restaurant in which to recuperate.

> Where: 3 al-Bahr al-Azam St. on the Corniche.
> Tel: 571-8675/6/7.
> When: 9am–6pm, except June, July, and August,
> 9am–9pm. During these three months, there is
> evening entertainment, which features dances
> from pharaonic times, belly dancers, and tan-
> nura dancers. Closed the first half of Ramadan.

Entrance fee: Prices as of the summer of 2006 are: foreigners LE119; Egyptians LE44. Children under nine pay half price, children under five enter free. Look for discount coupons in newspapers and magazines.

Age group: Although the Pharaonic Village is for all ages, children aged 7–12 will particularly enjoy this outing.

Taha Hussein Museum and Ramtan Cultural Center

Taha Hussein (1889–1973), although blind from childhood, became one of Egypt's most revered literary figures and scholars. Born in Upper Egypt, he received his first doctorate from Egyptian University (now Cairo University) in 1914. In 1918, he received another PhD in ancient history, Greek, and Latin from the Sorbonne and continued his education in Oxford, Madrid, and Rome. He wrote more than fifty books of educational theory, philosophy, history, literature, and literary criticism.

Taha Hussein was not only a prolific writer and a professor of ancient history and Arabic literature but was also involved in politics, which caused him much aggravation in his life. He complained that Egyptians, including himself, were too absorbed with politics and that they could think and talk of little else. He wrote: "Life is not all politics; it has some other substance that we should neither ignore nor belittle." In 1950, when he became minister of education, he promoted free education in elementary and secondary schools. A great thinker and a pioneer of enlightenment, he spoke out for his beliefs, which often made him enemies. He spoke out for women's emancipation, a controversial issue causing heated debate, and the views he expressed in his book on pre-Islamic poetry got him into trouble with the religious authorities. His career suffered as a result of his literary attack on Saad Zaghloul, but he wrote: "It is easy to endure vilification and slander, and I have resolved to bear all such vileness as long as there is hope that in the end we can arrive at the truth."

Upon the revision of this edition, Taha Hussein's house is closed for renovations. The following description gives the reader some idea of what was in the house. As you enter the gates, a bust of the great man sculpted by Faruq Ibrahim greets you. To the right is Taha Hussein's residence; to the left is an identical house built for his son that is now the Ramtan Cultural Center (Ramtan means two oases: Taha Hussein considered the two houses sharing a garden an oasis for him and his son).

Entering the residence is like walking into a time machine and being transported back into the 1940s. It feels as if Taha Hussein, with his beloved

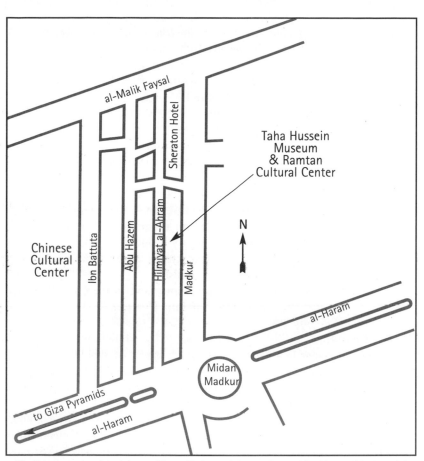

al-Malik Faysal

Sheraton Hotel

Taha Hussein
Museum
& Ramtan
Cultural Center

N

Chinese
Cultural
Center

Ibn Battuta

Abu Hazem

Hilmiyat al-Ahram

Madkur

al-Haram

Midan
Madkur

to Giza Pyramids

al-Haram

Giza:
al-Haram St.

wife Suzanne beside him, will walk from his study and hold out his hand in greeting. It is not difficult to imagine the footsteps of politicians and artists that converged every Sunday in the large reception hall. The rooms contain personal belongings of Taha Hussein and his family—furniture, paintings, books. Paintings by famous Egyptian artists such as Muhammad Nagi and Raghib Ayyad hang on the walls. Throughout the house are a number of sculptures, the most important being the bust of Taha Hussein by Abd al-Qader Rizq. Rare records of works by such famous composers as Bach and Mozart and over 6,000 books in Arabic and various foreign languages are in his personal library.

Upstairs, the beds made and waiting for their occupants produce a melancholy longing for the past. A hallway display case has medals and decorations bestowed on Taha Hussein by presidents and kings of Arab and foreign countries. The most prestigious is the Order of the Nile, which he received in 1965. He was 77 years old when he received this highest distinction that Egypt awards its citizens.

Where: 1 Hilmiyat al-Ahram St., off al-Haram St.
Tel: 583-4869.

When: 10am–3pm. Closed Mondays
Ramtan Cultural Center: Every Thursday 12 noon–2pm the center is open for children to draw and paint, and every day from June to September it is open 10am–2pm for children's arts and crafts. Professors from different fields give lectures in Arabic every Sunday evening. Call for program.

Library: A reading library is open to all.
The subject matter is varied and books are in Arabic and English.

Statue: On the roundabout next to the Cairo Sheraton is a statue of Taha Hussein.

Nagi Museum

"Life ought to resemble a piece of art, which the artist should shape like a jewel, and improve upon it, incessantly, to try to make of it the masterpiece toward which he aspires." —Muhammad Nagi to a friend

Muhammad Nagi's home, hidden away from the well-traveled Pyramid Road, has been converted into a museum where his paintings and memorabilia remain in relative seclusion from public knowledge. However, ask most Egyptians, and they will know the name of the artist Muhammad Nagi.

Nagi was born in Alexandria and obtained his law degree from the University of Lyon, France, in 1910. He studied painting at the Academy of Art in Florence, Italy, from 1910 to 1914. He met Claude Monet and went to France to study with him. In 1924 he was appointed to the diplomatic corps. He served in Brazil and Paris, and went to Ethiopia in 1932 for one year, which greatly influenced his painting and portraits. He wrote afterward: "There are colors that are truer than nature, for they correspond to the state of the soul . . . . While improving upon my paintings from Abyssinia, I found again this first vision of the distant soil of Abyssinia on the African continent. The idea of the tropical sun forced me to rethink my idea of the color yellow."

Muhammad Nagi was interested in expressing his ideas of beauty through painting and he was famous for his use of color, light, and shadow. The art of

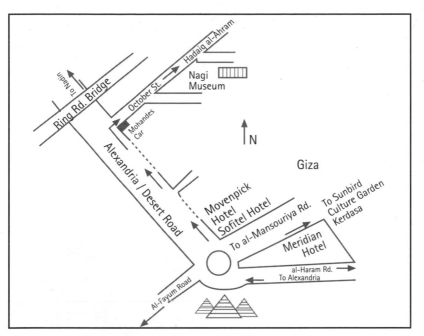

Giza: Pyramids

the ancient Egyptians and their use of color fascinated him. From 1937 to 1939, Nagi was director of the Fine Arts School in Cairo, and he became the first director of the Museum of Modern Art in 1939. He accepted the nomination of director of the Egyptian Academy in Rome and became cultural counselor at the Rome Embassy in 1947. Interested in fresco and heavily influenced by Raphael, Nagi completed a wall-painting called "The Alexandria School" at the Governorate Building in Alexandria in 1952. He built his private studio near the pyramids the same year and wrote in his journal: "I imagine the repose of my soul in the proximity of the desert and the pyramids. The profusion of flowers, vegetables, and fruits blesses my existence with a well-being that one cannot find in the big cities." He died in his studio in 1956, and the Ministry of Culture turned the studio into a museum in 1968.

Where: **9 Mahmoud al-Gindi St., Hadaiq al-Haram. Tel: 383-3484.**

When: **10am–5pm in winter, 10am–6pm in summer, 10am–1pm on Thursdays. Closed Mondays.**

Entrance fee: **Foreigners LE2; Egyptians 50 piasters.**

Facilities: **Bathrooms. There are no stairways and there is a wheelchair ramp.**

Age group: **For older children and teenagers interested in** art. There is a lovely garden if smaller children are bored while others in the group wish to tour the museum. During the summer, fine arts workshops are held for children of all ages. Contact the supervisor of cultural activities, 383-3484.

NADIM: National Art Development Industries of Mashrabiya

This institute produces woodwork and *mashrabiya* of high quality and on a large scale. The founder, Dr. Assad Nadim, was interested to revive traditional woodworking crafts. Educating people in the historical significance of this craft has been a priority as well. The institute has opened its doors to students who wish to see the making of *mashrabiya* and the intricate handwork that it entails. However, please make an appointment before going if your desire is to learn and observe, as this is a factory and without prior notification, you might be disappointed.

Where: In the Abu Rawash Industrial Zone. Take the Cairo–Alexandria Desert Road heading out of Cairo. The exit to NADIM is on the right, after the McDonalds and before the toll station. Tel: 539-1601 through 1608; Fax; 539-1609.

When: 9am–1pm or by appoinment. Closed Fridays.

Web site: *www.nadim.org*

Mashrabiya

The latticework window covers called *mashrabiya* soften the austere stone of Islamic houses. When the protruding, handcrafted, wooden *mashrabiya* grilles are part of the architecture, the harsh coldness of the stone no longer seems uninviting. Apart from beautifying the house, *mashrabiya* controls light, filters air, and allows privacy for the inhabitants.

Hundreds of years ago, one element that artisans had plenty of was time: in one square meter, two thousand small wood pieces fit together like a puzzle to form a patterned grille. And what machines now do was once done by fingers, toes, lathe, and bow. When glass windows became popular, the unique Egyptian tradition of *mashrabiya* almost became extinct. Fortunately, the technique and popularity of *mashrabiya* screens and picture frames has kept the art from becoming lost.

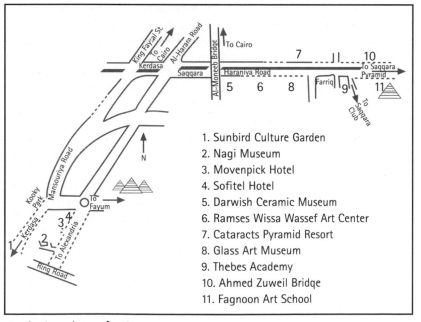

1. Sunbird Culture Garden
2. Nagi Museum
3. Movenpick Hotel
4. Sofitel Hotel
5. Darwish Ceramic Museum
6. Ramses Wissa Wassef Art Center
7. Cataracts Pyramid Resort
8. Glass Art Museum
9. Thebes Academy
10. Ahmed Zuweil Bridge
11. Fagnoon Art School

Saqqara - Harraniya Road and Kerdasa

Outskirts of Giza
Sunbird Culture Garden

"Aw, Mom, do we have to leave?" Can there be a better recommendation about an outing! These words were heard over and over again by the young people in our group—the adults were hesitant to leave even after staying on for four hours. Layla Sedek is no stranger to teaching students and foreigners about the rich traditions of her country, Egypt. She was a tour guide for over twenty years. After retirement, she was not able to give up the idea that we all need to know more about these traditions within in an enjoyable environment. Madame Sedek transformed her farm into an ethnological, outdoor museum with recreational facilities. There are areas to play volleyball and ping-pong, stage a play, or wander along the perimeter of the botanical gardens and discover what vegetables, fruits, and trees are native to Egypt. Have you ever seen a henna tree or the loufa plant? Madame Sedek explains, "All the crops that we grow are without chemical fertilizer; they grow naturally and are seasonal. They may not be perfect in size and color—that is what makes them natural. Most people don't see this anymore." Everything is labeled in Arabic, English, French, and German.

The meticulous processes of describing the lifestyle of farmers in the Delta or Bedouin life in the deserts have been the goal, including descriptions of religious celebrations and marriage and birth ceremonies. See a replica of a farmhouse in the Delta, arranged as if it is still occupied. Try your hand at weaving a basket, pet the rabbits, study the many ways land is irrigated in Egypt, or just sit under a date tree and listen to the birds. There is a new Ancient Egypt area that shows examples of how plants and herbs were used during that time. (In the spring, you can even spot a sunbird for which the garden is named.) This is a great place for birthday parties, class trips, or outdoor meetings, especially for families and groups.

Where: 25 Mansouriya Road, Giza. From King Faysal Street, turn on right on Mansouriya Road, go under a flyover and follow the sign to Kerdasa, it is about 4 kilometers from here. A large blue decorated sign with the street number, 25, is in clear view from the road. Tel/fax: 795-8147; mobile: 012 211-7552.

When: It is open everyday by appointment.

Cost: Prices are available by calling Madame Sedek, who can arrange food, music, and dancing horses.

Guides: Professional guides are available to take the children and adults through the exhibits to explain everything.

Age recommendation: Young children to 12 years.

Kerdasa

The green fields of the Egyptian countryside offer a welcome respite from the bustle of Cairo as one drives toward Kerdasa. Rows of cabbages, beans, and alfalfa line the road and date palms sway under the steady watch of the nearby pyramids. On arrival, Kerdasa might look like a tourist trap with store after store selling an array of *gallabiya*s and carpets, but if you are in the mood and have the patience, an investigation might lead to intriguing stories just waiting to be told.

Sitting on a pile of carpets, ask Hagg Muhammad about the origins of Kerdasa and his many theories will guide your imagination and interest. He traces the origin of Kerdasa as a trading post for caravans crossing the desert to and from Libya. He also hints that Kerdasa supplies Libya with certain cloth used in making Muammar al-Qaddafi's shawl! Abd al-Fattah, a carpet weaver, believes the city was an encampment for Amr ibn al-As and his army in the seventh century. He proudly confided that members of the Hashemite tribe of Jordan settled in Kerdasa, his mother being one of their descendants. Whether this is true or not, linguist Gerd al-Naggar explains that the name Kerdasa does indeed mean a gathering place, as the verb *kardasa* means to heap up, pile up, crowd, or flock together.

Today, Kerdasa is a village of heaps and piles of tapestries, carpets, *gallabiya*s, kaftans, and shawls that line the streets. However, just behind the storefronts or through an alleyway, a dark entrance opens onto weavers bent over broad looms that consume small rooms. Their fingers deftly pass the shuttles strung with burgundy or emerald cotton between the warp threads. A radio blares popular melodies and rich hued skeins of thread hang from the beamed ceiling, cascading onto wooden benches and dusty floors. Atef has written his name in thick black ink near his loom, and on each peeling wall, the word Allah is painted boldly, reminding us of blessings. In the corner, a teapot boils.

Where: From Cairo, turn right (west) off al-Haram Street onto the Kerdasa Road (Maryutiya Road), cross al-Malik Faysal Road, and continue west for 5.7 kilometers. Turn left before the large white building that juts out to the road. Kerdasa is also accessible from 26th July Corridor leaving Mohandiseen.

When: Stores are open 11am–7pm every day.

Age appropriateness: This trip is fun for all ages.

Darwish Ceramic Museum

Dr. Nabil Darwish dedicated his life to pottery. He was a prolific potter and produced over 3,000 pieces in twenty-five different styles. He is best known for his work with black clay. Internationally recognized, Dr. Darwish often received delegations from abroad, who noted the connections between his pottery and traditional heritage. He stated, "During my search in my homeland for appropriate raw materials needed for creating pottery which is both functional and beautiful, the voices of my aesthetic forbearers from the early and late dynasties arose within me. . . . I spent a long time contemplating the pottery of the early dynastic era, studying the human feeling and the natural style of implementation which is reflected in their work. The clarity and the simple use of materials by them permitted the natural integration of human feelings."

Where: **On the Saqqara-Harraniya Road, just past the new highway, on the way to Saqqara Pyramid. There is a large sign on the right. Tel: 381-5294.**

When: **7am–6pm every day. Ring doorbell, if no one answers, Mrs. Darwish may be on an errand. Do return another day or call for an appointment.**

Ramses Wissa Wassef Art Center

This working museum brings alive ancient crafts in the hands of today's artists. Ramses Wissa Wassef developed this center to create a place for local village children to express what they see in their environment through weaving tapestries, but the center now also hosts adults and young people, who both weave and make pottery.

Ramses Wissa Wassef, a Copt from a prominent family, studied in Paris at the Ecole des Beaux Arts. Encouraged by the great Egyptian sculptor Mahmoud Mukhtar to pursue his interest in art, Ramses became professor of art and history of architecture at the Faculty of Fine Arts in Cairo.

Ramses's concern for Egypt's architecture led him to observe painfully: "What I could not explain was why our own civilization would produce such coldness and ugliness to replace the wealth of indigenous architecture. I used to like walking through the old parts of Cairo, but even there hideous fungus-like 'modern' buildings are going up, insults to human sensibility. And it is even sadder when it happens in the open countryside." Some of his own architectural achievements can be seen in the Mahmoud Mukhtar Museum (in Gezira), in two churches in Zamalek and Heliopolis, and in the Art Center in Harraniya.

In 1941, Ramses and his wife Sophie began to experiment with weaving,

Example of tapestry weaving at Ramses Wissa Wassef Art Center

wool, and natural dyes. By 1950, he had bought land outside of Cairo near the village of Harraniya, where his main goal was to provide an opportunity and artistic outlet for children in Harraniya village. Believing children to have an innate gift for composition, he set down three rules: no cartoons or drawings, no imitation of other works of art, no criticism or interference from adults. "Human freedom," he wrote, "never has as much meaning and value as when it allows the creative power of the child to come into action. All children are endowed with a creative power, which includes an astonishing variety of potentialities. This power is necessary for the child to build up his own existence."

Where: On the Saqqara–Harraniya Road, past the new highway going toward Saqqara. Tel: 381-5746, 012 312-1359.

When: Showroom open 10am–5pm every day. Workshops open 10am–12 noon and 2–5pm in winter, 10am–1pm and 3–5pm in summer; closed Thursday afternoon and all day Friday.

Facilities: Museum with tapestries from the first generation weavers and Ramses Wissa Wassef at the back of the compound. Pottery, weaving, batik, and tapestry are for sale.

Web site: *www.wissa-wassef-arts.com*

Glass Art Museum

Heavy trucks and fast cars rumble past the iron gate of the Glass Art Museum, but few stop to inquire about the aqua-green sculptures in the windows. If you are not in a hurry, take a few moments to pause and enter another world. Behind the gate, the tall date trees cast mellow shadows over the glass art and garden sculptures. It is time to indulge in the love of glass and art that the late Major General Zakariya Al Khanani and his wife, Aida Abdel-Kerim spent their lives to create. Both artists in their own right, they studied glass techniques used by the ancient Egyptians and eventually, converted their atelier and home into a museum to celebrate the sculptures, memorabilia, and works of glass art. Aida Abdel-Kerim continues to work on the premises with other artists and some sculptures and glass object d'art are for sale.

Where: **Harraniya Road in the direction of Saqqara, opposite the Cataract Pyramids Resort.**
Telephone: **381-5955, 381-5562.**
When: **11am–4pm daily except Sundays. The door is usually locked so knock and ring the door bell.**
Web site: *www.glassartmuseum.com*

Fagnoon Art School–Sabil Om Hashem

Freedom of space to paint, explore, think, and create is attainable in Cairo. On the road to Saqqara, children and adults have the opportunity to experience

Fagnoon Art School. Harraniya Road

226

all this in the fresh country air. During the weekends and every day, you can organize individual or group lessons in painting, pottery, woodcrafts, iron bending, and silk painting. There is even an oven to bake bread Bedouin-style. Parents are welcome to stay with their children.

Fagnoon is an Arabic word meaning something that does not exist. This is creativity at its essence—imagination, discovery, creation. Fagnoon's vision is to give people space to use their imagination and create something new, and through use of different techniques discover and experiment with different art forms.

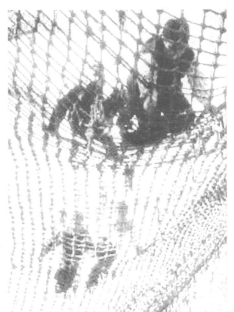

Where: Saqqara Road, Sabil Om Hashem, exactly 12 kilometers east of al-Haram St. Drive past the turn-off to the Saqqara Country Club, continue past Egypt Carpet Institute and Nut Carpet School. The art center is just around the bend in the road, after Ahmed Zewail Bridge.

Telephone: 815-1633, 012 214-7136; Fagnoon Fallah, 815-1369.

When: Morning to sunset.

Fees: LE30 for first two activities, LE10 for each activity thereafter.

Web site: www.fagnoon.net

Cultural Centers
Chinese Cultural Center

10 Ibn Battuta, off al-Haram St. Tel: 581-8203. This cultural center has an excellent information section. Pamphlets and material on everything from Chinese history to traditions are available. A good source for students who need to know more about China. Open 8:30am–2:30pm. Closed Thursdays and Fridays.

Maadi

Springtime in Maadi. It happens early, a bridge between the brief cool months of winter and the harshness of the summer heat. Few districts in Cairo enjoy this time of year as much as the residents of Maadi. Flowering purple jacarandas, red flame trees, and showers of burgundy bougainvillea gently invite us to stop for a moment and remember the metamorphoses.

Maadi was an extremely important site for Neolithic culture in ancient Egypt, from roughly 4000 to 3500 BC. In the area of the satellite station, archeologists have found evidence of a settlement with huts and storage pits, as well as a rectangular structure that has been interpreted as an early temple. Nearby, there were cemeteries not only for humans but also for dogs and gazelles, which perhaps is early evidence for animal cults. The artifacts of the Maadi culture show connections to Upper Egypt and the Early Bronze Age in Palestine. Maadi was strategically located on the north–south route, and served as a trading center for goods moving between Syro-Palestine and Upper Egypt. Maadi also had trade connections with the copper mining area of southern Sinai, and evidence has been found of small-scale copper industries in Maadi. Recently, excavated sites in the eastern Delta revealed that the Maadi culture spread through Lower Egypt in the early Neolithic period. Then, bit by bit, the culture of Upper Egypt took over, and by 3500 BC, Maadi culture disappeared. Plans are being discussed for a museum in Maadi that would display artifacts of the Maadi culture, so watch for future announcements.

Like all areas of Cairo, Maadi has changed. It has experienced rapid urbanization, especially in the past ten years, as grand villas and spacious gardens

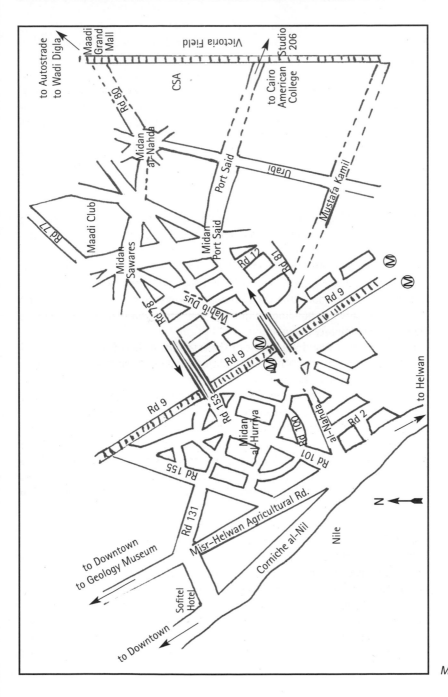

Maadi

have been destroyed to make way for high-rise apartment buildings. Fifteen years ago on leaving Old Cairo, one drove south toward Maadi along abundant farming land on the Nile road. Today, only patches remain of the rich, fertile farmland, now mostly covered by apartments of bricks, steel, and cement. Once considered a true suburb of Cairo, Maadi is no longer on the periphery.

Urbanization began to take hold when the railroad connected Maadi to Cairo. Until then, the narrow strip of fertile land on the east bank of the Nile supported orchards and vineyards, where the yearly inundation of the river guaranteed a fruitful soil. Beyond, the desert and wadis fanned out to the Muqattam Hills. In 1904, when the railroad expanded to Maadi, developers recognized the investment opportunities in this new area.

Land-grabbing seems to be a human affliction, and in Maadi the story is no different than anywhere else. A speculator could buy land at LE42 a feddan and six months later, after the arrival of the railroad, sell it to the Delta Light Railway Company (later the Egyptian Delta Land and Investment Company) at LE200. But fortunately, times were different then, and the developers of Maadi initiated a code, embodied in the *Cahier des charges*, which set out rules such as the ratio between building height and the size of garden. In other words, there was community planning.

Before the First World War, most of the residents of Maadi were British and Egyptians. After the war, other nationalities—Italians, Greeks, Lebanese—built marvelous villas, and the gardens bloomed continually. It was rare in those days for foreigners to arrive in Egypt to work for only a year or two, as they usually do now: the foreigners came to stay, raise their children, and even possibly retire. This is what furthered community planning and improvement. After the 1952 Revolution, property was liquidated, people left, and Maadi seemed to slumber for several decades, but now this once-sleepy Cairo suburb is a favorite residential area for expatriates. To find out more about the history of Maadi, read Samir Rafaat's book, *Maadi, 1904–1962: Society and History in a Cairo Suburb*.

Maadi has the population of a city but the feeling of a village. There are several major shopping districts and malls, but a trip to the well-known Road 9 is like walking through a village square with a variety of shops, galleries, and restaurants tossed together in a surprisingly delightful mishmash. You can enjoy a peaceful felucca ride on the Nile or a bicycle ride in Wadi Digla, and a variety of recreational opportunities abound in Maadi, such as state-of-the-art entertainment and movie centers. Although high-rise buildings are quickly taking the place of villas and gardens, Maadi's tree-lined streets are still a quiet antidote to the clamor of its neighbor, Cairo.

Petrified Forest

On the old road to Ain Sukhna, there was an entrance to the Petrified Forest, a protected area (Cairo is fast approaching), this fascinating place lent itself to investigation and the study of acres of petrified wood strewn across the sand, including a few whole trees embedded in the sand. (See Wadi Digla, below, for a detailed explanation.) Scattered among the petrified

Petrified tree

wood are reddish-brown nodules of chert, which form in limestone. When broken, chert has a fine cutting edge like flint: the ancient Egyptians used these rocks as tools and weapons (you can see examples in the Geology Museum). From Carrefour take the Ring Road to the Ain Sukhna exit, make a U-turn, and go straight. (Do not take the new road to Sukhna.) The entrance to the protectorate is at the top of the hill on the left. It is open seven days a week. There is some debate in governmental circles if the area will be preserved.

Wadi Digla

By Janice Hill-Garing

Just a short drive east of Digla in Maadi lies Wadi Digla. A wadi is a canyon carved by water. Looking at the desert, it is hard to imagine the torrents of water necessary to carve out a magnificent canyon such as the Wadi Digla. However, these processes have taken place over the course of millions of years and under different climatic conditions. Even today, Egypt sometimes experiences catastrophic rains, which cause flash floods to rage down its wadis. The force of this water would be awesome to behold—from a safe distance.

Arriving at Wadi Digla, you leave the millions of people of Cairo behind and enter a quiet refuge of solitude. For all its close proximity to Cairo, the wadi can absorb its visitors and give them privacy. Many groups make regular use of the wadi for outdoor activities. The Boy Scouts and Cub Scouts take camping trips. The Hash House Harriers and other cross-country racers hold their races on the rugged hillsides. Bikers pedal up the canyon road. Other groups just spend the day picnicking and exploring, staying until evening to watch the myriad stars come out, especially during the meteor showers of August and November.

A desert canyon is a geologist's paradise, with no superfluous vegetation obscuring the rocks. The walls and hills of the wadi are upper Eocene in age,

Wadi Digla

about 50 million years old. This fossiliferous limestone provides great opportunities for fossil study. Common marine fossils include many varieties of mollusks such as oysters, clams, scallops, and snails, which are easily recognizable, as they have not changed much through time. Do not be deceived by the white snail shells that you see scattered on the surface. These modern desert snails, amazingly, live under the ground. You can also find echinoderms of the sea urchin family. They are rounded, about the size of your fist, with an imprint like that of the sand dollar on top. Nummulites are the characteristic fossil of these rocks. Billions of these foraminifera floated around in the ocean, hence they are found all through the rocks: they are lens- or coin-shaped, ranging from the size of an eraser head to a 25-piaster coin.

Common crystalline minerals include dog's tooth calcite, which formed as filler in cracks in the limestone. Its sharp and jagged points look just as they are named. Another common desert mineral is anhydrite, which formed during evaporation. It looks somewhat similar to calcite, but crumbles easily. The hills are coated with desert varnish, a dark mineral film formed in desert regions by solar radiation, which causes ground water to evaporate and form iron oxides on the surface of the sand. This varnish actually protects the sands of the hills from wind erosion, but vehicles travelling over it quickly destroy this protective cover.

Petrified wood can also be found lying on the surface of the wadi. It has been eroded out of the Oligocene-aged sandstone rocks of the Petrified Forest just to the north and carried down into the wadi. How did petrified wood form in the middle of the desert? You will notice that the wadi is made up of limestone rocks, which means that the ocean once covered this whole area. Then later the land areas rose up, perhaps through earthquakes, and the ocean level fell. Low, marshy lands with trees appeared after the ocean receded, which are the source of today's petrified wood. However, there are billions of trees living and dying in this world, but not very much petrified wood: petrified wood forms only when trees are buried in mud saturated with mineralized water. This special kind of mud appears when there are volcanoes nearby. When a volcano explodes violently, it spews out clouds of ash that bury the land and trees in a thick layer. Volcanic ash is full of minerals that dissolve in the water. The water slowly dissolves the tree and replaces the wood with silica, a mineral that is the same as quartz and very hard. Later the softer ash and mud weather away, but the very hard, petrified wood remains. So we can see that this area was once an ocean, then a marsh covered with trees, with volcanoes nearby, and now a desert. Walking in the wadi is like traveling through time.

Wadi Digla can actually be divided into two parts. The lower wadi is accessible via the road out of Digla, under the autostrade. A blue sign that reads "Wadi Digla Protectorate Road" marks the actual entrance. Conditions vary, and it often requires a four-wheel drive vehicle. The road runs along the bottom of the canyon and ends when you reach the waterfall area, about a 45-minute drive. You can hike up through this narrow canyon, around pools of water that are about two feet deep in the springtime, and reach the upper wadi.

The upper wadi is accessible from the Ain Sukhna road, marked on the right by a blue sign: "Wadi Digla Protectorate." This access road has been paved and improved recently, enabling very large trucks to use it for transporting quarry materials and garbage. A dirt road turns off from this paved access road at a bus recycling yard and now runs through a massive garbage dump. The upper wadi gives you glorious vistas and sunset views. The road stops at the edge of the narrowly carved and hidden canyon separating the upper and lower wadi.

As with many places in Cairo, it is better on your first visit to go with someone who has been there before: roads and landmarks are constantly changing. Always be sure to carry extra water and an emergency kit when traveling and exploring.

Where: **Go to Wadi Digla Country Club. Facing the entrance turn left (east) and drive alongside a drainage ditch until the road ends. You will see a rock wall. That is the entrance to Wadi Digla.**

Entrance fees: **Foreigners (per person) LE5, car LE5, overnight LE10; Egyptians (per person) LE3, car LE3, overnight LE10; Membership for both Egyptians and foreigners: monthly LE50; annually LE300.**

Protect Wadi Digla: **Wadi Digla Protectorate is unique not only for its natural beauty and for its ecological importance but for the fact that it came into** being through community action: the Egyptian government responded favorably to community lobbying to protect this natural environment. There are challenges in the future to preserve this area from encroachment of the city. Dumping of garbage, burning of tires, and polluting industries pose a serious threat to this delicate desert wilderness. We need to regard the desert as a record of the world's evolution—natural and human alike.

What you can do to help: When visiting Wadi Digla, take a plastic bag to collect garbage. Respect the delicate ecological system.

The Tree Lovers Association (TLA)

The Tree Lovers Association, founded in 1973, is a non-governmental organization working with a vision to encourage the preservation and promotion of trees and nature conservation in Egypt. Its objectives are fulfilled by an action-oriented program of environmental awareness as well as campaigns to protect and promote natural resources in a sustainable manner for future generations. In 1997 the TLA gained active membership in the International Union for the Conservation of Nature based in Switzerland. The TLA has widened its scope since 1998 to support public initiatives for the establishment of protectorates. The declaration of Wadi Digla in June 1999 came as a result of these efforts. The association cooperates with academic institutions, local authorities, governmental agencies, the media and other non-governmental organizations which act for environmental and urban improvement.

The Tree Lovers Association has established Ezbet al-Ward public botanical garden to replace a rubbish dump in Basateen. An amphitheater allows the TLA to invite schools and institutions for informal environmental awareness programs and tree walks to identify 40 species of trees and plants. It is involved in the prevention of the destruction of around 5,000 Eucalyptus street trees in the governorates of Qualyoubia, Ismailia–Abbassiya Road, and Musturud Abu Zaabal Road in cooperation with the official authorities. It is responsible for the formation of the Wadi Digla Protectorate Management committee in collaboration with EEAA and academic institutions. The TLA has declared the sycamore tree as Maadi's official tree marking the 100th anniversary of Maadi on May 11, 2004. TLA is presently working to consider the sub-

urb as an urban man-made protectorate to safeguard its natural and architectural heritage.

Activities:	Annual Maadi tree walk, annual gardeners day, monthly lectures, environmental education and planting in schools, seasonal pruning of trees in streets, planting on squares, campaigns to implement building codes, protection of green spaces, protection of the Nile and its islands.
For more information:	Tel: 519-5240, 358-0099 or write to ZeitounS@aol.com; Tree Lovers Association, P.O. Box 592, Maadi, Cairo, Egypt.

Felucca Ride

On the Corniche, before the Grand Café Restaurant, there are two felucca docks. A sail in the late afternoon while the sun is setting is a sure remedy for any stressful day. Agree on a price per hour with the boatman and go out on the river for an hour or three. Most people add a tip at the end of the trip.

Studio 206

Got a dream? Studio 206 is testament that dreams can come true as long as the other ingredient is hard work. Noha Sayedalahl, founder and visionary of Studio 206, has experienced both, and with powerful results: a community cultural center for Egyptians (and foreigners). Studio 206's purpose and mission is to "develop individual creativity and expression," in the belief that in helping each person tap into their natural creative energy, all of society will experience an economic and spiritual awakening as a result. To promote creativity workshops are offered in fine art, design, crafts, dance, acting, cooking, and history. There are lectures and discussions in psychology, philosophy, comparative religion, education, alternative medicine, literature, history, fine art, social issues, and the environment, with the intention to enable exchange of ideas between members of the community. The showroom exhibits young talents as well as established artists. In addition, Studio 206 hosts and cooperates with other cultural groups such as Zakhareef, Pen Temple Pilots, Greenpeace, Care International, and Lions. Volunteer work constitutes an important objective. There are opportunities for volunteers at the charity art workshops for children in Beni Suef and Cairo, visiting orphans, and helping at the Sinai Art Festival.

Studio 206 is an artist-run cultural center where culture is defined according to E.B. Tylor's definition: "that complex whole which includes knowledge, belief, art, morals, law, custom, and any other capabilities and habits acquired by man as a member of society."

Where: Villa 14/18; Road 200, Digla Tel: 519-5713.
When: 10am–10pm daily except Friday.
Facilities: The venue for all activities is a beautiful 300-square-meter villa with three classrooms, a garden, library, cafeteria, crafts shop, and 24-hour security.
E-mail: noha@omeldonia.com
Discussion groups: *www.groups.yahoo.com/group/studio206*, *www.groups.yahoo.com/group/comparativereligion*, *www.groups.yahoo.com/group/Egypt_photographers*.

Community Services Association

The Community Services Association (CSA) is an international community center, which offers various classes, including exercise, cooking, and language classes, tours, counseling, support groups, and orientation for newcomers to Egypt. There is a complete Fitness Center, as well as a newly opened Serendipity Center for health and wellness. The second Monday of every month from 10am–12 noon is a free lecture in a Spotlight on Egypt series. There is a library with a large selection of books for both adults and children. A family membership is $20 a year, or LE equivalent. Every Wednesday at 11am there is a Children's Reading Hour for three to five year olds. There is a Book Lovers Meeting every second Wednesday from 1:30–3pm. CSA also has a café, gift shop, and small bookstore.

A newsletter is distributed on a monthly basis listing the classes. Children's classes are offered in art, yoga, pre-ballet and ballet, and taekwondo. The classes change, and many times special courses such as CPR are scheduled. Child psychologists are available through CSA at the Maadi Psychology Center, #16 Orabi Street (corner of Road 14), and an appointment can be made by calling 359-2278 or 010 657-0691 (mobile).

Where: **4 Road 21. Tel: 358-5284/0754, 768-8232.**
When: **9am–9pm Sunday through Wednesday; 9am–5pm Thursday. Closed Fridays. Library opens Sunday through Wednesday 9am–8pm, Thursday 9am–5pm. Closed Fridays. In the summer, hours are shorter.**
Web site: *www.livinginegypt.org*

Community Youth Soccer, Basketball, and Baseball Leagues

An opportunity for children and youth to learn a new skill or improve in their favorite sport, this community service is open to all. Some schools in Cairo also participate as teams, so ask the sports director at your school. Otherwise, look for the advertisements at the  Community Service Association or Cairo American College community relations office (755-5555). Registration for soccer is in late August; registration for basketball is in early November; registration for T-ball (beginning baseball) and baseball is in mid-January. The soccer and baseball leagues accept children from 6 to 14 years of age. The basketball league accepts children from 8 to 12. Teams consist of boys and girls of the same ages. Depending on the sport and age group, games are played at either Cairo American College or Victory College Field.

Victory College Field

Victory College Field is a haven for recreational opportunities. Sports such as soccer, rugby, cricket, and softball are open for anyone who wants to join the league. Also there is remote control auto racing, skate boarding, and a playground provide a chance to get outside and participate. Visit Community Service Association for more information or check their magazine for details.

Summer Enrichment Program at Cairo American College

Cairo American College (CAC) offers a summer program at the CAC campus in three two-week sessions. There is a Preschool Program for ages three to five, a Day Camp for ages six to eight and nine to eleven, as well as classes in a wide range of academic subjects and sports for ages six to eight, nine to eleven, twelve to fourteen, and fifteen and older. There is also a separate Soccer Camp for ages seven to twelve and twelve and up. Fees vary from $65 (ten-hour class) to $315 (seventy hours of preschool). See the website for information. A summer session brochure is put out in the spring, and a Summer Program office opens in early May.

Where: CAC, 1 Midan Digla.
Tel: 755-5555, fax: 519-6808,
or e-mail: summer@cacegypt.org
Web site: *www.cacegypt.org/summer/index.html*
When: Early June to early August.

Khayal Fine Arts Studio
Children and adults can take advantage of the art lessons and field trips. They also have a farm at Dahshour where children can see baby animals, bake bread, and participate in outdoor activities. For older children, teenagers, and adults there are sketching field trips to historical monuments and the Egyptian countryside.
Where: 5 Road 253, Digla, Maadi
Tel: 520-1615, 010 560-4020.
Web site: *www.khayalstudio.com*

Serafis Cultural Society
This group invites professionals to lecture about Egyptology, quantum physics, philosophy, and self-improvement. They offer cultural trips and seminars on health issues.
Where: 34 Road 218, Digla, Maadi. Tel: 521-2104
When: 6–9pm. Closed Thursdays, Fridays, and Saturdays.
Web site: *www.serafis.net*

Maadi Public Library–Integrated Care Society
A brand new, state-of-the-art library opened on July 1, 2002, to the delight of the Maadi community. Spacious, with opportunities galore to access the Internet, do computer work, and read, this library supports the arts, literature, and technology. There are reading, CD, audio-visual, periodical, and art rooms. An Internet café is connected to the cafeteria. The theater has its own entrance with the capacity for 210 people. All computer research can be done in Arabic as well as English.
Where: Al-Nasr St., New Maadi. There are signs throughout Maadi that lead to the library. Tel: 145-8457, 245-8457, 345-8457.
When: 9am–8pm. Closed Mondays.
Membership: For yearly subscription: LE50 for adults, LE25 for students. Bring passport with proof of residency or ID and two photographs.

Internet Café: LE2 for one hour use; pay in the lobby.
Computer Lessons: Call the library for all levels of lessons from
introduction to computers to Excel and Adobe
Photoshop.

Egyptian Geology Museum
The Egyptian Geology Museum offers the opportunity to study geology through the ages by focusing on Egypt. For those trying to gain an understanding of minerals, rocks and fossils, vertebrates and invertebrates, and the development of the earth through its geological phases, the museum helps to simplify and clarify things. A noteworthy point is that one can study millions of years of the earth's history from what has been discovered in Egypt. Science teachers throughout Cairo should take advantage and plan their geology lessons around a trip to this museum: to have such an excellent, well-organized museum available is a treasure indeed.

The Egyptian Geology Museum opened in 1904, in downtown Cairo in a building constructed specifically to exhibit geological specimens. There the exhibits remained until 1982, when the building was demolished during the construction of the Cairo Metro and the museum was transferred to its present site.

The exhibits begin as you enter the compound. Along the outside wall, ancient grinding tools and rocks from Egypt are on display. It is possible to touch and handle these tools, as well as examples of igneous and metamorphic rocks, mineral ores, and invertebrate fossils, all from Egypt. At the entrance of the museum, take a moment to survey the layout and orient yourself. There are three major galleries, with miscellaneous displays along the front and back walls. The gallery to the right displays invertebrate fossils, the central gallery contains vertebrate fossils, and the gallery to the left has minerals and rocks. Each gallery contains three long cases: one along each wall and one down the center.

As you enter on the right, there is a display of semiprecious stones. The raw stone prior to being polished is shown alongside the polished stone. Turquoise from Sinai, lapis lazuli, emerald from Wadi Dabba, jasper, garnet, agate, and opal are but a few. To the left, there is a case showing amber and how insects, air, slivers of wood or leaves are caught in the resin from coniferous trees, which then hardens over millions of years to become amber. There is also a collection of fossils that belonged to the family of Muhammad Ali.

Inside the door on the right is a large glass case containing parts of the fossil skeleton of *Paralititan stromeri*, the second largest dinosaur to ever walk the earth. Its discovery in Bahariya Oasis was announced in May 2001.

Paralititan stromeri lived about 99 million years ago, during the Late Cretaceous, in hot, wet mangrove swamps along the edge of the ancient Tethys Sea. This dinosaur was a plant-eating sauropod, more than eighty feet long and weighing perhaps as much as seventy tons.

Paralititan stromeri was discovered by a team from the University of Pennsylvania that went to Bahariya following up on the work of a little known German paleontologist, Ernest Stromer. He had discovered a number of dinosaur fossils in Bahariya in 1911, and had them shipped to Germany for study. The specimens and his work were destroyed in the bombing of Munich in April 1944.

The Invertebrate Gallery is where you will find the same fossils and petrified wood as you would when walking through many locations throughout Egypt. The displays of this gallery are divided into three themes: the stratigraphic sequence, which displays fossils from Cambrian to recent; Egyptian geology, which exhibits Egyptian stratigraphic sequence; and the classification of invertebrate organisms.

The majority of the fossils on display in the Vertebrate Gallery come from the Fayoum, which has rich fossil-filled sedimentary deposits from the Oligocene era, roughly 31 to 37 million years ago. Fossils of plants and water birds indicate that the Fayoum at that time had a freshwater swamp environment with tropical forests. There is a helpful geological model of the Fayoum in the center of the gallery.

Prominent in a standing case on the left is a fossil skeleton of Moerithium, a primitive elephant. On the right are cases with skulls belonging to Arsinoitherium, a double-horned early relative of the elephant. Behind them, along the wall on the right, are skeletal bones of Arsinoitherium. A geological model of the Fayoum is set up in the middle of the aisle. Beyond it are fossil shells of early Oligocene tortoises, and cases of fossilized fish.

Toward the back, in a standing case on the left, is a cast of a fossil skull from Aegyptopithecus, probably the most primitive ape yet discovered. It was found in 1966 in late Oligocene deposits in the Fayoum, and dates back about 32 million years. This animal was quite small, probably weighing about 6 kilograms, and monkey-like, with a long tail. Its teeth and jaw, however, are those of an ape. Aegyptopithecus is the oldest ape ancestor known; the next species in ape evolution is Proconsul, whose remains date to about 20 million years ago. There is a plaster cast of a Proconsul skull next to that of Aegyptopithecus in the case. Also in this case are casts of skulls of early hominids, or ancestors to modern humans: Australopithecus (who lived around three million years ago), Homo erectus (one million years ago), and also Neanderthal (55,000 years ago), now known to have been genetically distinct from the line leading to modern Homo sapiens. There are also stone tools, as well as a case of bone and horn tools from these early hominids. The vertebrate fossil collection is quite complete: there are even saber-tooth tiger skulls from the La Brea Tar Pits in Los Angeles in the last case against the wall on the left.

The Minerals and Rocks Gallery is the section farthest to the left from the entrance. Questions to ask are: What is a mineral? What is the difference between minerals and rocks? How are the differences identified? Begin with the two cases in the front, where a collection of minerals is classified according to physical properties, such as color, metallic luster, florescent character, transparency, hardness, cleavage, and streak character. Another section arranges minerals according to chemical composition: native elements, oxides, sulfides, halides, carbonates, sulfates, and phosphates. The minerals found in Egypt are divided according to area—Eastern Desert, Western Desert, and Sinai.

The rock specimens exemplify the three main groups of rocks—igneous, sedimentary, and metamorphic. Each group is subdivided: for example, sedimentary rocks are subdivided into clastic rocks (such as shale and sandstone) and nonclastic rocks (such as limestone and coal). Along the wall, you can compare minerals, rocks, and fossils found in Egypt from the Pre-Cambrian, Cambrian to Jurassic, and Recent periods.

Other cases worth studying are the meteorite collection and the gold collection, and a must-see are the ancient Egyptian artifacts and implements dating back to the late Paleolithic and Neolithic periods. In addition, you can see examples of the ores that the ancient Egyptians pulverized to make colorful paints to use on temple walls, which are still vivid today. For example, their red came from hematite or iron oxide, yellow from yellow ocher, green from malachite, and blue from azurite. Look for the moon rock from Taurus Littron Valley and the Egyptian flag carried to the moon by Apollo XVII.

Where: Agricultural Road. From Maadi to downtown on the Corniche, a large blue and yellow sign marks the entrance of the Egyptian Geological Museum. This is the entrance on the Corniche, but there is no parking on this busy street. Continue until you reach the roundabout. Turn right, and keep to your right. There is a sign that directs you to the Agricultural Road. Do not go onto the on-ramp, which is Zahraa St. Keep to the right and take the Agricultural Road. (If you continue on this road, you will end up in Maadi.) The sign on the gate reads "River Transport Authority": this is the other entrance to the museum. Coming from downtown Cairo, take a left at the roundabout next to the Crystal Nile Dinner Boats, and follow the remainder of the directions above. There is plenty of parking space. Tel: 524-0916/0917.

Metro: El Zahraa Station. The museum is about one block to the north.

When: 9am–2:30pm. Closed Thursdays and Fridays.

Entrance fee: Free.

Facilities: No stairs. There is a bathroom in the building next to the museum.

Guides: Geologists from each specialty of the museum are continually available for questions. They are most happy to give explanations and are pleased to be consulted. The librarians are very helpful as well.
There is a guidebook available: just ask.

Library: A library is open to all for research and reading. Books cover geology in Egypt and other parts of the world. If you are a lover of rare books, this is a haven. Just to whet your appetite, there is a 22-volume set written in 1887, *Memoirs of the Geological Survey of India*. The librarian complained that not one person had ever looked through them. Books, periodicals, and journals are in Arabic, English, Chinese, Japanese, French, Turkish, and other languages. There is a library of reference and research about geology in Egypt. Geological maps of all areas of Egypt are for sale.

Heliopolis and Matariya

M atariya—the original Heliopolis—is a very ancient city: Cairo by comparison is a mere youth. Of course, most people have long forgotten old Heliopolis, the ancient Egyptian city of On. The Greeks called it Heliopolis, meaning 'City of the Sun,' because it was the cult city of the sun god Re. Today, the only trace of the city that Plato visited and lived in is an obelisk erected by Senusret I almost four thousand years ago.

Memphis, on the west bank of the Nile, and Heliopolis, on the east bank, were the two major ancient Egyptian cities at the apex of the Delta. They flourished and survived for thousands of years, but when the Greeks built their new capital at Alexandria on the Mediterranean coast, the importance of both declined. The Greek geographer Strabo traveled to Heliopolis in 24 BC and wrote that the city was completely deserted: "I also saw large houses in which the priests lived; for it is said that this place in particular was in ancient times a settlement of priests who studied philosophy and astronomy; but both the organization and its pursuits have now disappeared. The houses of the priests and schools of Plato and Eudoxus were pointed out to us, for Eudoxus went up to that place with Plato [about 380 BC] and they both passed thirteen years with the priests as is stated by some writers."

When the Arab commander Amr ibn al-As arrived in Egypt in AD 640, he first camped on the plain of Heliopolis with 15,000 men. He defeated the Byzantine forces that marched out of the fortress of Babylon and when they retreated, he followed them, camped near the fortress, besieged it, and subsequently established his new city of al-Fustat nearby.

Heliopolis was to witness another major battle before it drifted into the footnotes of history: the battle between Napoleon's army and the Ottoman Turks occurred here in March 1800. Napoleon had left the army in the charge of General Kléber and returned to France. General Kléber successfully defeated the Ottoman offensive at Heliopolis, although he was assassinated three months later in Cairo.

In 1906, the name Heliopolis resurfaced, to become a familiar one to Cairenes. A Belgian industrialist, Baron Empain, established the Heliopolis Oasis Company with the intention of creating a new town in the desert area east of Matariya. It was a time when the influx of Europeans and British was at its height, and the Baron envisioned building a new city of the sun. He began by constructing his own grand residence—what is now known as the Baron's Palace. A few blocks from the Baron's Palace is the great Basilica: both were designed by the French architect Alexandre Marcel. The Baron Empain and his family are buried in the Basilica; the design is based on Istanbul's Aya Sofya.

Heliopolis, Matariya, and Medinat Nasr are often overlooked as areas with places of interest, but they have many sites that are worth investigation. We begin with the October War Panorama, which is closest to central Cairo, and end with the Obelisk in Matariya, following an approximate loop back toward central Cairo.

October War Panorama

Inside the well polished cylindrical building, tableaus depict some of the great battles fought in Egypt. The massive wall sculptures illustrate King Narmer's battle to unite Upper and Lower Egypt, Ahmose chasing the Hyksos out of Egypt in 1570 BC, the Battle of al-Mansura in AD 1250 when the Mamluk Prince Baybars al-Bunduqdari defeated the Crusaders, the Battle of Port Said in October 1956, and the Great Suez Crossing in 1973. Each tableau has an explanation beneath it in Arabic and English.

Up a winding and slippery staircase, there is seating arranged on a revolving platform that circles around a three-dimensional mural. Headphones are distributed before the program begins, if your language is not Arabic. The narrator describes the Egyptian victory at the Suez Canal after the storming of Israel's Bar Lev line. The narration pronounces the glorious 1973 victories over the Israeli occupation of Sinai. The show lasts about twenty minutes.

Downstairs and to the right is another auditorium in which authentic film footage of the 1967 and 1973 wars against Israel is shown. Afterward, an animated, three-dimensional diorama recreates the battle at the Suez Canal in 1973. The program lasts approximately twenty minutes. After the shows, you can go to the front of the museum and look at—and climb on—the authentic airplanes and tanks.

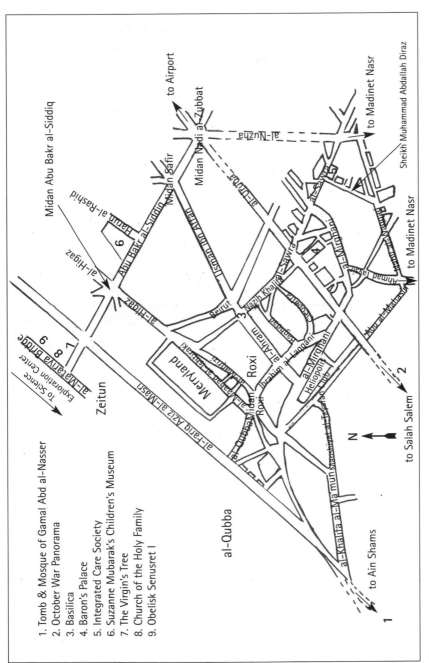

1. Tomb & Mosque of Gamal Abd al-Nasser
2. October War Panorama
3. Basilica
4. Baron's Palace
5. Integrated Care Society
6. Suzanne Mubarak's Children's Museum
7. The Virgin's Tree
8. Church of the Holy Family
9. Obelisk Senusret I

Heliopolis

Where: Salah Salim St. Coming from Central Cairo, turn right before the museum, which is clearly marked by the tanks and airplanes parked in front of the building. There is ample parking in the rear. Tel: 402-2317.

When: Morning programs: 9:30, 11, 12:30; evening programs: summer 6, 7:30; winter 5, 6:30. Closed Tuesdays.

Entrance fee: Foreigners LE20, Egyptians LE3. All children under 15 are admitted free. Admission is free on October 6.

Language: The program and film are both in Arabic. Headsets are available in English, Dutch, Spanish, and Japanese for the program, but there are no headsets for the film.

Facilities: Snacks are available. The bathrooms are clean.

Caution: Floors are well polished and slippery.

Library: A small reading library about the military and government is open to all; the titles are in Arabic.

Anwar al-Sadat's Memorial and Tomb of Unknown Soldier

In Madinat Nasr, on Tariq al-Nasr, just past the International Conference Center, a pyramid-shaped memorial commemorates the October victory of 1973. But the monument to Sadat's greatest triumph was also the scene of his assassination. In 1981, while sitting in the stands viewing a military parade here, he was attacked and killed. Although Sadat is buried in his village, Mit Abu al-Kom, the monument is a lasting dedication to his service to Egypt.

Anwar al-Sadat was born on December 25, 1918 to a poor family in the village of Mit Abu al-Kom in the Delta governorate of Minufiya. His father was Egyptian and his mother Sudanese. When he graduated from the Military Academy in 1938, he was posted near Alexandria, where he soon became involved in the Free Officers Movement, led by Gamal Abd al-Nasser. In the revolution of 1952, Sadat was the officer who announced the news of the revolution to the country over the radio. In 1970, when Nasser died, Anwar al-Sadat became president of Egypt.

Anwar al-Sadat inherited a demoralized Egypt struggling to overcome a weak economy, the loss of the 1967 war against Israel, growing corruption, and the breakdown of Pan-Arabism. Sadat began to reform the stagnant economy by reintroducing capitalism and encouraging foreign investment to revive the private sector. In 1971, he tried diplomatic negotiations to restore Sinai to Egypt and to settle the Palestinian refugee situation, but when that failed, Egypt and Syria attacked a surprised Israel on October 6, 1973. The Arabs viewed the invasion as an honorable victory, although Sinai and the Golan Heights were not regained. Ultimately, Sadat made an unprecedented trip to Israel in 1977 and offered peace for return of land captured in 1967, thus angering other Arab states. This led to US President Carter's invitation to Camp David, where a summit was held with the Israeli premier, Menachem Begin. The Egyptian–Israeli Peace Treaty of 1979 was the outcome.

The Baron's Palace

How many times have you passed this palace and wondered why it seems forgotten and desolate? The children ask if there are ghosts and want to know more. Unfortunately, the Baron's Palace is not open to the public, but you can stop and have a good look from outside the fence. In the spring of 2005, the Ministry of Housing replanted the garden. To celebrate, summer musical evenings gave some Cairenes the opportunity to enjoy the gardens.

Baron Palace

Baron-General Edouard Louis Joseph Empain, a Belgian-born industrialist, had the vision to construct a new city outside of Cairo, which he called Heliopolis. To promote the area, Baron Empain built his own palace in the undeveloped desert east of Matariya in 1907.

Alexandre Marcel, a French architect known for his exotic designs, was responsible for designing the Hindu-style exterior of the palace. The temples of Angkor in Cambodia particularly inspired Marcel. The grand exterior pagoda depicts Hindu gods, mythical creatures, elephants, gargoyles, goddesses playing musical instruments, and Buddha posed serenely in his lotus position. French designer Georges-Louis Claude, who had decorated the Oriental Pavilion at the Royal Palace of Laeken in Belgium with Alexandre Marcel, decorated the once sumptuous interior, now completely bare of furnishings.

One can only imagine the extravagance of the palace—massive gilded doors, elaborate ceilings, fresco murals. The garden surrounding the palace was wondrous: terraced and filled with exotic vegetation and marble statues, it greeted European royalty and Egypt's most influential rulers.

After the death of the baron in 1929, who is buried in his Byzantine-style basilica, three generations of Empains lived in the palace. Then it was sold in 1957 by foreign investors and is now the property of the Egyptian government, and home to an ever-growing family of bats. After half a century of deterioration, defacement, and no water for the gardens, this Hindu palace is but a rattling skeleton in its own desert, a treasured historic landmark crumbling amid gossip and ghosts.

Where: **Uruba St. and Ibn Battuta St., on the road to the airport before al-Sawra intersection.**

More information: *www.egypttoday.com* **(June 2005 back issue).**

Integrated Care Society

Founded by Suzanne Mubarak in 1977, the Integrated Care Society opened its doors to provide opportunities for children to explore and to challenge themselves through art, computer studies, dance, music, and cultural activities. The library is well stocked with books in Arabic and English. There are three computer labs providing ample space and a quiet environment for learning. Musical instruments and lessons are provided as well. Varied summer programs offer supervised activities from June to mid-September, and a change of programs occurs every two weeks. Registration begins in May.

Where: **Cultural Center Building, 42 Sawra (Abdallah Daraz intersection), Ard al-Golf. Tel: 417-2084/5/6/7/8, fax: 417-1787.**

When: **All summer programs for children. Winter programs for adults.**

Ages: **Groups are divided into 6–9 years and 10–15 years.**

Web site: *www.ics.org.eg*

Suzanne Mubarak Children's Museum

Opened on May 30, 1996, by Suzanne Mubarak, the patron of Egyptian children, this museum is dedicated to encouraging children to observe through interactive displays. The children begin their tour by walking through a botanical garden with plants and trees labeled with information about the species. Inside the museum, a television with nine screens displays images of Egyptian children and their environment. Next, an exposition of the ancient Egyptian civilization shows what it would have been like living during that time. There are interactive displays of irrigation techniques, agricultural supplies, garment manufacturing, writing hieroglyphics, and even a mechanical pyramid: press a button to answer the question, lift a lid, or feel the texture.

The tour continues through the River Nile Hall, the Desert Hall, and the Red Sea Hall. In each room children have the opportunity to observe the various regions, environments, and their problems. In the River Nile Hall, musical patterns and folksongs characterize three Egyptian communities: Nubia, Lower Egypt, and Upper Egypt. In the Desert Hall, children can touch a picture and see a short film on a particular desert animal. An explanation of Egypt's three deserts—Sinai, the Eastern Desert, and the Western Desert—and films about desert minerals, stones, and resources are most informative. They can also observe through a submarine the environs of the Red Sea: there is a discussion of the seriousness of a damaged sea environment and pollution. All labels are in easy-to-read Arabic, which lends itself well to a field trip for Arabic classes.

After the museum tour is over, there are more activities in the Discovery Hall, which involve identifying different elements such as fossils and stones. The Handicraft Hall and the Art Hall are next to the Discovery Hall. Drawing, painting, and weaving equipment are provided for experimentation. Next, the Information Hall contains CD-ROMs, video and tapes cassettes, and pictures in the fields of history, geography, the environment, and sciences.

Where: 34 Abu Bakr al-Siddiq St. Coming from Midan Nadi al-Zubbat, the next major crossroad is Harun al-Rashid. There is an enormous red sign at the entrance, which is difficult to see because of the trees. Tel: 639-9915, fax 632-6126.

When: 9am–2pm. Closed Mondays; open on national holidays.

Entrance fee: LE5. Children under two enter free.

Visits: Groups are guided through the museum at intervals, which allows plenty of time to see the exhibits without distractions. First, go to a tree-covered pavilion. There is a waiting area here, as well as a concession stand and toilets. Backpacks are checked outside the museum. Cellular telephones must be turned off. The tours take approximately an hour and a half.

Facilities: Sidewalks, ramps, and elevators facilitate movement throughout this museum.

Guides: Call ahead to request a guide who speaks English.

Parking: There is ample parking for cars and buses.

Tomb and Mosque of Gamal Abd al-Nasser

Gamal Abd al-Nasser died in 1970 after serving as Egypt's president for sixteen years. Nasser was born in Alexandria in 1918, though his family was originally from the Asyut governorate in Upper Egypt. He graduated from a prestigious secondary school, entered law school, and was then accepted in the Military Academy. The army commissioned him in 1938 and he fought in the war against Israel in 1948. An ardent nationalist, he organized the Free Officers movement, which overthrew King Farouk in 1952 and established Egypt as a republic.

Nasser's vision for Egypt confronted colonialism, transforming the government and the country in social revolution, which quickly took shape as the revolution focused on eliminating corruption in the government, promoting free education, better health care, and land reform. Nasser's policy of socialism nationalized industry and banking, and introduced price control and subsidization of commodities to bring about more economic equality between the social classes. He nationalized the Suez Canal, had the High Dam built at Aswan, and abandoned Egypt's claims on Sudan.

His vision for the Middle East was of Arab unity, which brought him adoration within the Arab masses. He forged a pact between Egypt and Syria in 1958, but by 1961 the union collapsed, which was a major setback for Pan-Arabism. Three years before Nasser's death, Egypt fought Israel in a new war and lost Sinai, which greatly demoralized the Egyptians, but they refused to let him step down, and he continued in office until his death in 1970.

Where: This memorial, which includes Nasser's tomb, a mosque, and a school is open to visitors. As you drive away from Midan Roxy in Heliopolis toward Ain Shams University on al-Khalifa al-Mamun St., the mosque/tomb is on the right. It is near a military complex, so photography outside the building is forbidden, but it is allowed within the gardens.

When: 9am–4pm every day.

Web site: *http://nasser.bibalex.org* (devoted to documenting the life and work of Nasser).

Book: *Nasser: His Life and Times* by Anne Alexander (AUC Press, 2005).
Parking: None. It is best to go by taxi or have a driver who can come back and collect you.
Tip: There is a box at the entrance of the tomb, where donations for the poor are welcome.
Bust of Nasser. Shawarbi Street, Downtown.

Al-Qubba Palace

Al-Qubba Palace is Egypt's official guest house for visiting heads of state. It was built by Khedive Mohammed Tewfik, who ruled Egypt from 1879 to 1892. In 1917, when King Fuad took the throne, al-Qubba Palace became the official residence of the royal family. It was also the main residence of King Farouk. The palace, hidden behind six-meter-high walls, has four hundred rooms, and is surrounded by seventy acres of gardens.

Suzanne Mubarak Science Exploration Center

This interactive science and technology center opened in the Hadayeq al-Qubba district in July 1998. The objective of the museum is to encourage children to explore science by providing them with opportunities to learn about theories of physics, space, and the environment through hands-on experiments.

Unfortunately, the center has not been maintained. Whereas this center was a favorite in past editions, at the time of writing it has not lived up to its potential.

Where: Near Nuqrashi Secondary School, at corner of al-Wafa St. and al-Safa wa-l-Marwa St., Hadayeq al-Qubba.
When: 9am–4:30pm. If you are an individual or family visiting the museum, it is better to go in the afternoon, when the school groups have left, or on Fridays.
Entrance fee: Free.
Organization: Guests and schools view the museum at intervals to allow maximum time for experiments. Displays and experiments are in Arabic and English.
Summer programs: Call for information: Tel: 257-0793, 259-7537; Fax: 453-4926.

Metro: The nearest Metro stop is Kobri El Kobba.
Parking: There is parking on the street near the museum.

Saad al-Khadem and Effat Nagui Museum

Except for Manal el-Jesri's article in *Egypt Today* (August, 2001, p. 28–30), it would be highly unlikely that this museum would appear here. In fact, this article was the first to notify us that such a museum exists. Not a well-known museum or in an easily accessed part of Cairo, it is unique in that the three-story villa filled with paintings by Saad al-Khadem and Effat Nagui has been bequeathed to the Egyptian people by its owners. Both husband and wife built a distinguished reputation in the world of Egyptian modern art. A trip to this museum is for the serious art student. Paintings are labeled in Arabic and English.

Where: 12 Karim St., off Selim al-Awwal St., Saray al-Qubba. Tel: 258-3703.
When: 10am–6pm. Closed Mondays.
Entrance fee: Free. You will be asked to leave an ID.
Metro: Saray al-Qubba Station.
Summer Program: In July and August, classes in folk art are offered to children. Call for the exact schedule.

The Virgin's Tree

The Holy Family fled from Palestine into Egypt to escape Herod, who had ordered Jesus killed. The story goes that here at Matariya the Virgin Mary, upon hearing Herod's soldiers approach, hid with the child beneath the branches of a magnificent balsam tree; the soldiers did not notice them and left. Another version of the story tells of a spider weaving its web like a curtain between the branches, hiding the Holy Family.

Since that time, the balsam tree died and a sycamore fig tree grew in its place, and it is this tree, estimated to be at least one hundred years old, that is now known as the Virgin's Tree, or Shagarat Maryam. In a nearby well, the water is said to have sprung up to Christ's touch when Mary needed water to wash his clothes. The water is believed to have healing properties.

Upon entering the walled-in area, you will find besides the tree and the well, a small museum with Coptic artifacts, a room with photographs of places in Egypt the Holy Family is believed to have traveled, and a souvenir shop.

Where: Follow al-Matariya St. past al-Qubba Palace (built by Ismail Pasha's son, Khedive Tewfik;

The Virgin's
Tree

this is Egypt's main guesthouse for visiting heads of state). Drive almost 2.5 kilometers, then turn right on the street before the Church of the Holy Family. The Matariya Tree is two blocks farther on. A visit to the Suzanne Mubarak Science Museum, the Virgin's Tree, and the Obelisk of Senusret I is possible in one day, as the sites are relatively near to one another. Or from al-Uruba/Salah Salim St. (coming from the direction of the airport), turn right onto Abu Bakr al-Siddiq St., follow it past Suzanne Mubarak Children's Museum (on right) over bridge and turn right onto Matariya Street.

When: 10am–4pm.
Entrance fee: Foreigners; LE12, residents LE6; Egyptians: LE2, students LE1.
Metro: El Matariya Station.
Parking: There is parking along the street.
Photography: No camera or video charge.
Facilities: Clean toilets but ask for the key.

Obelisk of Senusret I

This obelisk is the last standing part of the Heliopolis cult temple of Re, the sun god and preeminent deity of ancient Egypt. There is evidence for Re's cult at Heliopolis from at least the very beginning of the Old Kingdom, and it probably goes back even earlier. Re eclipsed and absorbed Atum, the original god of Heliopolis, the creator god, who was born at Heliopolis out of the waters of chaos. The family of gods that Re/Atum first created is called the Heliopolitan Ennead (from the Greek word for 'nine,' as there were nine gods in the family). Atum is thought of as an old man, while Re is the sun at its prime.

Sun god Re

Obelisk of Senusret I

The obelisk was one of a pair set up at the doorway of the temple of Re built by King Senusret I, the second king of the Twelfth Dynasty, in approximately 1940 BC. It is cut out of a block of pink Aswan granite, and is about 22 meters high and weighs 120 tons. On each side of the obelisk is an identical hieroglyphic inscription giving the five names of the king, and stating that he set up this obelisk as part of the celebration of his *heb-sed*, a festival carried out after the king had reigned for thirty years. The inscription reads: "Horus (Long) Live the Renaissance, King of Upper and Lower Egypt Kheper-ka-re, Two Ladies (Long) Live the Renaissance, Son of Re Senusret, Beloved of the Souls of Heliopolis, given life forever. Horus of Gold (Long) Live the Renaissance, the good god Kheper-ka-re. First Occasion of the Heb-Sed. He made (it) to be given life forever."

The ancient cult site of Heliopolis was roughly square in shape, measuring about 1,000 meters on each side. Large mudbrick walls, 13 meters wide

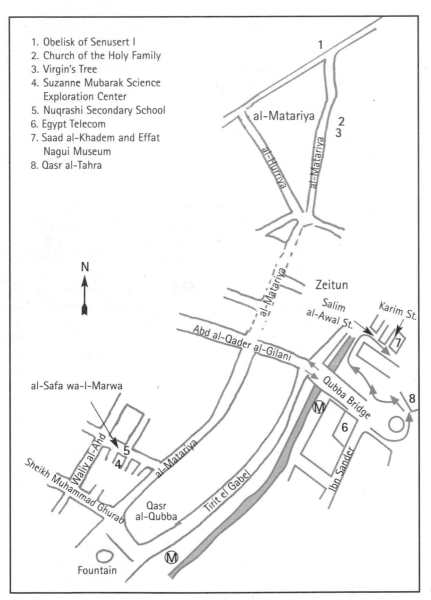

1. Obelisk of Senusert I
2. Church of the Holy Family
3. Virgin's Tree
4. Suzanne Mubarak Science Exploration Center
5. Nuqrashi Secondary School
6. Egypt Telecom
7. Saad al-Khadem and Effat Nagui Museum
8. Qasr al-Tahra

N

al-Matariya

Zeitun

Salim al-Awal St.

Karim St.

Abd al-Qader al-Gilani

al-Safa wa-l-Marwa

Qubba Bridge

Sheikh Muhammad Ghurab

Waliv al-Ahd

al-Matariya

Tirit el Gabel

Ibn Sander

Qasr al-Qubba

Fountain

Matariya

and at least 5 meters high, surrounded the sacred area. There was one gateway in the east and another one opposite in the west. Aligned between these two gates was the temple, containing numerous altars for offering to the sun. Also, there was the sacred *benben* stone, in the shape of a squat obelisk, sym-

The Heliopolitan Ennead

Re/Atum created the first male/female pair, Shu, the god of air, and Tefnut, the goddess of moisture. They created the earth god Geb and the sky goddess Nut. These two then created the god Osiris and his sister/wife Isis, whose son Horus ultimately became king of Egypt. Every human king of Egypt was considered to be an incarnation of Horus, and thus the descendent of the sun god. This divine ancestry of the king provided the most important basis for his unquestioned power in ancient Egypt. Re also provided the king with the assurance of an afterlife. Just as the sun dies each night when it sets, but is born again the next morning, the king will always be born again after death.

Atum

bolic of the mound on which Atum/Re first appeared. The obelisk that you see was erected on the right side of the temple entrance. There was a matching obelisk on the left side, which apparently fell down in AD 1158.

After the Ptolemies built the city of Alexandria as their capital and cult center, the importance of Heliopolis waned. Many monuments were taken from the temple to Alexandria, including two obelisks of Tuthmosis III of the Eighteenth Dynasty, one of which ended up in New York's Central Park and the other on the bank of the Thames in London. When the Greek geographer Strabo visited Heliopolis in 24 BC, the ancient city was virtually deserted. As you enter, there are inscribed architectural blocks on the ground, as well as an anthropoid, or human-shaped, clay coffin. Clay coffins were very common in ancient Egypt, but rarely is one displayed. On the left, there are two nicely preserved false doors, now set in glass cases. Beyond them are other ancient pieces, sadly some of them are submerged in ground water. The park around the obelisk is very pleasant and has sitting areas. If you have questions, ask the antiquities inspector at the booth inside the gate on the left.

Where: From the Virgin's Tree on al-Matariya St. pass through Midan al-Misalla and continue on. When you are parallel with the obelisk turn left. If you need directions, ask for *al-misalla*, meaning 'the obelisk.'

When: 8am–5pm every day.

Entrance fee: Foreigners: LE12, residents and foreign students LE6; Egyptians: LE1, Egyptian students 50 piasters. (You could just look at

the obelisk from the gate without buying
a ticket.)

Photography: No camera charge.

Obelisk at EgyptAir Terminal

Going to or from the EgyptAir terminal at Cairo Airport you can see Cairo's
third obelisk. Like the Gezira obelisk, it was originally set up by King Ramesses
II as one of a pair at his royal city in the Delta, Per-Ramesses. Later in the
Twenty-first Dynasty, the obelisk was taken to the site of Tanis, and set up
along the approach axis of the great temple of Amun. When the obelisk was
found, it had fallen and broken into two. You can clearly see where it has been
mended. The obelisk is made of Aswan granite and stands approximately fifty
feet high.

On each side of the tip of the obelisk Ramesses II offers to a deity, and a
similar scene appears on each side at the bottom of the obelisk's shaft. All the
sides of the obelisk have a vertical hieroglyphic inscription. One side of the
obelisk has the king's full set of five names, while the other three sides have
three of his names and then reference to his victories over foreign countries.

Web site: *www.pbs.org/wgbh/nova/lostempires/obelisk*
(how ancient Egyptians shaped, transported,
and erected obelisks).

The Pyramids at Giza and Saqqara

No exploration of Cairo would be complete without a visit to the famous pyramids at Giza and Saqqara, although they are outside the confines of the city proper. These pyramids date to the period called the Old Kingdom, approximately 2686 to 2160 BC, encompassing the Third to the Sixth dynasties. At this time the ancient Egyptian king lived in and ruled from the city of Memphis on the west bank of the Nile, roughly opposite Maadi. The foundation of Memphis as the capital of ancient Egypt was the beginning of

The Giza Pyramids—left to right: Menkaure, Khafre, Khufu

pharaonic history. Although in later times the king did not always live there, or locate his burial nearby, Memphis remained the capital city of Egypt until the Ptolemies built Alexandria.

Since the Giza pyramid complex is closer to Cairo, and is one of the Seven Wonders of the World, perhaps this is the best site for children to visit first. There are other pyramid fields, such as Abu Sir and Dahshur, and other monuments at Giza and Saqqara other than those described below. This chapter is meant only to serve as an introduction to the pyramid sites and present children with a small, selected number of the most important monuments.

Remember to prepare for a rough and rugged day when you go out to the pyramid sites. Have good, sturdy, closed walking shoes. Long trousers are best even in the summer to avoid scraped knees. In the summer, have a hat, sunglasses, sun lotion, and lots of water. In the winter, be sure to have a good coat, and even take along a woolen hat; the desert can be extremely cold and windy. There are usually vendors with cold drinks at both sites, particularly in the summer. Both sites have minimal bathroom facilities.

Who Built the Pyramids?

Egyptian peasants paid their taxes to the crown by performing labor for the king. Since the majority of the ancient Egyptian population were peasants, a vast labor force was at the king's disposal. Particularly in the late summer and fall when farmland was covered by the inundation, a large segment of the population was free to work in pyramid construction. These workers lived in settlements near the pyramid, and were fed and clothed at the crown's expense.

The Giza Pyramids

Giza is a one-period site. All the most important monuments here date from the Fourth Dynasty, roughly 2600 to 2500 BC. Specifically, the three main pyramids at Giza date to the reigns of three kings: Khufu, Khafre, and Menkaure. (You may run across the Greek forms of these names—Cheops, Chephren, and Mycerinus.) Khufu built the Great Pyramid, his son Khafre built the second pyramid, and Khafre's son, Menkaure, built the third pyramid.

Each pyramid at Giza was part of a building complex with set structures. A valley temple, built at the edge of cultivation, served as the entrance, and was used for part of the funeral rites. A closed corridor, called a causeway, led from the valley temple to the mortuary temple, which was built against the east face of the pyramid. A corridor entered the pyramid on the north face. After the king was buried, the pyramid was sealed, but each day priests went into

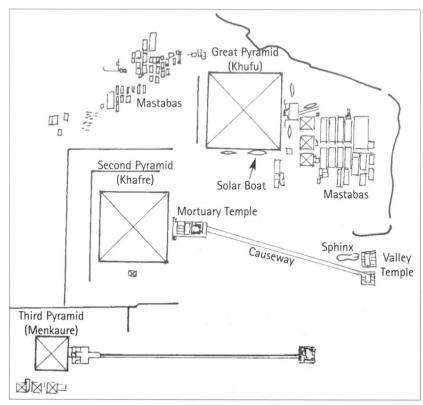

The Giza Pyramids (after Hart, 1991)

the mortuary temple to offer provisions for the king's soul, or *ka*. Other elements were sometimes added to this complex: smaller pyramids for queens, a small symbolic pyramid on the south side, pits for boat burials, and mastaba tombs for relatives and officials of the king.

In the early Fourth Dynasty, the form of the royal burial site changed from the step pyramid complex, like the one you can visit at Saqqara, to a complex with a true pyramid, with smooth sides. This change in shape reflects a shift to the importance of the sun and the solar cult in the religious beliefs on which the afterlife of the king was based. While a step pyramid served as a 'staircase,' a true pyramid was a 'sun-ray ramp' for the king's ascension to heaven. The sides of the pyramid are likened to sun rays in one of the Pyramid Texts: "Heaven has made the sun rays hardened for you that you may ascend to heaven." The various structures in a true pyramid complex are aligned on an east–west axis, following the course of the sun's rising and setting.

Where: **At the end of Pyramid Rd. (Sharia al-Haram), on the plateau past the Mena House Hotel.**

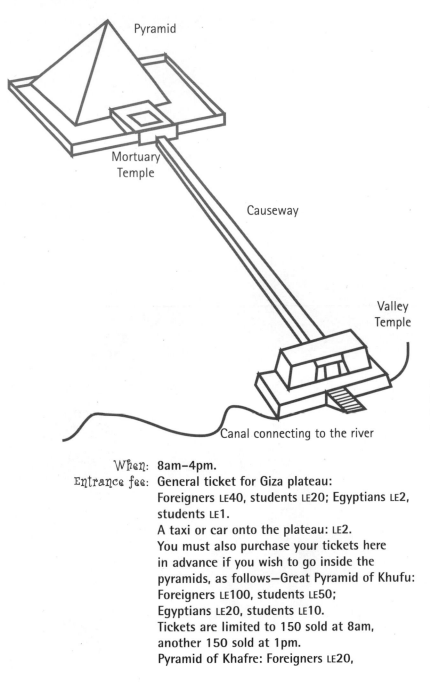

Plan of a Pyramid Complex (after Mendelssohn, 1976)

When: 8am–4pm.
Entrance fee: General ticket for Giza plateau:
Foreigners LE40, students LE20; Egyptians LE2,
students LE1.
A taxi or car onto the plateau: LE2.
You must also purchase your tickets here
in advance if you wish to go inside the
pyramids, as follows—Great Pyramid of Khufu:
Foreigners LE100, students LE50;
Egyptians LE20, students LE10.
Tickets are limited to 150 sold at 8am,
another 150 sold at 1pm.
Pyramid of Khafre: Foreigners LE20,

The Giza Pyramids: Khufu, with Khafre around the corner

students LE10; Egyptians LE2, students LE1.
Pyramid of Menkaure closed in Fall 2005.

Photography: Allowed outdoors only. Forbidden inside pyramids and tombs.

Web site: *www.gizapyramids.org/code/emuseum.asp* (a Giza archives project).

How Were the Pyramids Constructed?

The location of a pyramid needed to be chosen carefully. The pyramid had to be built on a good outcropping of rock so that as much stone as possible could be quarried right at the pyramid site. Much of the bottom part of the Great Pyramid is actually solid bedrock, which saved quarrying and dragging many blocks of stone. As the pyramid grew, ramps were used to drag blocks up and put them in place. Rather than being straight ramps, they probably wrapped around the pyramid. At the completion of the pyramid, it was cased from top to bottom in white Tura limestone (sometimes red Aswan granite for the lower courses), the ramps being removed as the casing blocks were put in place. The very tip of the pyramid, the pyramidion, was sometimes covered with gold.

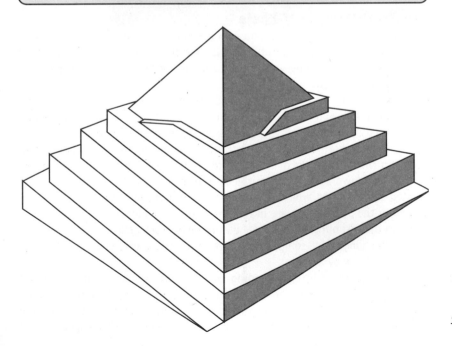

Pyramid with construction ramps (after Siliotti, 1997)

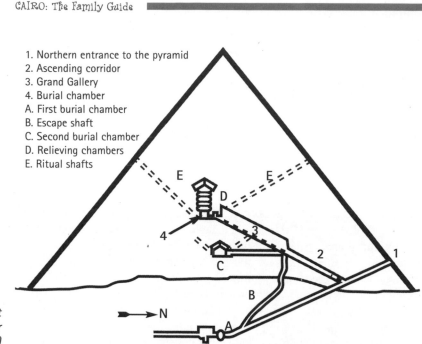

1. Northern entrance to the pyramid
2. Ascending corridor
3. Grand Gallery
4. Burial chamber
A. First burial chamber
B. Escape shaft
C. Second burial chamber
D. Relieving chambers
E. Ritual shafts

The Great Pyramid (after Hart, 1991)

The Great Pyramid of Khufu

The Great Pyramid originally stood 156 meters high when it was completed, and its base covered an area of five and a quarter hectares. It is estimated that 2,300,000 blocks of stone were used to build the pyramid, and on average, each block weighs two and a half tons.

The parts of the pyramid that you will see inside are marked with numbers on the plan, followed by an explanation. Other parts of the pyramid included in the discussion but which you cannot see are marked with letters.

1: This is the northern entrance into the pyramid. You must be very careful going up the huge blocks of stone on the outside of the pyramid, and especially going down again after your visit. Before you begin, notice the smooth, slanted casing blocks, which remain at the very bottom of the pyramid. Once you enter the pyramid you are in the descending corridor that originally went down to the first burial chamber (A) cut in the bedrock below the pyramid. The plan was changed for some reason, and a second burial chamber (C) built higher up in the pyramid.

2: You connect with the ascending corridor, which leads to the horizontal corridor and into the second burial chamber (C). The plan of the pyramid changed again, and this burial chamber was also not utilized. This is probably the hardest section of the climb, as you are bent over in a small space, going up at a steep angle. Note that at the junction of **1** and **2**, there are still plugging (or portcullis) blocks in place.

3: The Grand Gallery is unique: you will not see its like in any other pyramid. The theory is that this space was created to store the plugging blocks that would be slid into the ascending corridor to close it. The workers who did this escaped through shaft **B**, and out of the pyramid through the descending corridor **1**. Then this corridor was plugged with blocks from the outside. Contrary to Hollywood movies, workers were not left in the pyramid to die! Note the cuts around the bottom of the Grand Gallery walls: these were for wooden scaffolding that held the plugging blocks up near the ceiling of the gallery. Notice the use of corbeling to close the ceiling—placing blocks closer and closer together until a roof is formed.

4: You enter the burial chamber through a small antechamber. The chamber is lined with red Aswan granite, and the sarcophagus is of red granite as well. Above the ceiling, a series of small rooms (**D**) helps reduce the enormous weight of the pyramid structure above. Graffiti found on the blocks of the small rooms mention the year 19 of the reign of King Khufu, so it must have taken that many years to build the pyramid up to this point. In both the north and south walls of the burial chamber you can see a 20-centimeter opening (**E**). These were ritual shafts for the king's soul to ascend to heaven. The northern shaft was aligned with the North Star, the southern shaft with the stars of Orion's belt.

After leaving the Great Pyramid, go around to the south side to visit the Solar Boat Museum. Along the way, the ruins of the mortuary temple are on the east side of the pyramid, and the small queens' pyramids are at the southeast corner.

The Solar Boat Museum

In the 1920s, three boat-shaped pits were found near the mortuary temple of King Khufu. Except for fragments of gilded wood and pieces of rope, they were empty. Two rectangular pits discovered on the south side of the pyramid in 1954, however, revealed (in the easternmost pit) the boat that is on display in this museum. The sealed, airtight pit had preserved the wood of this beautiful boat, which had been dismantled and laid out in pieces; it has been reassembled in this museum. A special probe was put into the second pit in 1987, revealing that it also contains a boat, but the pit has yet to be opened.

Upon entering the museum, you will be requested to cover your shoes. First, you will see the pit in which the boat was discovered, and then you go upstairs to a circular ramp to walk around the boat, which is simply stunning.

The flat-bottomed boat has no keel. The planks of the hull are fourteen centimeters thick, joined by pegs and ropes that run through the planking. From

The solar boat

the top ramp, when you are level with the boat, you can see these ropes. There are five rowing oars one each side, and a steering oar on each side of the keel. A large state boat like this, however, was actually towed by smaller boats, as illustrated in numerous tomb scenes. There is a deckhouse on the foredeck made of wooden screens with poles to hold up an awning. This is where the captain of the boat stood. A watermark on the hull seems to indicate that the boat was used at least once. A theory is that this boat brought the king's mummy from Memphis.

The boat is now called the solar boat, although this may be a misnomer because scholars are not sure exactly what function this boat had. Generally, there were five boat pits placed around a pyramid. Three boats were for the three pilgrimages the deceased was to make to the old cities of Sais and Buto in the Delta and Abydos, the cult center of Osiris, in Upper Egypt. The other two boats were for the king to accompany the sun god: one boat to cross the sky by day and the other to traverse the underworld by night.

Entrance fee: **Foreigners LE20, students LE10; all Egyptians LE2. These fees are in addition to the general entrance fee you paid to go onto the Plateau.**

When you leave the Solar Boat Museum, go straight down the road between the Great Pyramid of Khufu and the second pyramid of Khafre, arriving at the valley temple of Khafre's pyramid and the Sphinx. Go into the valley temple and then after your visit, the Sphinx is in close view.

The Valley Temple of the Pyramid of Khafre

This valley temple is one of the best preserved in Egypt, and will give you a good idea of what a valley temple and the adjoining causeway were like. When this temple was built, it was right at the edge of cultivation and reached by a canal. It was built of limestone blocks quarried right here in Giza, and then cased with blocks of Aswan granite. This outside casing has been lost, thus causing the rather sad appearance of the temple exterior.

Inside the temple, the walls and pillars are of granite, and the floor is of alabaster. Enter the vestibule before the main pillared hall. The famous seated statue of King Khafre and the falcon, which is now in the Cairo Museum, was found in the square pit in the floor. It is thought that at some point the temple priests buried it for safekeeping. It is the only statue remaining of the twenty-three statues of the king that originally stood in the pillared hall. Notice the rectangular cuts in the floor around the walls in the pillared hall. Each one held a statue of the king, used in a funeral ritual called the 'Opening of the Mouth': on each statue, a different part of the king's body was touched with a different implement, so that he could function again in the afterlife. This ritual derives its name from the fact that the first part involved touching the mouth with an adze—a carpenter's tool—tipped with meteoritic iron. This enabled the deceased to speak and eat again.

After these funeral rituals were completed, the king's body was carried out the back door of the valley temple (on the right side) and up the causeway to the mortuary temple. You can walk a short way up the causeway and get an idea of what it was like. When complete, the causeway was roofed with stone slabs. Narrow, horizontal slits at the top of the walls emitted just enough indirect light to be able to see. You can see these same slits at the top of some of the blocks in the valley temple, which was also roofed with stone blocks. The interior walls of the causeway were carved with relief scenes of the king and deities.

Outside the temple, on the north side of the causeway, sits the Sphinx.

The Sphinx

The Sphinx is a colossal representation of King Khafre. It is twenty meters high and fifty-seven meters long. On its head is the *nemes*, the royal headcloth, and originally it had a uraeus, a rearing cobra, above the forehead. The Sphinx also wore the ritual beard of the king, portions of which are now in the British Museum in London and the Egyptian Museum in Cairo. The king was often portrayed as a lion in ancient Egyptian art, for the lion represents dominance and power. In this way, King Khafre, positioned next to his valley temple, not only guarded the necropolis, but facing the east greeted his divine father, the sun, as he rose each day.

The Sphinx and the Great Pyramid

The Sphinx is carved out of an outcropping of bedrock left in the area quarried for stone blocks to build the valley temple. The stone of the head is of much better quality than the stone of the body, which is why the head is better preserved.

Between the forelegs of the Sphinx is the 'Dream Stela' of King Tuthmose IV of the Eighteenth Dynasty, dating to about 1400 BC. When Tuthmose was a young prince riding in the desert, he became hot and fell asleep in the shadow of the Sphinx. He had a dream in which the Sphinx spoke to him and said that if he cleared away the hot sand pressing against the Sphinx, the Sphinx would reward him by making him the next king of Egypt. The text on the stela says that the prince remembered the dream when he awoke and had the sand cleared away. Later Tuthmose IV did become king of Egypt—but it helped that his older brother, the crown prince, died!

Saqqara

Saqqara is on the desert plateau just west of the site of the ancient city of Memphis. Because of its proximity to the capital city, Saqqara was the most important necropolis in the Memphite area. High officials of the king had their tombs built here beginning in the First Dynasty, and the site was used extensively for private tombs in the Old and New Kingdoms. During the Third, Fifth, and Sixth dynasties, the kings of Egypt built their pyramids at Saqqara.

The name Saqqara comes from the name of the hawk-headed deity of fertility and agriculture, Sokar, whose cult was based at Memphis. Another divine animal important at Saqqara was the Apis Bull, the animal incarnation of the

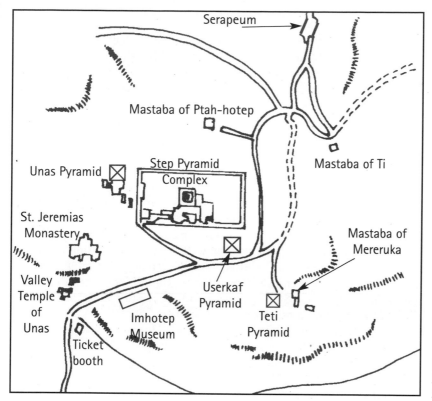

Map of Saqqara (after Siliotti, 1997)

god Ptah of Memphis. When each incarnation of the Apis died, it was buried in a special catacomb at Saqqara known as the Serapeum.

Where: Roughly 20 kilometers south of Giza. From al-Haram Road take the Harraniya–Saqqara Road. Turn right at the Saqqara sign and continue straight ahead until the ticket booth, where the farm land ends and the plateau begins.

When: 8am–4pm.

Entrance fee: Foreigners LE35, students LE20; Egyptians LE2. General ticket includes everything at the site. Taxi or private car LE2.

Photography: No photography allowed inside tombs.

Web sites: *www.ancient-egypt.org/saqqara* and *http://france.strabon.org/louvre* (database of Saqqara site and collections).

The Imhotep Museum

Immediately after the ticket booth at Saqqara, turn right into the parking lot of the Imhotep Museum. Newly opened in April 2006, the Imhotep is the first of many planned regional site museums. It is a gem! On display are monuments excavated at Saqqara but never displayed before. Seated around a scale model of the Step Pyramid Complex, your visit begins with a short video in the Visual Setting Hall, after which you proceed into the museum.

The museum is relatively small and the pieces beautifully displayed. There are two large halls in a row, and each of these has a smaller room off on the left and right. The two large halls are devoted to Imhotep and the Step Pyramid Complex, while the other four rooms each have a separate theme.

The centerpiece in the first large hall is the base of a statue of King Djoser that honored Imhotep by having his name and titles inscribed on the base. Just inside the door against the wall in the second large room is a famous bronze statuette of Imhotep holding a papyrus roll on his lap. The most interesting piece in this second room is a tall, boundary stone that had been set up at the Step Pyramid enclosure. Notice the snakes on the side that would have protected the sacred area.

To the right of the first large room is Saqqara Monuments, which displays the most recent finds from excavations, including the Golden Mummy. Across on the left side of the large room is the Lauer Library, with a display of the personal effects of Jean-François Lauer, the French architect who spent his life working at Saqqara.

To the right of the second large room is a room named Saqqara Styles, which exhibits wood and stone statuary from private tombs at Saqqara and the tools that were used to produce them. The statues, particularly those from the mastaba of Ptah-hotep, are masterpieces. In the room called Saqqara Tombs, on the left, are funerary pieces from both royal and non-royal tombs. At the far end of the room is the mummy of King Merenra I of the Sixth Dynasty, the oldest royal mummy known from ancient Egypt. It was found by Auguste Mariette in 1881, and has been languishing ever since in the basement of the Egyptian Museum. Mariette's handwritten card describing 'the find' can be seen in the very front of the case.

When: Museum hours are daily 9am–4pm.

Tickets: Foreigners LE15, students LE10; Egyptians LE2, students LE1.

Facilities: Cafeteria, gift-shop and bathrooms.

The Step Pyramid at Saqqara

The Step Pyramid Complex

The Step Pyramid Complex was built to house the burial and funerary cult of King Djoser of the Third Dynasty. The Step Pyramid is the first and oldest ancient Egyptian pyramid, although it is stepped, not a 'true' pyramid with smooth sides. The Step Pyramid complex is also the world's first architectural monument constructed entirely in stone, dating to approximately 2780 BC. The actual building of the complex is attributed to the official Imhotep, who was vizier (next in command under the king) and held the title 'Chief of all the Works.' In later pharaonic times, Imhotep was deified as a sage and physician.

The complex was built of local limestone and then faced with the high quality limestone quarried at Tura, across the river. It is in the shape of a large rectangle, and the perimeter of the enclosure walls measures almost two kilometers. The exterior of the walls is decorated in the *serekh*, or niched-façade, style that imitated the walls of the king's palace as well as a ceremonial enclosure known as the 'Fortress of the Gods.' These structures were built of mud brick and the recessed paneling is a stylized attempt to reproduce in brick a primitive structure made from reed matting.

The Step Pyramid, rising above all the other buildings, dominates the entire complex. The other structures are either tied to the funerary cult of the king (such as the mortuary temple and the South Tomb) or else were built for a symbolic reenactment of the Heb-Sed Festival. This festival was held to renew a king's reign after he had ruled for thirty years. The actual Heb-Sed Festival would have been celebrated at Memphis; these Heb-Sed structures were placed in Djoser's mortuary complex so that symbolically, for eternity, he could renew his kingship.

Excavation of the complex began in 1924, and from 1926 until his death in 2001, just a day after his ninety-ninth birthday, French architect Jean-Phillippe Lauer was in charge of its restoration. A section of each part of the complex has been restored as authentically as possible. Ancient blocks are fitted back together; when one is missing, a new block is quarried at Tura, cut with the same types of copper tools that were used by the ancient Egyptians.

In the text that follows, details are given about each place marked on the map.

1: The only entrance into the complex is in the southeast corner of the enclosure wall. Go in and walk down a long corridor lined with engaged, fluted columns. These columns are carved to imitate the bundled reeds that would have been used as building material before construction with stone. The ceiling of the corridor is carved to imitate a ceiling made of palm logs, such as an early pre-stone building would have had. Look at the size of the limestone

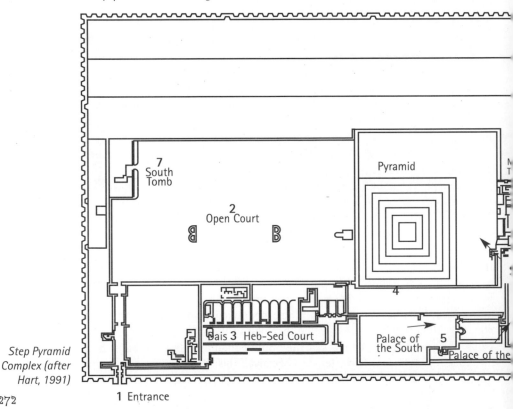

Step Pyramid Complex (after Hart, 1991)

blocks used in this building: they were cut to the same size as mud bricks. Having never built with stone, the builders cut the stone the same size as the bricks with which they normally built. The end of the corridor opens onto the large court in the center of the complex.

2: Originally, two large B-shaped stones were placed at either end of the eastern half of this court. They were symbolic boundary stones, and each half of one B-shape represented one of the four corners of Egypt. As part of the Heb-Sed Festival, the king ran around these stones holding a roll of papyrus

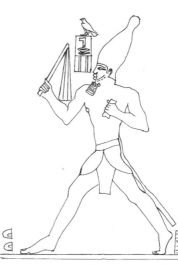

King Djoser running in the Heb-Sed

in his hand. The papyrus represented a will, stating his inheritance handed down by the gods. As the king ran, he proclaimed that he had taken possession of his inheritance, which was the land of Egypt.

3: Walking across the open court toward the pyramid, turn right and enter the Heb-Sed court on the eastern side of the enclosure. For the occasion of the Heb-Sed, the main deities of Upper and Lower Egypt would be brought to Memphis from their various temples and housed in shrines along the two sides of a court like this, called the 'Court of the Great Ones.' In the south end of the court is a square stone dais on which the thrones of Upper and Lower Egypt were placed back to back. First, the king would visit the deities in their shrines and give them the appropriate offerings. Then the gods would

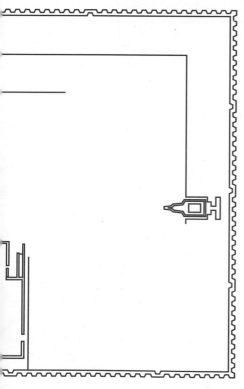

witness him being crowned, once with the White Crown of Upper Egypt, and once with the Red Crown of Lower Egypt. Note the unfinished standing statues of Djoser against the southeast wall of the court—see how chunky and heavy the style of these early pieces is.

4: Leaving from the north end of the Heb-Sed court, stop at the side of the pyramid. So much of the casing and inner blocks of the pyramid have fallen away at this point that it is possible to see its inner construction. The innermost core is a square mastaba covering the large shaft leading down to the burial chamber. For some reason, this mastaba was extended about three meters on each side. Then an addition was made on the east side to cover the openings of eleven shafts dug to bury members of the royal family. After this, the transformation of the mastaba into a four-step pyramid was begun, but before this work was completed, the plan was changed again to make a six-step pyramid. When complete, the pyramid was 60 meters high, and had a base of 140 by 118 meters. The reason for constructing a stepped pyramid is not clear, although it may well have been religious. Several of the religious spells in the Pyramid Texts mention "a stairway has been constructed for you [the king], that you may ascend to heaven."

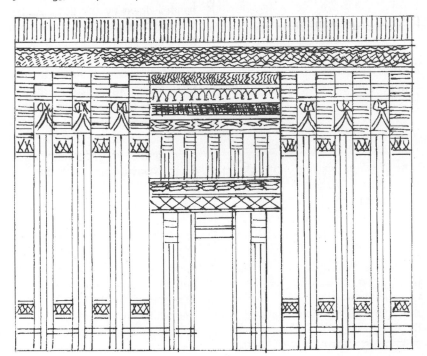

Serekh-façade decoration

*The façade of
the Palace of
the South*

Why Monuments Need to "Rest"

You might want to visit a tomb or pyramid at Saqqara or Giza that has been closed. This is because the monument needs to rest and recover from tourists! Each person who goes into a monument exhales and perspires between one-half and two cups of water moisture every hour. Depending on the weather, interior ventilation, and how long how many people visit a monument, several gallons of water can be left behind. This moisture can cause ancient paint to flake off, plaster to crumble, and even chunks of stone to break away.

5: Continue walking north and you will see on your right the partially reconstructed façades of two buildings. These are called the Palace of the South and the Palace of the North; it is possible that they symbolize two very early cult shrines. The façade of the Palace of the South has fluted columns and a decorative band called a *heker*-frieze running along the top. Inside on the walls are graffiti in black ink left by ancient Egyptian tourists of the New Kingdom, about 3,500 years ago. Note the very stylized handwriting in the cursive form of hieroglyphs called hieratic. One graffito dating to the Eighteenth Dynasty reads: "The scribe Ahmose came to see the Temple of Djoser. He found it as if heaven was in its midst, as if Re was rising in it. He [Ahmose] says: May all good and pure things come from heaven for the soul of Djoser, deceased, may heaven rain fresh myrrh, may it drip incense."

6: Turn to the west and walk over to the mortuary complex on the north side of the pyramid. Just before the mortuary temple, you will come to the *serdab*, a small, enclosed room containing a statue of King Djoser. (The statue in place now is actually a plaster copy—the original is in the Cairo Museum.) The two small, round holes that you peer into were to allow the *ka* (the soul of the king, which inhabited the statue) to see, hear, and smell the ritual offerings made for him in his afterlife. The mortuary temple is badly ruined. The large hole in the ground is the descending corridor down to the burial chamber under the pyramid. This corridor was used when the mummy of the king was carried into the pyramid to be buried. Excavators found nothing in the burial chamber; thieves had stolen the king's mummy. The direction of north had religious meaning for the ancient Egyptians, and spells of the Pyramid Texts mention the king joining the North Star. This explains why the mortuary temple was placed on the north side of Djoser's pyramid, and the entrance corridor into the pyramid on the north as well. Even in later pyramids, when the mortuary temple shifts to the east side, the pyramid entrance remains on the north. At this point, you have almost finished your tour of the Step Pyramid Complex. Walk back all the way to the other end of the open court where a wall topped with uraei, or rearing cobra heads, can be seen in the southwest corner.

7: This is the façade of the south tomb. Twenty-eight meters below the ground is a burial chamber, much smaller than, but otherwise identical to, the one under the pyramid. The reason for this chamber is not fully understood; it may be symbolic of very early kings' burials, which were actually made in the south of Egypt at Abydos. The chamber was empty when it was discovered. Later pyramids retain this feature and place a small pyramid on the south side of the main pyramid.

If you want to visit the Pyramid of Unas, go up the stairs here, and walk over the enclosure wall. If Unas is closed, return to your car and drive north to the Pyramid of Teti.

The Pyramid of Unas

The pyramid of Unas dates to the very end of the Fifth Dynasty, roughly 2350 BC. This pyramid is important because it was the first to be inscribed with Pyramid Texts. These religious texts go back to the very beginnings of pharaonic culture, but were not written on pyramid chamber walls until the Pyramid of Unas. From then on, until the end of the Old Kingdom, these religious spells were written in the pyramids of kings, and slightly later, those of queens as well. The spells of the Pyramids Texts ensure that the king wakes up after death, ascends to heaven, and joins the gods.

The Pyramid of Unas

The Pyramid of Unas is very small and ruined. Originally, it was slightly more than forty meters high; now it is half that size. This is an easy pyramid to enter, so if you did not visit one of the pyramids at Giza, try this one. The descending corridor into the pyramid is just eleven meters long, and then it continues horizontally for another eighteen meters. Halfway along the horizontal part are three spaces where you can actually stand up straight. These once held three granite slabs—called portcullis blocks—that were lowered down and blocked the passageway after the king was buried.

Name of King Unas in a cartouche

Name of King Unas with the title 'Osiris'

Enter the antechamber, with an area of storage chambers on the left and the burial chamber on the right. The antechamber, as well as most of the burial chamber walls, are carved with Pyramid Texts in vertical lines of hieroglyphs. Look for the name of Unas in his cartouches (but please don't touch the hieroglyphs: touching damages them). The first part of the name of Unas is written with a desert hare, which was read as *wn* in ancient Egyptian. The horizontal zigzag line below it repeats the *n* sound. Then there are two vertical signs; a flowering reed for *i*, and a folded bolt of cloth, *s*. The whole name thus reads *wnis*. We do not know exactly how the name was pronounced, though: ancient Egyptian was a partially Semitic language and, as in Arabic, vowels were not written. If you have sharp eyes, you will notice that in the burial chamber two signs are repeated above the name of Unas, the throne and the eye, signs that represent the name of the god Osiris, the king of the underworld. Adding this to Unas's name meant that he had 'become an Osiris'; he had died and been resurrected.

Notice that the walls just around the black granite sarcophagus are deco-

Function of the Mastaba

The mastaba had to fulfill two specific functions: protect the body and provide a cult place for the deceased. A vertical shaft went down from inside the mastaba to a burial chamber just large enough for the sarcophagus and accompanying objects. This shaft was filled up with rubble and closed after the burial. The cult for the deceased focused on the false door with offering table in front. The false door, a stylized door carved in stone, was provided for the soul, or *ka*, to pass through and receive offerings each day.

The scenes carved on the mastaba walls fall roughly into two categories: scenes of daily life on the estates of the deceased, and scenes of offering for the cult of the deceased. Since the agricultural pursuits on the estate provided the offerings for the cult, the two types of scenes are naturally interrelated.

rated with the *serekh* façade, which also appeared on the outside of the enclosure walls of the Step Pyramid Complex. This motif represents the king's palace, and here in the burial chamber it marks his house of eternity. Also notice that the ceiling is carved with stars; only a royal monument has a ceiling decorated in this way.

The Pyramid of Teti

Teti was Unas's successor and the first king of the Sixth Dynasty. His pyramid was originally about twelve meters higher than that of Unas. The plan of the descending corridor and the interior chambers is virtually identical to that of Unas, but slightly larger. As you walk along the horizontal part of the corridor you will come to three spaces that were for the portcullis blocks that were lowered down to seal the corridor once the king was buried. The sarcophagus in the burial chamber is basalt with a single band of hieroglyphic inscription. At the southeast corner of the sarcophagus is a hole in the floor for the king's canopic box. The walls behind the sarcophagus are decorated with a *serekh*-façade design, representing the king's palace for eternity.

Just as in the Pyramid of Unas, Pyramid Texts to assure the king's resurrection and afterlife cover the walls of the antechamber and burial chamber, but not the walls of the storage chambers to the left. The huge limestone blocks carved with Teti's Pyramid Texts were badly damaged and have been restored. Note the ceiling blocks decorated with stars.

When you come out of Teti's Pyramid, walk across and visit the mastaba, or private tomb, of his vizier, Mereruka. The mastaba of Mereruka is the largest and most famous at Saqqara.

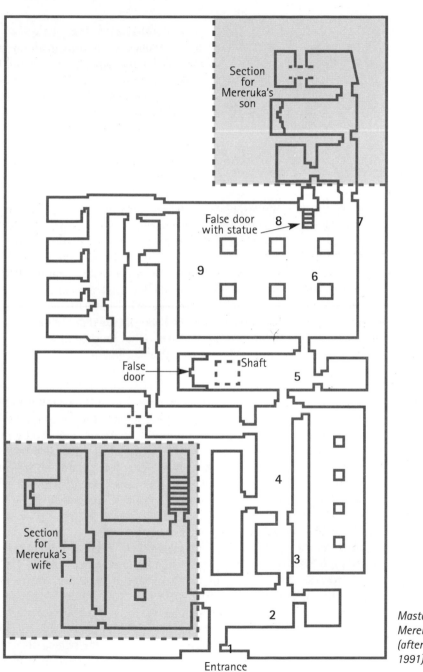

Section
for
Mereruka's
son

False door
with statue 8

7

9

6

False
door

Shaft

5

Section
for
Mereruka's
wife

4

3

2

1

Entrance

*Mastaba of
Mereruka
(after Hart,
1991)*

279

Entrance into the mastaba of Mereruka

The Mastaba of Mereruka

High officials were buried in mastaba tombs near the pyramid of the king they served. Mereruka was vizier, the highest official of the land, under King Teti, and so received a large, impressive mastaba next to the king's pyramid. In addition, Mereruka just happened to be married to the king's daughter! In this mastaba are rooms not only for Mereruka but also for his wife and their son.

Walk through the mastaba following the accompanying floor plan. Particularly interesting scenes are marked on the plan and described below. The scenes were carved in raised relief, meaning that the stone was cut back around the figures, so that they stand out. Off the main rooms leading to the mastaba's large pillared hall you will see that the decoration on the walls was sometimes hurriedly finished, or not finished at all. Small storage rooms, however, were meant to be left undecorated.

As you go through Mereruka's mastaba you will notice a change in subject matter in the wall scenes. Active outdoor scenes such as fishing and fowling in the swamp are in the outermost room. Other outdoor scenes such as animal husbandry and agriculture follow these scenes. The inner rooms have domestic scenes concerned with the furniture, clothing, and jewelry of the deceased. Closest to the false door are the scenes of slaughter and the offering bearers with food. All these figures are oriented toward the false door, where these goods would be offered. As you walk through the door of the mastaba, note the figure of Mereruka on both sides, accompanied by a list of all his official titles.

1: Immediately on your right in the doorway is a scene of Mereruka painting the seasons of the year. In one hand, he holds a shell full of paint and in the other a paintbrush. The picture he is painting is on an easel in front of him. The seasons are symbolized by seated gods, with the name of the season written above.

2: The two long walls in the first room both have scenes in the swamp. Mereruka and his wife on a papyrus skiff are the focus of the scene on the right-hand wall. On both walls notice the details of the crocodiles and hippopotamuses under the water and the birds and their nests in the swamp plants.

3: In the bottom row, under scenes of craftsmen, are four dwarfs with pieces

The Ancient Egyptian Calendar

The earliest calendar devised by the ancient Egyptians was based on the three seasons of the agricultural year: inundation, emergence (the land coming back out of the floodwaters), and deficiency (of water). Each of these seasons lasted for four lunar months (note that in front of each season in Mereruka's painting is an enclosure with four crescent moons) of thirty days each, with five or six extra days at the end of the year. The beginning of the calendar year was in mid-July, when the rising waters of the inundation were first noted. Over time, the Egyptians developed a more schematic calendar for administrative purposes, but religious dates and festivals were always determined by the old agricultural calendar. The ancient calendar is still used today by the Coptic Church and by many farmers in their cycle of sowing and harvesting crops.

of gold jewelry. The size of the jewelry is completely out of proportion to the people. Dwarfs in ancient Egypt seem to have held household positions concerned with linen and jewelry, as if these tasks fitted their small size.

4: The overseers of the estates are being brought in to see what taxes they owe. They kneel down in front of scribes, who are busy writing. One tax evader is being held to a pole and beaten!

5: Here is the shaft that goes down to Mereruka's burial chamber. After he was buried, it was filled in and covered over. Notice Mereruka's false door above it in the west wall. His burial was plundered by ancient tomb robbers, but parts of his mummy were still in the stone sarcophagus when excavators found it.

6: This pillared hall is the focal point of the mastaba. Look straight ahead at the dramatic statue of Mereruka, as it seems to stride right out of the niche in which it is carved. An offering table is set on steps in front of him. Notice the stone ring in the center of the room. Cattle brought in to be slain as offerings were tied up here.

7: Over the doorway into the part of the mastaba belonging to Mereruka's son are rows of boys and girls playing and dancing. The children in your group might recognize games that they play. On the wall to the right of the doorway, Mereruka sits with his wife and plays the board game *senet* against his son.

8: Different animals are being fed. Notice that some men are feeding a very fat hyena. In the Old Kingdom, Egyptians experimented with trying to domesticate all kinds of animals, and one of these was the hyena. They may have used hyenas for hunting, and kept them well fed so that they would not eat the game animals, but scholars are not sure.

9: Mereruka sits on his bed, leaning against the pillow while his wife plays the harp for him. Note the fly whisk that he holds in one hand.

Appendix 1

Community Service

There are plenty of opportunities for community service in the Cairo area. As teenagers often want to improve their community and environment, but do not know where to start, and parents may not know where to begin to look for an organization their teenager might best fit, the following list provides a starting point. It is important that parents first make sure that the organization the teenager is interested in does want volunteers and that they have a training program. Volunteer programs have specific objectives and guidelines for the teenager to follow. It is necessary that the parent be involved in making the initial contact with the service organization, understanding the service and learning what their son or daughter can offer.

Charitable Organizations

Al Nur wal Amal Association (Light and Hope). Have a gift shop of their products. Tel: 671-6424.

Awladi Orphanage. Behind Cairo American College. Tel: 521-2598; or call Mona, who speaks English: 516-5560.

Bashayer Workshop, Helwan Community Service Center. 27 Tariq ibn Zayad St., off Abd al-Rahman St., Helwan. Tel: 554-2491. Helps women through literacy programs.

Befrienders. Tel: 344-8200.

Bulaq Social Service Association. 1 Ramlat Bulaq St., Bulaq.

CARE Egypt: 526-0096, ext. 162/163, *www.care.org.eg.*
Caritas. Tel: 590-5148/8391.
Children's Orphanage for Boys, 9 Dar al-Salam St., facing Ain Shams Police
    Station. Tel: 523-1998.
Children's Orphanage for Girls. Tel: 257-3549.
Coptic Benevolent Association, Aghsan al-Karma for the Mentally
    Handicapped. Tel: 362-6102.
Ebnati Care Society, Sixth of October City, 6th District–Central, Egypt.
    Tel: 831-1503. Mailing address is 4 Saraya Street, Dokki, Giza, Egypt.
Egyptian Association for Society Consolidation (EASC), works with street
    children, welcomes donations and volunteers. Misr-Fayoum Road, Giza,
    Tel. 376-2202.
Egyptian Association of Social Defense, 91 Ain Shams St. Tel: 490-2238.
Egyptian Red Crescent. 23 Galaa St. Tel: 575-0558
Egyptian Volunteer Center, 119 Nile St., Dokki, Cairo. Tel: 749-1414.
Fat'het Kheir Volunteers al-Moqattam. Tel. 505-4536, *www.fathetkheir.org*
    (Arabic/English).
Friends of Children with Cancer. Tel: 358-3625, 012 279-1226.
General Evangelical Caring Home for Boys. Tel: 556-2803.
Hope Village. Tel: 261-5199; Nasr City Hope Village 272-4563, 270-2023:
    ask for Ashraf.
Mother Theresa Orphanage. Tel: 512-6385.
Nahdit al-Mahrousa, 7 Haret Salem, off Sheikh Rehan St., Abdeen, Cairo, Tel:
    792-0195.
Resala Club, 0777-7100 (free Internet), needs donations for orphans.
Right to Live Association for the Mentally Handicapped. Tel: 267-1729, 266-1271.
SOS Children's Village. Tel: 274-2286.
Tukul Craft Center for Refugees, All Saints Cathedral, behind Marriott Hotel,
    Zamalek.

Environment
Association for the Protection of the Environment, 7 Suliman al-Sayyid St.,
    near Heliopolis Hospital. Tel: 510-2723.
Friends of the Environment Association, Youth Club, 22 Ahmed Bek Gharbo
    St., Zizinia, Alexandria. Tel/Fax: 584-5759.
Maadi Environmental Rangers. Tel: 358-5694, 519-9723, 359-1223.
Tree Lovers Association, P.O. Box 592, Maadi, Cairo. Tel: 358-0099, 519-
    3819, 519-5240.
Zabbaleen Environmental and Developmental Program. Tel: 518-2723,
    358-0757.

Animals

Animal Friends. Tel: 378-2043, 380-9175.

Animal Lovers. Tel: 519-1043.

The Egyptian Society of Animal Friends, 30 Khorshed St., Road 293, New Maadi. Tel: 702-1142, 010 535-8651.

Society for the Protection of Animal Rights in Egypt (SPARE). Tel: 381-3855, 012 316-2912, *www.sparealife.org.*

Shop to Help Others

Kids of all ages love to shop. Why not let their money help others by frequenting stores and community bazaars that help others help themselves?

Egypt Crafts: Marketing Link Egypt Crafts is a non-profit group launched to support craft producers throughout Egypt by increasing income of community groups and preserving Egyptian arts. Participants include the Bedouin Women's Community, the Orthodox Youth Association of Akhmim, the Nubian Heritage Preservation Association, the Sinai Wildlife Project, the Association for the Protection of the Environment, and many more. Ask for a brochure for complete information of all the participants and the program. 27 Yehia Ibrahim (off 26th July Street), First Floor, Apt 8, Zamalek. Tel: 736-5123. Or visit *www.fairtradeegypt.org.*

Tukul Crafts is a project to promote self-reliance through developing skills of Sudanese refugees. Tel: 736-4836.

Hadayik al-Maadi Shop, 18 Road 162, Hadayik al-Maadi.

Diocesan Craft Shop, All Saint's Cathedral, Zamalek, Tel: 738-0821, ext. 229. Open Monday–Thursday, Saturday: 9:30am–6pm; Friday and Sunday: 11am–4pm.

Appendix 2
Libraries of Cairo

Cairo has many libraries, although some are in the most unsuspected places, such as the October War Panorama or the Entomology Museum. If there is a library at a museum, it is noted at the end of the section in the entries of this book. In addition, many cultural centers offer library facilities highlighting their country's literature and culture. In the summer months, all libraries throughout the Cairo area have a 'Reading for All' program, promoting reading through competition. Mobile libraries are dispersed throughout the city. Inquire at each library for membership fees and opening times.

Public Libraries
Ain al-Sira Library for Children. Magra al-Uyun St. Tel: 531-3546.
Ain Shams Cultural Club Library. 6th October St., near Zahraa Police Station, Ain Shams. Tel: 294-1623.
Al-Bahr al-Azam Library for Children. Al-Bahr al-Azam St., near Giza Police Station. Also has a library for adults.
Arab al-Hammad Library for Children. Lutfi Sayyid St., Arab al-Hammadi Garden, al-Waili.
Great Cairo Library. 15 Muhammad Mazhar St., Zamalek. Tel: 736-2271/2278.
Helwan Library for Children. 6th October St., near Helwan Kabritage.
Khalid ibn Walid Library for Children. Midan Kitkat, Imbaba. Also has a library for adults. Tel: 311-8950.

Maadi Public Library. El-Nasr Street, New Maadi. Tel: 345-8457.
Medinat al-Salam Library for Children. Atlas Building, Medinat al-Salam.
   Tel: 278-4708.
Medinat Nasr Library for Children. Makram Ebeid St., Zone 6, Medinat Nasr.
Mubarak Library. 4 al-Tahawiya St, Giza. Tel: 336-0291/0294.
National Library and Archives. Nile Corniche after Conrad Hotel, Bulaq.
New Maadi Library for Children. Nasr St., in front of Supermarket al-
   Ahram, New Maadi.
Shubra al-Kheima Library for Children. Midan al-Muahada, 1st May St.,
   near Musturud Bridge, Shubra al-Kheima. Also has a library for adults.
6th October Library for Children. 6th October Garden, Agouza. Also has a
   library for adults.
Zeitun Library for Children. 5 Tawfiq Khalil St. Tel: 603-0340.

Major Cultural Center Libraries
American Research Center in Egypt (ARCE) Library, 2 Simon Bolivar Square,
   Garden City. Tel: 794-8239, 795-8683, 796-4681.
American Studies Library, US Embassy, 5 Latin America St., Garden City.
   Tel: 797-3529, 795-8927.
British Council Library. 192 al-Nil St., Agouza. Tel: 303-1514.
Goethe Institute. 5 Abd al-Salam Arif St., Downtown. Tel: 575-9877.

Other Libraries
Amideast. 23 Musaddaq St., Dokki. Resource library.
   Tel: 337-8277, 338-3867.
Arab Music Institute. Ramsis St., Downtown.
Community Services Association. 4 Road 21, Maadi. Tel: 358-5284/0754,
   768-8232.
Education Museum and Document Library. Falaki St., Downtown.
Egyptian Geology Museum. Agricultural Road, Old Cairo.
Entomology Museum. Ramses St., Downtown.
Geographic Society. In Ethnology Museum, 2nd Floor.
Integrated Care Society. 42 Sawra St., Heliopolis. Tel: 417-2084-8.
Music Library. Opera House Complex, Gezira.
October War Panorama. Salah Salem St., Heliopolis.
Sohair Osman Library. Opera House Complex, Gezira.
Taha Hussein Museum. 1 Helmiyat al-Ahram St., Giza.

Web Sites

Egyptian Library Network. *www.library.idsc.gov.eg.* This site contains 140
 libraries across Egypt with about one million titles.

Online Bookstore. *wwwcairobookmark.com.* Order books online, pay in cash
 when book is delivered to your door.

Appendix 3
Sporting Clubs with Programs for Children with Special Needs

Parents do not need to be members
Cairo Sporting Club, near Gezira Sheraton, Gezira. Tel: 748-9415.
Gezira Club, Gezira. Tel: 735-6000/6006, 736-5270.

Parents need to be members
Heliopolis Club, Heliopolis. Tel: 417-0061/2.
Medinat Nasr Club, Medinat Nasr. Tel: 635-1833.
Shooting Club, Dokki. Tel: 337-3337/4535.
Imbaba Sporting Club for the Disabled. Imbaba.

Appendix 4
Web Site Directory

If it is too hot to be a tourist, or you are traveling abroad and feel homesick, here are some Web sites that will keep you connected and remind you of magnificent Cairo. All Web sites below are cross-referenced within the text of the book, with the exception of "Just for Fun."

What's on in Cairo
www.egycalendar.com – calendar of conferences held monthly in Egypt
www.croc.filbalad.com – Arabic/English guide to restaurants and events
http://groups.yahoo.com/group/wazzup_in_Cairo/ – people of Cairo inform the people of Cairo of events, workshops, openings, exhibitions, and performances
http://weekly.ahram.org.eg – good section of weekly event listings
www.egypttoday.com – monthly listing of events in an online magazine
www.aucegypt.edu/tools/calendars.html – schedule of events at AUC

About Egypt
www.egyptedantan.com/egypt – Photographs of Egypt 100 years ago

Museums
www.gem.gov.eg – Grand Egyptian Museum

www.egyptianmuseum.gov.eg/ – Egyptian Museum
www.discoverislamicart.org – The Discover Islamic Art
  Virtual Museum
www.ancient-egypt.org/saqqara/ – Saqqara Pyramids
www.copticmuseum.gov.eg – Coptic Museum
www.mkhalilmuseum.gov.eg/ – Mr. and Mrs. Mohammed Mahmoud Khalil
  Museum
www.agri.gov.eg/MainMenule.aspx?Id=zoo.htm&ph=1600 –
  Giza Zoo, Botanical Gardens, Agricultural Museum (information on
  museums is out-of-date)
www.wissa-wassef-arts.com – Ramses Wissa Wassef Art Center
www.glassartmuseum.com – Glass Museum

Famous Egyptians in history (each has a museum in Cairo)
http://almashriq.hiof.no/egypt/700/780/umKoulthoum/ – Umm Kulthoum
http://nasser.bibalex.org – Gamal Abd al-Nasser

Ancient Egypt
www.animalmummies.com/project.html – *Animal mummies*
www.mcdonald.cam.ac.uk/Projects/Amarna/home.htm – Ongoing project at
  Tell al-Amarna

Organizations that focus on art and culture
www.cairooperahouse.org – Cairo Opera House
www.groups.yahoo.com/group/studio206 – Studio 206
www.egyptmusic.org – MAKAN and Egyptian Center for Culture and Art
www.khayalstudio.com – Khayal Studio
www.fagnoon.net – Sabil Om Hashem
www.serafis.net – Serafis Culture Society
www.culturewheel.com – El-Sawy Culture Wheel
www.swiss-club-cairo.com – Swiss Club in Cairo
www.livinginegypt.org – Community Service Association

NGOs in community service
www.care.org.eg – CARE Egypt
www.fathetkheir.org – Fat'het Kheir (volunteer organization – Mokattam
  Hills)
www.sparealife.org – Society for Protection of Animal Rights in Egypt
www.fairtradeegypt.org – Fair Trade Egypt, Egyptian crafts
www.ritsec.org.eg – Regional Information Technology and Software

Engineering Center is a non-government organization that provides
technical, professional, and developmental services

About Egypt

www.eternalegypt.org – Eternal Egypt, Supreme Council of Antiquities
www.egs-online.org – Geographic Society
www.arce.org – American Research Center
www.ees.ac.uk – Egypt Exploration Society
www.coptic.org – Guide to Coptic churches, organizations, youth programs
www.egy.com – History of Cairo from monuments to people by Samir
  Raafat
www.library.idsc.gov.eg – List of all libraries in Egypt
www.pbs.org/wgbh/nova/lostempires/obelisk/ – How ancient Egyptians
  shaped, transported, and erected obelisks

Database, researching and documentation of ancient Egyptian to present

www.bibalex.org/English/researchers/cultnat.htm and *www.cultnat.org/*
  CULTNAT from Bibliotheca Alexandrina and Ministry of Communication
  and Information Technology, Center for Documentation of Cultural and
  Natural Heritage
www.globalegyptianmuseum.com – Global Egypt Museum (GEM) database
  of worldwide museum collections of objects from pre-historic to present
  in Egypt includes eight languages and activities for kids.
http://france.strabon.org – Database of Saqqara site and collections
www.usaid-eg.org/detail.asp?id=292 – Before and after renovation views
  of Bab Zuweyla

Miscellaneous

www.thetownhousegallery.com – The Town House Gallery
www.akdn.org/agency/aktc_hcsp_cairo.html – Al-Azhar Park
www.icm.gov.eg/E_island_art_center.html – Gezera Art Center, Islamic
  Ceramics
www.mevlana.ws – Site about Mevlavi Jelaluddin Rumi, Whirling Dervish,
  Sufism
www.cairo-airport.com – Schedule of arrival and departure flights at Cairo
  International Airport
www.egyptair.com.eg - Schedule for EgyptAir

Books online
www.cairobookmark.com – Order books online, delivered to your door

Just for fun
www.earth.google.com – A bird's eye view of your house!

Appendix 5

Timeline
of Egyptian History

Date	Period	Ruler	Event	Monument
Prehistoric (Predynastic)				
ca. 4000–3500 BC			Maadi Culture flourishes in Lower Egypt	
just before 3100		Narmer	Battle in Delta	Narmer's Palette
Pharaonic (3100–332 BC)				
ca. 3100–2680	Early Dynastic (Dyn. 1–2)		Memphis becomes capital of Egypt	
ca. 2680–2181	Old Kingdom (Dyn. 3–6)	Djoser (Dyn. 3)		Step Pyramid, Saqqara
		Khufu, Khafre, Menkaure (Dyn. 4)		Giza Pyramids
		Unas (Dyn. 5)	First use of Pyramid texts	Pyramid at Saqqara
ca. 2181–1991	First Intermediate Period (Dyn. 7–11)	Nebhepetre Mentuhotep (late Dyn. 11)	Reunites Egypt after bloody struggle	
ca. 1991–1786	Middle Kingdom (Dyn. 12)	Senusert I		Temple with two obelisks at Heliopolis
ca. 1786–1552	Second Intermediate Period (Dyn. 13–17)		Egyptian Delta invaded by Hyksos from Syro-Palestine	
ca. 1552–1069	New Kingdom (Dyn. 18–20)	Hatshepsut (Dyn. 18)	Expedition to Punt	
		Tuthmose IV (Dyn. 18)	Clears sand from Giza Sphinx	

Date	Period	Ruler	Event	Monument
ca. 1358–1340	Amarna Period	Akhenaten (Dyn. 18)	Aten worship	Royal city at Tell al-Amarna
		Tutankhamun (Dyn. 18)		Tomb in the Valley of the Kings
		Ramesses II (Dyn. 19)		Colossal statues at Memphis; obelisks at Per-Ramses in the Delta
ca. 1069–664	Third Intermediate Period (Dyn. 21–25)	Psusennes (Dyn. 21)	Buried at Tanis	
	Dyn. 21–22		Obelisks of Ramesses II moved to Tanis	
ca. 664–332	Late Period (Dyn. 26–31)			
Greek (332–30)				
332		Alexander the Great	Takes Egypt when he defeats the Persian Empire	
331			Founds city of Alexandria	
305–30	Ptolemaic			
30 BC			Death of Cleopatra VII	
Roman (30 BC–AD 395)				
AD 14–37		Tiberius		
24			Strabo visits Heliopolis	
98–117		Trajan		
100				Fortress of Babylon
Byzantine (395–642)				
2nd–3rd cent. (?)				Church of St. Sergius built inside Babylon
457–74		Leo I		
470				Monastery of Apa Jeramias founded at Saqqara
Islamic (642–1805)				
640		Umar	Arabs enter Egypt under Amr ibn al-As	al-Fustat founded

Date	Period	Ruler	Event	Monument
642			Capture of Babylon	Mosque of Amr ibn al-As
658–750	Umayyad			
750–868	Abbassid			
861				Roda Nilometer
868–905	Tulunid	Ibn Tulun		
876–879				Mosque of Ibn Tulun
905–935	Abbasid			
935–969	Ikhshidid			
969–1171	Fatimid			
969–975		al-Muizz		
969			al-Qahira founded	
970–972				Mosque of al-Azhar
975–996		al-Aziz		
988			al-Azhar becomes a university	
1035–1094		al-Mustansir		
mid-11th cent.				Ben Ezra Synagogue
1087				Bab al-Nasr and Bab al-Futuh
1092				Bab Zuwayla
1160–1171		al-Adid		
1168			Burning of al-Fustat	
1169			Saladin comes to Egypt	
1171–1252	Ayyubid			
1171–1193		Saladin		
1176				Northern Enclosure of the Citadel
1218–1238		al-Kamil	First ruler to live in the Citadel	
1252–1382	Bahri Mamluk			
1260–1277	Baybars I			Mosque 1267–69, Lion Tower, Citadel.
1280–1290		Qalawun		
1284–1285				Mosque of Qalawun

Date	Period	Ruler	Event	Monument
1296–1298		Lajin		Restores Ibn Tulun Mosque
1310–1340		al-Nasir Muhammad		
1315				al-Ablaq Palace
1318–1335				Mosque of al-Nasir Muhammad
1345-1361	Sultan Hasan			Mosque of Sultan Hasan
1382				Khan al-Khalili
1382–1517	Burgi Mamluk			
1501–1516		al-Ghuri		
1504–1505				Complex of al-Ghuri
1507				Aqueduct intake tower
1517–1805	Ottoman			
1528				Mosque of Sulayman Pasha
1798–1801		Napoleon Bonaparte	French Occupation	
1799			Rosetta stone discovered	
1800			French troops defeat Turks at Heliopolis	

Modern Islamic Rule (1805–Present)

Date	Period	Ruler	Event	Monument
1805–1848		Muhammad Ali		
1811			Slaughter of the Mamluks	
1814				Gawhara Palace
1822			Champollion deciphers hieroglyphs	
1824				Mosque of Muhammad Ali
1827				Harem Palace
1848		Ibrahim Pasha		
1848–1854		Abbas I		
1849				Shepheard's Hotel opens
1851				Cairo Ramses Train Station
1854–1866		Said Pasha		
1863–1879		Ismail		

Date	Period	Ruler	Event	Monument
1866			First Egyptian stamp issued	
1869				Suez Canal opened
1872				Opera House, Abdin Palace
1879–1892		Khedive Tawfiq		al-Qubba Palace
1882			British Occupation	
1891				Giza Zoo founded
1892–1914		Abbas II Hilmi		
1894			Mustafa Kamil founds Egyptian National Party	
1897				Sakakini Palace
1898			Khalig Canal filled in: becomes Port Said St.	
1901				Manial Palace
1902			Fish Gardens open to the public	
1904				Baron Empain Palace
1908			Mustafa Kamil dies	
1917–1936		Fuad I		
1919			AUC founded	
1922			Howard Carter discovers Tutankhamun's tomb	
1923			Hoda Sharaawi unveils	
1923				Arab Music Institute
1924			Saad Zaghoul becomes Prime Minister	
1927			Saad Zaghoul dies	
1936–1952		Farouk		
1936			Tomb of Psusennes discovered at Tanis	
1945			Naga Hammadi Gnostic texts discovered	
1952			British attack Ismailia Police Station, Jan. 25 Black Saturday Riots, Jan. 26	

Date	Period	Ruler	Event	Monument
1952			Revolution of 23 July	
1952–1954		Muhammad Naguib		
1954			Solar boat discovered at Giza	
1954–1970		Gamal Abd al-Nasser		
1958–1970			Construction of the Aswan High Dam	
1961				Cairo Tower
1965			Taha Hussein awarded Order of the Nile	
1967			6–Day War	
1970–1981		Anwar al-Sadat		
1971			Opera House burns down	
1972			Gawhara Palace burns	
1973			Arab-Israeli War	
1981			Sadat assassinated	
1981–present		Hosni Mubarak		
1987				Metro opens
1988				New Opera House opens Ring Road
1998			Groundbreaking for the Toshka Project	
2002				Bibliotheca Alexandrina
2004				Al-Azhar Park

Appendix 6
ACTIVE in Cairo

Art studios, dance studios, language and music centers, computer and sports
. . . you name it, so check out the list and sign up!

Art Studios and Music Centers
Art and Design School: 7 Baghdad St., Korba, Heliopolis. Tel: 415-9752. Art
  classes from drawing to graphic design.
Bedaya Art School and Conservatory: 93 Farid Semika St., Higaz Square,
  Heliopolis. Tel: 637-4233. Music lessons on most instruments, dance and
  gymnastic classes, too.
Cairo American College Summer School: 1 Midan Digla, Maadi. Tel: 519-
  6357. Lots of activities and classes, team and individual sports, art and
  photography classes. *Web site: www.cacegypt.org/summer/index.*
Community Services Association: 4 Road 21, Maadi. Tel: 358-5284, 358-
  0754. Art and craft classes and other activities for kids. Web site:
  www.livinginegypt.org.
Cre Art: 34 al-Israa St., off Lebanon St., Mohandiseen, first floor. Tel: 344-
  8433. Art classes.
Dina Sobhy: Nasr City. Tel: 012 362-0893. Mosaic and art classes.
Ecole de l'art: 10, 26th July St., Lebanon Square, Mohandiseen. Tel: 012
  319-5495. Art and crafts, sculpture, drawing and painting.
Fagnoon's Art School – Sabil Om Hashem: Saqqara Road, 12.5 km from al-
  Haram Road. Tel: 815-1014, 010 158-6715. Arts and crafts, outdoor activities.

Fagnoon Academy: 15b Taha Hussein St. Zamalek, Tel. 736–5826, 010 158–6715. Activities include painting, drawing, clay and woodwork, baking.

Francophone Art Academy in Cairo (AFCA): 37 Iran St., Dokki. Tel: 338-0205, 338-3199, 012 467-3435. Art classes. Web site: *www.afca.blogspot.com.*

Hoda Kamal: Maadi. Tel: 358-4526. Craft classes.

Il Penello Café: 2 Omar Ibn al-Khattab St., Abu Bakr al-Siddiq Square, in front of The English School, Heliopolis. Tel: 241-7603. Paint pottery.

Khayal Fine Arts Studio: 5 Road 253, Digla, Maadi. Tel: 520-1615, 010 560-4020. Art lessons and field trips, bake bread, and participate in outdoor activities. Web site: *www.khayalstudio.com.*

Kid's Island: 14 Muhammad Shafik St., next to al-Ghaba Club, ground floor, Heliopolis. Cooking and language classes, arts and crafts.

Maadi Music Center: 36A Road 206, Digla, Maadi. Tel: 521-1692. Private music lessons.

Onna Art Club: 9 al-Hadeed wal-Solb St., off al-Falah and Shehab Sts., Mohandiseen Tel: 305-1999. Arts and crafts, flower arranging, music, computers, and language classes.

Orange Art School: 3 al-Said al-Bakry St., fourth floor, flat 401, Zamalek. Tel. 736-6633. Art classes, painting, drawing collage. Ages 3–15.

Pharaonic Village: Corniche al-Nil, variety of art classes. Tel: 571-8675/6/7.

Plein Air: Ahmad Orabi Association, Km 28, Cairo–Ismailiya Road. Lots of activities for children and summer school. Tel: 012 322-9462, 010 188-2315.

Saad Zaghloul Cultural Center: The Center is to the right of the main entrance and in the basement of Bayt al-Umma. Tel: 795-6864. Lessons in art, theater, and films for children. There are monthly exhibits of the children's work.

Sayyida Zaynab Children's Cultural Park: Activities for children include film, theater, painting and drawing opportunities, rooms with computers, and playgrounds.

Studio 206: 14/18 Road 200, Digla, Maadi. Tel: 519-5713. Summer program for kids and arts and craft classes.

Cultural Centers, Computer, and Language Centers

British Council: 4 al-Minya St. Heliopolis. Tel: 452-3395, English language classes.

International Language Institute: 2 Muhammad Bayoumi St., off Mirghani St., Heliopolis. Tel: 291-9295. English language lessons for ages 5–15.

Maadi Public Library: 2 al-Nasr St., near Olympic Village, New Maadi. Tel. 754-8541. Computer and art classes.

RITSEC: 11a Hassan Sabry St., Zamalek. Tel: 339-1300, 735-2665. Computer classes for high school students.

El Sawy Cultural Wheel: Under the 15th of May Bridge, Zamalek. Tel: 736-6178, 735-4505 Movies for children, book exhibitions, and other events. Web site: *www.culturewheel.com.*

Serafis Cultural Society: 34 Road 218, Digla, Maadi. Tel: 521-2104. Lectures and cultural trips.

Swiss Club Cairo: Villa Pax, al-Gihad St., off Sudan St., Kit Kat Square. Tel: 314-2811 / 315-1455 / 010 300-9695. Activities for children. Web site: *www.swiss-club-cairo.com.*

Sport and Dance Centers

Creative Dance and Fitness Center: 13b Road 254, Digla, Maadi. Tel: 519-6575; 6 Amr St., off Syria St., Mohandiseen. Tel: 302-0572. Dance, gymnastics, and aerobics for youth.

Indji Solh Dance and Fitness Center: 1 Houssa Galal Square, Mohandiseen. Tel: 346-1517. All kinds of dance classes, drama classes. Ages 3 and up.

Katameya Tennis Center: Shafei Ranch, New Cairo City, fifth district. Tel: 758-0805. Tennis lessons.

Smash Tennis Academy: Behind Novotel Hotel, Heliopolis. Tel: 267-0897. Tennis classes.

Victory College Field: softball, soccer, rugby, Radio Auto Club. Contact Community Services Association in Maadi for information. Tel: 358-5284, 358-0754.

Appendix 7

Recommended Reading List

Compiled by Kelly Zaug

This recommended reading list is based on my experience as a bookseller and the requests of teachers and customers during my time in Cairo. All books are in paperback unless otherwise mentioned and are available in Cairo. The reading levels given at the end of each entry are as follows: Early readers (kindergarten to 2nd grade, ages 5–7); middle grade (late 2nd to 4th grade, ages 8–10); young adult (5th grade on up, ages 11+). Of course, these are only recommended guidelines and will vary greatly with each child's reading ability.

General History of Ancient Egypt

This is a tough category to make just a few selections for. Books on ancient Egypt would overflow bookstore shelves if we let them! These are just a few of the many that are available. Your local bookseller should be able to make some additional recommendations for you from their many selections.

Terry Deary and Peter Hepplewhite. *The Awesome Egyptians and The Awesome Egyptians Activity Book*. Scholastic Books, 1997 and 2004 (UK and US). Part of the terrifically funny *Horrible Histories* series, this book covers everything from pyramids and mummies to false beards and pharaonic acne. It's a very goofy look at ancient Egypt. Middle grade to early young adult.

Geraldine Harris and Delia Pemberton. *The Illustrated Encyclopedia of Ancient Egypt*. British Museum Press, 2005 (UK and US). This book, available in hardback only, draws on the vast resources of the British

Museum and is comprehensive in its scope. It's arranged alphabetically and covers almost everything between Abu Simbel and Zoser, and the new edition includes information on great Egypt websites for kids. Middle grade.

George Hart. *Eyewitness Books: Ancient Egypt.* Dorling Kindersley, 2004 (UK and US). This volume from the *Eyewitness* series provides good, solid content on ancient Egypt with great photos and interesting side notes. The same author has a paperback volume on ancient Egypt in the *Eyewitness Guides* series as well, but the contents are slightly different. Middle grade to early young adult.

Salima Ikram. *Gods and Temples*; *Land and People*; *The Pharaohs.* Hoopoe Books, 1997–1998 (Egypt and UK). These books are part of the *In Ancient Egypt* series by Dr. Ikram and Hoopoe Books. They combine authoritative but simple texts and great photographs to introduce young enthusiasts to ancient Egypt. Early to middle grade.

James Putnam. *Amazing Facts About Ancient Egypt.* Thames & Hudson, 1994 (UK); Harry N. Abrams, 1994 (US). This is just a cute, small, humorous book that everyone will like. It contains facts from the practical to the wacky. Middle grade on up.

Emily Sands. *Egyptology* and *Egyptology Handbook*: A Course in the Wonders of Egypt. Candlewick, 2004 and 2005 respectively (UK and US). These fun novelty books are the work of a fictional Egyptologist named Emily Sands who vanished into the Egyptian sands in 1927. There are papyrus pull-outs, pop-up art, minibooks, and foldout maps and an envelope in the back with period postcards, ticket stubs and so on that will charm even a jaded reader. All ages.

Scott Steedman. *The Egyptian News.* Walker Books, 1997 (UK); Candlewick Press, 2000 (US). This lively book presents information about ancient Egypt in a tabloid newspaper format. It's sure to keep the attention of the most unmotivated reader. Middle grade to early young adult.

General Activity Books

Another difficult category in which to make selections. The British Museum Press in the UK and Dover Publishing Company in both the US and the UK have many activity books, including punch-out masks, origami sarcophagi, and coloring books on ancient Egypt. These are some of the more sophisticated kits and books that I've found to be good fun.

Mira Bartok and Christine Ronan. *Ancient Egypt and Nubia Stencils.* Collins Educational 1995 (UK); Goodyear Books, 1994 (US). One of the few activity books that includes information about Nubia—something sorely lacking in most books on Egyptian history. Middle grade.

Marian Broida. *Ancient Egyptians and their Neighbors*. A Capella Publishing, 1999 (UK); Chicago Review Press, 1999 (US). This is an excellent resource for parents and teachers looking for activities related to the ancient Near East. Also covers the Hittites, Nubians, and Mesopotamians. Middle grade.

Janet Coles. *Fun with Beads: Ancient Egypt*. British Museum Press, 1995 (UK); Viking Childrens Books, 1995 (US). Excellent set that includes thousands of Egyptian-style beads, wire, hooks, project book, and everything else needed to make great ancient Egyptian-style jewelry. Not recommended for children under 10 years old. Middle grade to adult.

Avery Hart and Paul Mantell. *Pyramids: 50 Hands-On Activities to Experience Ancient Egypt*. Williamson Publishing Company, 1997 (UK and US). Not just about pyramids, this terrific activity book encourages children to not just read about it, but to do it! Includes games, recipes, and tons of how-to projects. Middle grade.

Linda Honan. *Spend the Day in Ancient Egypt: Projects and Activities That Bring the Past to Life*. John Wiley and Sons, 1999 (UK and US). This book is packed with activities organized by different themes in ancient Egyptian life and culture. Middle grade.

Jennifer Larson. *Egyptian Symbols: A Hieroglyphic Stamp Kit* and *Arabic Words and Patterns: 21 Rubber Stamps*. Chronicle Books, 2000 (US). These cool kits (with two different titles) come in a wooden box with a set of stamps, an inkpad, and a small booklet. Good for all ages, except children under 3 years old.

Diana Craig Patch. *Fun with Amulets*. Viking Childrens Books, 1995 (US). Use this kit to make oven-baked clay amulets to be used in various projects, from fridge magnets to necklaces. Not recommended for kids under 8. Middle grade to adult.

Catharine Roehrig. *Fun with Hieroglyphs*. Viking Juvenile, 1990 (US). Another good set of stamps with inkpad and book. The book has more activities and project suggestions than the Larson set. Middle grade to adult.

Hieroglyphs

Philip Ardagh. *The Hieroglyphs Handbook: Teach Yourself Ancient Egyptian*. Faber & Faber, 1999 (UK and US). A more in-depth, humorous look at hieroglyphs, both for reading and for counting. The author is a well-known children's history writer in the UK. Middle grade to young adult.

Mark Collier and Bill Manley. *How to Read Egyptian Hieroglyphs: A Step-by-Step Guide to Teach Yourself*. Hardback. British Museum Press, 1998 (UK); University of California Press, 1998 (US). This is a comprehensive, serious book to get yourself started reading hieroglyphs. Pretty difficult, but good for high-schoolers who are seriously interested in learning. Young adult to adult.

Roy Hollands. *Fun with Numbers in Ancient Egypt.* Hoopoe Books, 2000 (Egypt). Very fun, ingenious book teaching hieroglyphs and math at the same time. This book has good illustrations and fun activities. Early to middle grade.

Janice Kamrin. *Ancient Egyptian Hieroglyphs: A Practical Guide.* Harry N. Abrams, 2004 (US & UK). This definitive educational tool provides a systematic, step-by-step approach to learning ancient Egyptian hieroglyphs, complete with fun and increasingly challenging exercises and easy-to-reference sign and word lists. Young adult to adult.

———. *Hieroglyphs for Children.* Nahdet Misr, 2005 (Egypt). A great new addition to the 'teach-yourself' genre, this book features lively illustrations, exercises that gradually build on knowledge learned, and it includes a CD of hieroglyphs. Let's hope this nifty new book finds wider distribution soon! Middle grade to young adult.

Mummies

Judy Donnelly. *Tut's Mummy: Lost and Found* (Step into Reading). Random House, 1988 (US). Donnelly provides an exciting, yet easy-to-read, account of Howard Carter's discovery of Tutankhamun's tomb and ideas about what his funeral might have been like. Early readers.

Zahi Hawass. *The Curse of the Pharoahs: My Adventures with Mummies.* National Geographic Children's Books, 2004 (US). The "Pharaoh of Egyptology" debunks the horror stories surrounding Egyptian mummies with lively, passionate writing and storytelling. The full-color photos are superb and include clear close-up shots of mummies, statues, artifacts, sites, and a number of the scientist at work. Middle grade.

Salima Ikram. *In Ancient Egypt: Mummies and Tombs.* Hoopoe Books, 1998 (Egypt and UK). This book discusses how a mummy was made, what kinds of rituals were carried out by priests, and how people (and animals) were buried. An excellent book for younger kids who are good readers, part of a series written by Ikram and published by Hoopoe. Early readers to middle grade.

Joyce Milton. *Mummies* (All Aboard Reading). Grosset & Dunlap, 1996 (US). This book is an introduction for some of the youngest readers. The illustrations will satisfy their curiosity without grossing them out. Early readers.

Lila Perl. *Mummies, Tombs, and Treasures.* Houghton Mifflin, 1987 (US). Quite a thorough examination of the history of mummification in ancient Egypt, illustrated with lots of good photographs. Young adult.

Shelley Tanaka. *Secrets of the Mummies.* Madison Press Books, 1999 (UK and US). A very good book on mummification and the history of "mummy hunting." Several different Egyptian mummies (of people from different walks of life) are looked at and their lives speculated upon based on the results of the examination of their remains. This is one of my favorites in the category. Late early readers and middle grade.

Kelly Trumble. *Cat Mummies.* Houghton Mifflin, 1996 (US). This is a fascinating examination of the role of cats in ancient Egyptian religion. The author provides a good appendix and bibliography at the end. Middle grade to early young adult.

Pyramids

John D. Clare. *Pyramids of Ancient Egypt.* Random House, 1991 (UK); Harcourt Brace, 1992 (US, hardback only). Especially notable for its photographic reenactments using real people, this book touches on everyday life in ancient Egypt as well as the process of pyramid building. The photos are great, but one wishes they could have used real Egyptians! Middle grade.

David MacAulay. *Pyramid.* Houghton Mifflin, 1982 (US). Middle-grade kids will pore over the amazingly detailed pen and ink drawings in this book. MacAulay is a master at explaining the details of the backbreaking work put into the pyramids. Middle grade.

Anne Millard. *Best-Ever Book of Pyramids.* Kingfisher, 1998 (UK). *Mysteries of the Pyramids.* Larousse Kingfisher, 1995 (US). This book has different titles and cover looks in the US and UK, but the contents are the same. It describes the people and techniques needed for pyramid building. Also has short sections on pyramids in other cultures and time periods. Best for strong early readers through middle grade.

Alberto Siliotti. *Guide to the Pyramids of Egypt.* The American University in Cairo Press, 1997 (US and Egypt). This is a thorough yet readable book for someone who wants a little more meaty information on the pyramids and their funeral temples. It also includes contributions from Zahi Hawass, secretary general of the Supreme Council of Antiquities. Young adult and up.

Philip Steele. *I Wonder Why: The Pyramids Were Built.* Kingfisher Books, 2002 (UK and US). This is a good beginner's book answering lots of funny questions about the pyramids and the people who built them. Early readers.

Picture Books of Modern Egypt

Unfortunately, this is a category that is much neglected. While there are many beautiful coffee table-type books filled with images of Egypt, very few are specifically for children. These are the only few I am aware of, and any further suggestions to be added later would be welcome!

Jailan Abbas. *Festivals of Egypt.* Hoopoe Books, 1995 (Egypt and UK). This is a charming book that discusses all the festivals of Egypt, both Islamic and Coptic. It is illustrated with both photographs and drawings and is a good introduction to the sacred calendar of Egypt. Middle grade.

Khaled Eldash and Dalia Khattab. *Boushra's Day.* Frances Lincoln, 2002 (UK, hardback only). Part of a series on children around the world, this book follows Boushra, a 7-year-old Cairene girl on a typical school day. The photos are great—especially of dad selling papyrus and scarabs to tourists in his shop. Early readers.

Tim Loveless. *Pictures of Egypt: At the Market* and *Pictures of Egypt: In the Countryside.* Hoopoe Books, 1997 (Egypt and UK). These are two small books of captivating photographs of modern Egypt. They are aimed at the youngest of readers, even pre-schoolers, but the busyness and complexity will intrigue older ones, as will the explanations of the photos at the back of the books. Early (very) readers.

Arlene Moscovitch. *Egypt: The Culture*; *Egypt: The People*; *Egypt: The Land.* Crabtree Publishing, 2000 (UK and US). This set of three books are mainly meant for the school library market, but are thankfully available in paperback. Each one touches on both ancient and modern life and are illustrated with lively color photos. Middle grade.

Bruce Neale. *Young Guide: Alexandria*, Elias-Hoopoe, 1993 (Egypt only). This is an easy-to-read, short guide to the city of Alexandria. It is filled with wonderful drawings and interesting facts covering the history of the city and all the different places to visit. Early to middle grade readers.

Henry Pluckrose. *Picture a Country: Egypt.* Franklin Watts, 1999 (UK and US). This book is part of a series that I believe is also aimed mainly at schools. However, it is well illustrated with photos of many different parts of Egypt—Cairo, Dakhla, the Aswan Dam, Alexandria, as well as pictures of Egyptian money, foods, and people. Early readers.

Islam

Leila Azzam. *The Lives of the Prophets.* Hood Hood Books, 1995 (UK); Amideast, 1995 (US). Azzam bases her stories of the prophets of Islam, from Adam and Noah to Jesus and Muhammad, on the Quran and traditional Islamic writings. Through familiar characters, children can discover some of the similarities between Islam and Christianity. Middle grade to early young adult.

Suhaib Hamid Ghazi. *Ramadan*. Holiday House, 1996 (UK and US). *Ramadan* is full of incredibly beautiful watercolor illustrations, explaining the traditions and rituals of the holy month. The illustrator, Omar Rayyan, incorporates Islamic symbols and architectural motifs as well as lively, ethnically diverse images of people throughout the book. Early readers to early middle grades.

Umar Hegedüs. *Muslim Mosque*. A & C Black, 1997 (UK). This is an innovative book that helps children find out about Islam through the idea of a school class visiting a mosque. It depicts a visit to a mosque in the UK and is from a UK publisher, so some of the words and terms are in Modern Standard Arabic instead of Egyptian Colloquial, but the concepts explained are universal to Islam.

Denys Johnson-Davies. *The Battles of the Prophet Muhammad and Stories of the Caliphs*. Hoopoe Books, 1997 (Egypt and UK). These are just two of the many good children's books Denys Johnson-Davies has written or translated on Egypt and the Middle East. These two present stories and sayings of Muhammad and the early rulers of Islam in a lively format with good illustrations. I think boys especially would enjoy the *Battles of the Prophet Muhammad*. Middle grade.

———. *Rumi*. Hood Hood Books, 1997 (UK). Another one from Johnson-Davies, this time giving a brief biography of one of Islam's greatest poets and sages. It's part of a whole series called *Heroes from the East* by Hood Hood. Middle grade.

Mary Matthews. *Magid Fasts for Ramadan*. Houghton Mifflin, 2000 (UK and US). Magid is a young member of a modern Egyptian Muslim family, trying to understand the reasons for fasting during Ramadan. The book answers some serious questions about what religion requires, while demonstrating a warm, appealing image of family life. Early readers.

Shulamith Levey Oppenheim. *The Hundredth Name*. Boyds Mill Press, 1997 (UK and US). This is a heart-warming story about an Egyptian boy, Salah, and his camel, Qadiim. Through the example of his patient and devout father, Salah discovers the power of prayer and respect for God's creatures.

Philip Wilkinson. *Eyewitness Books: Islam*. DK Publishing, 2005 (UK and US). An introduction to the basic tenets of the faith, the history of its spread, the varieties of the cultures in which it flourishes, and highlights of the achievements of Islamic peoples, including the importance of Muslim scholarship during the European Middle Ages, Islamic architecture, the breadth of its trade, and various ruling empires.

Fiction

The following categories are all fiction stories, divided by their age groups. Again, this is a type of book where there are so many to choose from, narrowing it down to just a few for each age is very difficult. Also, Hoopoe Books has so many good books for the early readers and middle grade readers on Egypt and the Middle East, I can't hope to mention them all, but they are well worth seeking out. So, if you don't find your own favorite story about Egypt included here, don't despair—just add it on!

Early Readers / Picture Books

Eve Bunting. *I Am the Mummy Heb-Nefert*. Harcourt Brace, 2000 (UK and US). This book takes the form of an 'autobiography' of a mummy who was once the young woman Heb-Nefert. It is a lovely book, but slightly melancholy, as she contemplates who she was and what she has become. It is perhaps better for the older beginning reader, maybe closer to age 7 or 8.

Andrew Clements. *Temple Cat*. Clarion Books, 2001 (UK and US). A pampered temple cat in ancient Egypt longs to be like other cats, catching his own fish and roaming where he wills. Warm illustrations and the story of longing for adventure will appeal to kids.

Roy Gerrard. *Croco'Nile*. Farrar Straus Giroux, 2001 (UK and US). A young boy and his sister find a baby crocodile and then discover the delights and dangers of ancient Egypt in this book by an award-winning artist.

Florence Parry Heide and Judith Heide Gilliland. *The Day of Ahmed's Secret*. Puffin Books, 1990 (UK); HarperTrophy, 1995 (US). This book, illustrated by Ted Lewin, is absolutely one of the best children's picture books ever. Lewin captures the city of Cairo, its light, and its people perfectly. And the story is so heart-warming and simple you'll never forget it. I love this book!

Denys Johnson-Davies. This prolific author and translator has many children's books on the market, but his newest, *Goha the Wise Fool*, from Philomel (2005 US) is one of the best. This collection of 15 folk tales is beautifully illustrated with lively scenes, all created by Cairo's tentmakers. Although this is a picture book, it's best suited for middle-grade readers. Johnson-Davies also has sets of kids' books published by Hoopoe Books and Sunflower Books (both Egyptian publishing companies in Cairo). All are classic Arab tales revised and retold by Johnson-Davies and each book is illustrated by a different Egyptian artist with distinct, lively styles. *Thieves and Robbers* from Sunflower is especially eye-catching and fun with its (slightly) gruesome stories.

Betsy Lewin. *What's the Matter, Habibi?* Clarion Books 2004. (UK and US). This charming and funny paperback is worth every penny. Habibi the camel is down in the dumps and only a fabulous fez will brighten him up. Lewin masterfully conveys who is truly the boss in Habibi and Ahmed's warm and enduring friendship; the camel's self-satisfied expression as he returns from the bazaar speaks volumes.

Fred Marcellino. *I, Crocodile.* HarperTrophy, 2002 (US). This is a very funny, sort of sophisticated story about a crocodile kidnapped from Egypt by Napoleon in the eighteenth century, who is taken to Paris and becomes the toast of the town . . . until his appetites get away from him.

Elsa Marston. *Free as the Desert Wind.* Hoopoe Books, 1996 (Egypt and UK). It is Omar's dream to go with his father on the long camel drive from Sudan to Egypt. But Omar makes friends with one of the camels and causes quite a stir in trying to keep him from being sold at the market.

Robert Sabuda. *Tutankhamen's Gift.* Aladdin, 1997 (UK and US). This interesting take on the reigns of Amenhotep IV (also known as Akhenaten) and his younger brother, Tutankhamen, makes young Tut the hero. The illustrations are also neat, as they resemble the papyrus paintings one can buy all over Cairo.

Middle Grade Fiction

Enid Blyton. *Tales from the Arabian Nights.* Element Books, 1998 (UK). The most familiar and popular stories are condensed here by Blyton, a much-loved and prolific British author.

Tamara Bower. *How the Amazon Queen Fought the Prince of Egypt.* Atheneum 2005 (US). A vivid tale taken from an ancient Hellenistic scroll, this story of enemies who become friends, equals, and eventually lovers, is illustrated in a strikingly rich hieroglyphic style. It has been favorably reviewed by both *Booklist* and the *School Library Journal*.

John L. Foster. *The Shipwrecked Sailor.* The American University in Cairo Press, 1998 (Egypt, UK, and US). This tale, translated from hieroglyphs on a Middle Kingdom papyrus, would be interesting for readers of all ages, actually. The accompanying hieroglyphs and humorous watercolors by Lyla Pinch Brock will keep the reader's interest up throughout the book.

Kristiana Gregory. *Cleopatra VII: Daughter of the Nile* (The Royal Diaries series). Scholastic, 1999 (UK and US). This book has gotten great reviews from kids who like historical fiction. Gregory vividly recreates Egypt and Rome and puts a lively spin on the life of this most famous queen.

Claudia Logan. *The 5,000-Year-Old Puzzle: Solving a Mystery of Ancient Egypt.* St. Martin's Press, 2004 (paperback only in UK); Farrar Straus & Giroux, 2002 (hardback only in US). Follow a fictional family to Egypt in 1924 to an actual expedition in Giza led by Dr. George Reisner. A truly splendid picture book that comes highly recommended by *Publishers Weekly.*

Eloise McGraw. *Mara, Daughter of the Nile.* Puffin Story Books, 1990 (UK and US). A young Egyptian slave-girl is recruited to spy for both sides in the battle between Queen Hatshepsut and her brother. Gripping intrigue with a splash of romance, this book has been popular for many years. A companion book from the same author that might appeal more to boys is *The Golden Goblet,* in which a young Egyptian boy struggles to reveal a hideous crime and reshape his own destiny.

Jill Rubalcaba. *A Place in the Sun.* Puffin Books, 1997 (UK and US). Senmut is exiled to a life of hard labor in the gold mines of Nubia after accidentally killing a sacred dove with his sculpting chisel. Can his love of sculpting set him free from a life of heat and misery?

——. *The Wadjet Eye.* Houghton Mifflin, 2000 (US). Another fast-paced thriller from Rubalcaba. This time, a young man and his friend from Alexandria must search for his soldier father in Spain. With the protection of the Wadjet Eye, a gift from Cleopatra herself, they face one challenge after another as they cross the Mediterranean and enter the heart of the Roman Empire. This book seems to be especially popular with boys.

Young Adult Fiction

Some of the books I've chosen to include here are definitely for younger teens, while others you may recognize from the adult mystery sections of your favorite bookstores. I think there's a lot of crossover for mature teens, but I've chosen carefully, taking into consideration adult situations and language.

Agatha Christie. *Death on the Nile.* HarperCollins, 1995 (UK); Berkley, 2000 (US). A classic Christie mystery with Hercule Poirot at the helm. A tranquil Nile cruise is suddenly disrupted when one of the lovely passengers is found shot through the head. Thank goodness Poirot is taking his holiday in Egypt this season!

N.J. Dawood. *Sinbad the Sailor and Other Tales from the Arabian Nights* and *Aladdin and Other Tales from the Arabian Nights.* Puffin Classics, 1994 and 1996 (UK and US). These are the familiar tales of magic, trickery, and adventure, but translated directly from the Arabic specifically for younger readers. The translator was born in Baghdad and specializes in Arabic–English translations.

Roger Lancelyn Green. *Tales of Ancient Egypt.* Puffin Classics, 1995 (UK and US). Originally published in 1967, the stories in this book contain all the great myths of ancient Egypt—from Amun-Ra, creator of all the creatures in the world, to the many legends of Isis and her husband Osiris. This book is probably best for the 11 to 15-year-old set.

Elsa Marston. *The Cliffs of Cairo.* Hoopoe Books, 1998 (Egypt and UK). This book, set in the Cairo of the 1960s, is a fast-moving suspense novel that pits the wits of a teenage girl and boy against the ruthless world of international art smugglers. This is an action-packed book that both boys and girls will enjoy.

Elizabeth Peters. Rather than pick just a single title, I'd recommend the whole Amelia Peabody series by Peters. Set in Victorian England and Egypt, the books feature Amelia, the headstrong wife of an Egyptologist, and she's always getting into trouble of one sort or another. These mysteries are well researched and presented with a gracious sense of humor—everyone will like these mysteries.

Pamela F. Service. *The Reluctant God.* Fawcett Juniper, 1988 (US). These are the exciting adventures of a modern teenage girl, the daughter of an Egyptologist, and a teenage pharaoh, who lived over four thousand years ago. They should never have met . . . but they do, and soon find themselves running away from danger.

Zilpha Keatly Snyder. *The Egypt Game.* Yearling Books, 1994 (UK); Yearling, 1986 (US). The deserted storage yard behind a curio shop becomes the perfect place to play the 'Egypt game' for the main characters, Melanie and April. Soon after, more kids get involved in the game and strange things start happening to the players, culminating in the capture of a murderer. This book is for the younger end of the young adult age range, but don't let them be put off by the rather juvenile cover art.

Bibliography

General

Abu Al-'Izz, M.S., *Landforms of Egypt.* Trans. Dr. Yusuf A. Fayid. Cairo: The American University in Cairo Press, 1971.

Abu-Lughod, Janet L. *Cairo: 1001 Years of the City Victorious.* Princeton: Princeton University Press, 1971.

Aldred, Cyril, *Middle Kingdom Art in Ancient Egypt,* Alec Tiranti, London, 1969.

Aldridge, James. *Cairo: Biography of a City.* Boston: Little, Brown and Company, 1969.

Arnold, Dieter. *Lexikon der ägyptische Baukunst.* Zurich: Artemis Verlag, 1994.

Atil, Esin. *Renaissance of Islam: Art of the Mamluks.* Washington, D.C.: Smithsonian Institution Press, 1981.

Badawy, Alexander. *Coptic Art and Archaeology.* Harvard: Massachusetts Institute of Technology, 1978.

Behrens-Abouseif, Doris. *Islamic Architecture in Cairo.* Cairo: The American University in Cairo Press, 1998.

———. *The Minarets of Cairo.* Cairo: The American University in Cairo Press, 1985.

Berque, Jacques. *Egypt: Imperialism and Revolution.* New York: Praeger Publishers, 1972.

Butler, A. J. *The Arab Conquest of Egypt.* 2nd ed. Oxford: Clarendon Press, 1978.

Creswell, K.A.C. *The Muslim Architecture of Egypt,* vols. 1 & 2. New York: Hacker Art Books, 1978.

Coury, Ralph M. "The Politics of the Funereal: The Tomb of Saad Zagloul." *Journal of the American Research Center in Egypt* 29, 1992, pp.191–200.

Dasan, Veronique, *Dwarfs in Ancient Egypt and Greece*, Clarendon Press, Oxford, 1993.

De Bourguet, Pierre. *Coptic Art*. Methuen & Co. Ltd., London. 1971.

De Stefano, E. A. *Threads of Life: A Journey in Creativity*. Cairo: Ramses Wissa Wassef Arts Center, n.d.

Edwards, I.E.S. *The Pyramids of Egypt*. Revised ed. London: Penguin Books, 1993.

The Egyptian Geological Survey and Mining Authority. "Geological Map of Greater Cairo Area—Scale 1:100,000." *Ministry of Petroleum and Mineral Resources*, 1983.

Fahim, Mohammad, and Ali Zaghoul. *The Great Madrasa-Mosque of Sultan Hassan*. Cairo: Dar el-Maaref, 1974.

Fakhry, Ahmed. *The Pyramids*. Chicago: University of Chicago Press, 1961.

Glubb, Sir John. *Soldiers of Fortune: The Story of the Mamlukes*. New York: Dorset Press, 1973.

Gold of the Pharaohs. Catalogue of the exhibition of treasures from Tanis. City of Edinburgh Museums and Art Galleries, 1988.

Goldschmidt, Jr., Arthur. *Modern Egypt: The Formation of a Nation-State*. Boulder, Co.: Westview Press, 1988.

Habachi, Labib. *The Obelisks of Egypt*. Cairo: The American University in Cairo Press, 1988.

Harris, J. and E.F. Wente, eds. *An X-Ray Atlas of the Royal Mummies*. Chicago: University of Chicago Press, 1980.

Hart, George. *Pharaohs and Pyramids: A Guide Through the Old Kingdom*. London: The Herbert Press, 1991.

Hassan, Hassan. In the House of Muhammad Ali: A Family Album 1805–1952. Cairo: The American University in Cairo Press, 2000, p. 11.

Hayes, John R. (ed.). *The Genius of Arab Civilization: Source of Renaissance*, Cambridge: MIT Press, 1978.

Helck, Wolfgang and Otto Eberhard, eds. *Lexikon der Ägyptologie*. Wiesbaden: Otto Harrassowitz, 1975–86.

Ikram, Salima (ed.), *Divine Creatures: Animal Mummies in Ancient Egypt*, The American University in Cairo Press, 2005.

Karnouk, Liliane. *Modern Egyptian Art: The Emergence of a National Style*. Cairo: The American University in Cairo Press, 1988.

Khadduri, Majid. *Arab Personalities in Politics*. Washington, D.C.: The Middle East Institute, 1981.

Kubiak, W. B. *Al-Fustat: Its Foundation and Early Urban Development.* Cairo: The American University in Cairo Press, 1988.

Lambert, Phyllis, ed. *Fortifications and the Synagogue: The Fortress of Babylon and the Ben Ezra Synagogue.* London: Weidenfeld and Nicolson, 1994.

Landstrom, Bjorn. *Ships of the Pharaohs.* New York: Doubleday & Co., 1970.

Lane, E. W. *An Account of the Manners and Customs of the Modern Egyptians.* Reprint of 1895 ed. The Hague and London: East-West Publications, 1978.

Lane-Poole, Stanley. *A History of Egypt in the Middle Ages.* London: Frank Cass and Co. Ltd., 1968.

Lauer, Jean-Phillippe. *Saqqara: The Royal Cemetery of Memphis.* London: Thames and Hudson. 1976.

Lehner, Mark. *The Complete Pyramids.* Cairo: The American University in Cairo Press, 1997.

MacKenzie, Neil D. *Ayyubid Cairo: A Topographical Study.* Cairo: The American University in Cairo Press, 1992.

Mendelssohn, Kurt. *The Riddle of the Pyramids.* London: Cardinal, 1976.

Montet, Pierre, "Les obelisques de Ramses II," Kemi, 1936, vol. 5, pp. 104–114.

Murphy, Lawrence R. *The American University in Cairo: 1919–1987.* Cairo: The American University in Cairo Press, 1987.

Nassar, Rabbat, *The Citadel: A New Interpretation,* E.J. Brill, Leiden, 1995.

Nelson, Nina. *The Mena House.* Cairo: n.p., 1979.

Nothdurft, William and Josh Smith, *The Lost Dinosaurs of Egypt,* Random House, New York, 2002.

Porter, Bertha and Rosaline Moss. *Topographical Bibliography of Ancient Egyptian Hieroglyphic Texts, Reliefs and Paints,* vol. III, part 2, 2nd ed. Oxford: Griffith Institute, 1981.

O'Grady, Desmond, trans. *Ten Modern Arab Poets.* Dublin: Dedalus, 1992.

Rafaat, Samir. *Cairo the Glory Years.* Alexandria: Harpocrates Publishing, 2003, p. 22.

———. "The Mr. & Mrs. Muhammad Mahmoud Khalil Museum." *Egyptian Mail,* May 6, 1995.

———. "The Grand Vizier's Palace." *Cairo Times,* 7–13 June 2001, p. 25.

———. "Kobba Palace" *Cairo Times.* Feb 3–9, 2000, p. 25.

———. "Sakakini Palace." *Egyptian Mail,* April 5, 1997.

———. "Ramses Returns Home." *Cairo Times,* August 7, 1997.

———. "Garden City." *www.egy.com,* August 6, 1998.

Raymond, Andre. *Cairo*. Harvard University Press, 2000.

Raymond, A. and G. Wiet. *Les Marchés du Caire*. Cairo: IFAO, 1979.

Rodenbeck, Max. *Cairo: The City Victorious*. Cairo: The American University in Cairo Press, 1998.

Said, Rushdi. "Cenozoic." *The Geology of Egypt*. Amsterdam: Elsevier, 1972.

Reeves, Carole, *Egyptian Medicine*, Shire Egyptology, 1992.

Reeves, Nicholas. *The Complete Tutankhamun*. Cairo: The American University in Cairo Press, 1990.

Rizk, Yunan Labib, "A Time-honoured Institution," Al-Ahram Weekly, 28 February–6 March 2002, p. 24.

Robinson, J. M., ed. *The Nag Hammadi Library*. San Francisco: Harper & Row, 1977.

The Royal Mummies: The Egyptian Museum. Cairo: Egyptian Antiquities Organization Press, 1994.

Rizk, Yunan Labib. " Spotlight on the 'Dean.'" *Al-Ahram Weekly*, 27 January–2 February 2000, p. 24.

Saleh, Abdel-Aziz, *Excavations at Heliopolis*, vol. I. Cairo: Cairo University, Faculty of Archaeology, 1981.

Staffa, S. J. *Conquest and Fusion: The Social Evolution of Cairo AD 642–1850*. Leiden: E.J. Brill, 1977.

Stewart, Desmond. *Great Cairo: Mother of the World*. Cairo: The American University in Cairo Press, 1996.

Tamraz, Nihal. *Nineteenth-Century Cairene Houses and Palaces*. Cairo: The American University in Cairo Press, 1998.

Wiet, Gaston. " Lampes et Bouteilles en Verre Emaille." *Catalogue Général du Musée Arabe du Caire*. Cairo: General Egyptian Book Organization, 1982.

———. " Objets en Cuivre." *Catalogue Général du Musée Arabe du Caire*. Cairo: General Egyptian Book Organization, 1984.

Guidebooks

Antoniou, J. *Historic Cairo: A Walk Through the Islamic City*. Cairo: The American University in Cairo Press, 1998.

Baedeker, K. *Baedeker's Egypt, 1929*. Newton Abbot: David & Charles, 1974.

Bongioanni, A. and M.S. Croce, eds. *The Illustrated Guide to the Egyptian Museum*. Photographs by Araldo de Luca. Cairo: The American University in Cairo Press, 2001.

Cairo: The Practical Guide and *The Practical Maps*. Cairo: The American University in Cairo Press. Updated annually.

Gabra, Gawdat. *Cairo: The Coptic Museum and Old Churches*. Cairo: Egyptian International Publishing Company—Longman, 1993.

Lyster, William. *The Citadel of Cairo: A History and Guide*. Cairo: The Palm Press, 1990.

Mostafa, Mohamed. *The Museum of Islamic Art: A Short Guide*. 3rd ed. Cairo: General Egyptian Book Organization, 1979.

Richardson, D. *Egypt: The Rough Guide*. London: Rough Guides, 2000.

Russell, Dorothea. *Medieval Cairo and Monasteries of the Wadi Natrun: A Historical Guide*. New York: Thomas Nelson and Sons, 1963.

Saleh, Mohamed. *The Egyptian Museum and Pharaonic Sites*. Cairo: Egyptian International Publishing Company—Longman, 1996.

Saleh, Mohamed and Hourig Sourouzian. *The Egyptian Museum, Cairo: Official Catalogue*. Mainz: Philipp von Zabern, 1987.

Sattin, A. and S. Franquet. *Egypt: The Explorer Guide*. Cairo: The American University in Cairo Press, 2000.

Seif, O. and J. Spencer. *Khan al-Khalili: A Comprehensive Mapped Guide to Cairo's Historic Bazaar*. Cairo: The American University in Cairo Press, 1993.

Seton-Williams, Veronica and Peter Stocks. *Blue Guide: Egypt*. London: A. & C. Black, 1993.

Siliotti, Alberto. *Guide to the Pyramids of Egypt*. Cairo: The American University in Cairo Press, 1997.

Turing, P. *Egypt: A Concise Guide for Independent Travellers*. Thornton Cox, 1992.

Williams, C. *Islamic Monuments in Cairo: A Practical Guide*. 4th ed. Cairo: The American University in Cairo Press, 1993.

Ziock, H. *Lehnert & Landrock's Guide to Egypt*. Cairo: Lehnert & Landrock, 1956.

About the Authors

Lesley Lababidi is a mother, wife, friend, writer, and lover of Africa, where she has lived for thirty-five years. In 1989, she moved to Cairo to provide her three children with the opportunity to study Arabic and Islam. Lesley received her BS from the University of Colorado-Boulder. She is the author of *Paddle Your Own Canoe: An American Woman's Passage into Nigeria* (Spectrum, 1997) and *Silent No More: Special Needs People in Egypt* (AUC Press 2002), and she has updated and revised *Cairo: The Practical Guide* (AUC Press, 2006). She is the founder of Middle East North Africa Youth Leadership Initiative and Ma'an Foundation for Youth Leadership.

Dr. Lisa Sabbahy has a *Ph.*D. in *E*gyptian Archaeology from the University of Toronto. She moved to Cairo permanently in 1986, where she now teaches Egyptology at the American University in Cairo. Dr. Sabbahy's first book, *Ramses II: The Pharaoh and His Time*, was the exhibition catalogue for the 1985 premiere of the *R*amesses II show in the United States.

Jayme R. Spencer teaches information literacy at the American University in Cairo Library. Although a long-time resident of Cairo, showing Cairo to her four nephews when they were children gave her a different view of the city! She has written and lectured on many of the crafts and artisans of Cairo and is coauthor of *Khan al-Khalili: A Comprehensive Mapped Guide to Cairo's Historic Bazaar* (AUC Press, 1993).

Kelly Zaug has ten years of bookselling experience, including two working for the American University in Cairo Bookstores. While working as a bookseller in the US, she specialized in organizing special events for children, and in recent years she has been active with schools and reading groups in Cairo. She is a former member of the International Congress of Young Booksellers and the Great Lakes Booksellers Association board of directors. Kelly is now the publication director for the Egyptian Antiquities Project at the American Research Center in Egypt.

Janice Hill-Garing received her BS in Geology from the University of Texas in Austin and her MS in Geophysics from Stanford University.

Index